TREASURY SECURITIES

TREASURY SECURITIES

Making Money
With
Uncle Sam

Donald R. Nichols

Longman Financial Services Publishing
a division of Longman Financial Services Institute, Inc.

Publisher: Kathleen A. Welton
Senior Project Editor: Jack L. Kiburz

© 1990 by Donald R. Nichols

Published by Longman Financial Services Publishing
a division of Longman Financial Services Institute, Inc.

Printed in the United States of America

90 91 92 10 9 8 7 6 5 4 3 2 1

Library of Congress Cataloging-in-Publication Data

Nichols, Donald R., 1948–
    Treasury securities: making money with Uncle Sam/Donald R. Nichols.
        p. cm.
    ISBN 0-7931-0016-X
    1. Government securities—United States. 2. Investments—United
    States. I. Title.
HG4936.N53 1990
332.63 '232—dc20   89-13538
                                                                            CIP

Contents

Introduction

Today's investors face more befuddlements than they sometimes feel adequate to handle. For starters, they have access to more types of investments than any generation before them, and there are more financial institutions petitioning for investment dollars than many investors can sort out. Confounding their situation these days, it seems every place investors want to put their money is tainted by impropriety, if not impending collapse.

Yet people know they need to invest astutely today, even though there scarcely appears a sensible way to do so. The market they take stock of might not be a market they want to take stock in, what with eerie memories of the 1987 meltdown and fearsome expectations of a possible recurrence. They find little to bank on in the alarming ink of banking industry headlines. They wonder if corporate bonds will be junked by acquisition mania. They see the tax collector coming back for what little was left after 1986 tax reform, and investors are scarcely convinced seven will be a lucky number for continuing years of economic growth.

Looking upon these circumstances, investors are turning to the oldest, most secure, and most accessible group of investments available to them. As immune to default as possible, these securities stand aside from worrisome corporate bonds and bank-type deposits. Their interest and dividends are the definition of market level returns. Investors can use them as a steady support for an unsteady portfolio of equities. These securities have sustained investors throughout cycles of inflation, recession, and worse. Usually exempt from state and local taxes and sometimes deferred from federal tax, they are available in a battery of maturities and types offering singular features, and they are liquid in worldwide markets traded in billions of dollars every day.

These securities, of course, are bills, notes, and bonds issued by the United States Treasury and governmental agencies. Treasury and agency securities are more than safe havens and second choices, however, for in countless situations they are without question the best investment available. The foremost fact that commends Treasuries above competing investments is their backing by—or association with—the full faith and credit of the U.S. government. Taxing power of Uncle Sam distinguishes them in two practical ways. First, long-term investors can buy Treasury securities with confidence they will receive timely payments of interest and principal. Second, immunity to default makes Treasuries advisable any time the economy is particularly rocky.

The unchallenged quality of Treasury securities also makes them easier to manage than many investments. With their income and principal assured, investors manage Treasuries by selecting the types of issues that meet their needs and the maturities that fit the emerging economy. Unlike the case with other securities, investors don't have to research balance sheets, debt ratings, dividend policies, or other extensive material of investment analysis when making decisions.

Treasury securities are remarkably accessible and affordable. The Federal Reserve sells bills, notes, and bonds without commissions when they are newly issued, and government and agency paper is listed on public exchanges to be bought and sold through brokerages and banks. Prices start at $25 for savings bonds, range from $1,000 to $5,000 for notes and bonds, and ascend through $10,000 for T-bills to $25,000 for some government agency securities. Purchased indirectly via mutual funds, whole portfolios of Treasury and agency securities cost $1,000 to $2,500 and sometimes less.

Plain vanilla Treasuries meet a number of investor tastes and preferences, whether for current income, capital stability, or capital gains. The many types of Treasuries add versatility to a portfolio. Some, like the well received zero coupon CATS and TIGRs, fit best with retirement plans. Others, such as **flower bonds** or tax anticipation notes, serve estate and corporate tax management. Securities from government agencies offer a variety of alternatives, often with higher yields than direct Treasury debt and with more assurance against default than corporate securities. Still others, such as mortgage-backed agency securities, offer differing types of payments than customarily associated with Treasury issues. In general, there is at least one type of Treasury or agency security that can meet any given portfolio purpose.

You'll meet all of them in this book. As with any type of investment, a little knowledge goes a long way in maximizing the benefits of Treasury and agency securities in your portfolio. There are a few eccentric twists to these securities, but for the most part they are simple, safe, and well worth the learning of a few principles.

Section I of this book discusses each type of Treasury and agency security as a self-contained topic deserving its own chapter. Each chapter starts by describing what the security is and follows with a broad discussion of its advantages, disadvantages, and uses. You'll also learn specifics—where to buy, how to read quotations, how to calculate yields. Beyond basics, each chapter in Section I also discusses key subjects such as where a specific bill, note, or bond serves your portfolio or how a Treasury or agency issue might supplement or replace another investment you were considering.

Section II covers useful topics in the management of Treasury and agency securities. It discusses which Treasuries best fit changing economies, how to use them for retirement planning, staging them for current income, and other matters that will help you make the most of your investment.

In short, this is a fundamental text for the individual investor, and that's a diverse group of people. It includes people who ordinarily gravitate to other investments and want to learn more about income alternatives, just as it includes the growth investor seeking alternatives to corporate securities. He or she might be an active trader or a coupon clipper, an economy watcher, or someone who simply wants an investment that does what it is supposed to do while getting on with life. The individual investor might be retired or anticipating a distant retirement in accounts for which Treasuries are perfect. In addition, the individual investor might be a small business manager for whom Treasuries enhance cash flow, fund pensions, or aid elsewhere in management. If you're an investor, you can benefit from knowing more about Treasury and agency securities.

SECTION

I

Understanding Treasury and Agency Securities

1

The Basics of Treasury and Agency Securities

No area of personal, business, or national investment is untouched by United States Treasury and **agency securities** and their markets. The Treasury market is the place where individuals and businesses attend to short-term or long-term needs for investment, where nations exercise their financial clout, where refugees defend against their own economies, where our own Federal Reserve system conducts countercyclical monetary policies, where toddlers get their first savings bonds from doting grandparents, and where gangsters launder cash.

Treasury securities of all types come into being because the U.S. government and federal agencies need to borrow money for their operations. Thus, the essential characteristic of Treasury securities is that they are loans to the issuer, whether the issuer is our national government or federal agencies operating under the aegis of national authority. For our national government, Treasury bills, notes, and bonds are fund-raising alternatives to taxes. For federal agencies, agency paper likewise provides operating funds as an alternative, addition, or supplement to funds that might be received from tax revenues or other sources. For all parties who borrow by issuing Treasury and agency securities, financial markets give national and international access to investors worldwide who provide capital by purchasing their debt.

Investors benefit in many ways from the availability of Treasury and agency securities. Because the Treasury and government agencies are heavy borrowers, investors have access to a constant stream of new securities. Treasury securities are the highest quality instruments available in any financial market anywhere, for they are direct debt of the U.S. government and are universally considered to be immune from default. Agency paper is also considered to be of unimpeachable quality even though not all federal agencies have a direct claim upon backing by Uncle Sam. Investors also benefit from a fully liquid secondary market for Treasury and agency debt. Hundreds of billions of dollars of these securities trade each day, permitting investors to buy and sell in regulated, efficient, well established markets.

STRUCTURE OF THE MARKET

What we commonly call "the market" for these securities is actually a meeting of two markets, the primary and secondary. The primary market comprises Treasury and agency securities at the time they are originally issued by the Treasury through the Federal Reserve. Secondary markets comprise institutions and investors who buy and sell these securities after they are originally issued. Operations of the primary and secondary markets go on simultaneously, and many participants are active in both. As a result, they function continuously in what effectively behaves as a single market.

The market for Treasury and agency securities resembles a pyramid. At the apex of the market stands the Federal Reserve system. "The Fed" is the nation's central bank, chief monetary authority, and agent for the Treasury Department in issuing new Treasury bills, notes, and bonds. All Treasury securities originate from the Fed, and all transactions in Treasury securities after they are issued are cleared through the Fed.

Slightly further down this financial pyramid is a layer of **primary dealers.** These include selected large commercial banks and investment houses that have been granted primary dealer status by the Fed. They undertake several indispensable functions. First, they bid on all new issues of Treasury and agency debt brought to market. Second, they bid on and distribute all new issues of debt from federal agencies. Third, they hold substantial inventories of existing Treasury and agency securities and are obligated to maintain liquid markets in those securities. Primary dealers act as a principal rather than an agent in all of their transactions. That is, they buy securities for and sell securities from their own accounts to their customers.

The numerous patrons of primary dealers occupy the broad base of this pyramid. They include other primary dealers, firms that specialize in government securities, and financial institutions of all types nationally and internationally. Also included are all parties who are not primary

4

dealers or major money center institutions, such as banks, S&Ls, mutual funds, brokerages, pension funds, corporations, and, to a lesser degree these days, individual broker-dealers. Once you descend beyond the level of primary dealer, all other parties in Treasury markets are customers, not dealers, and, as you will have noticed, there are as yet no personal investors in this scheme.

Personal investors occupy an irregular position in the pyramid of the market, for they can, in limited respects, deal directly with the Fed and primary dealers. As we discuss individual securities, you will see that personal investors can buy new issues of Treasury bills, notes, and bonds directly from the Federal Reserve at its regular auctions. However, investors can only buy from the Fed, and can buy only new issues brought to market.

Personal investors can't sell securities back to the Fed, with the exception of savings bonds, and they can't buy existing Treasury securities from the Fed. In addition, many full-service brokerage firms or large banks are primary dealers of Treasury and agency securities. As the customer of a primary dealer's retail subsidiary, you can buy and sell Treasury and agency securities from a primary dealer.

For the most part, however, personal investors are customers of a primary dealer's patrons. Looked at another way, personal investors buy and sell Treasury and agency securities with an intermediary acting as their agent, not as a principal. Most investors buy and sell Treasury and agency securities through a brokerage and occasionally obtain Treasuries through their local bank. Unless the bank or brokerage is also a primary dealer, it will take your order to another financial intermediary to be executed and will charge you a fee for executing your order.

Another point that we will emphasize repeatedly: It's best to work with the retail subsidiary of a primary dealer or a firm specializing in Treasury securities, for you will be working more closely with the source and eliminating needless intermediaries. Most full-service brokerage firms are primary dealers whose registered representatives would be happy to make your acquaintance. You can buy or sell directly through their inventories without paying someone else to do it for you.

OVER-THE-COUNTER NETWORK

The market for Treasury and agency securities doesn't exist in a physical location, as does a commodity or stock exchange. Instead, the market exists only as an electronic network of computers linking dealers, brokers, and customers worldwide. This computer network is called an **over-the-counter (OTC) market.**

Although scattered, the OTC market is remarkably efficient. Primary dealers and broker-dealers who trade in Treasury and agency securities make a market—specify prices at which they will buy and sell—by entering their transactions on terminals. Compatible terminals at other locations spread the information. When you wish to make a transaction, you can identify securities, prices, trading volume, and other particulars through a broker or agent who has access to this electronic network. That party will place your order.

Financial media summarize the results of the previous business day's transactions throughout the OTC market for Treasury and agency securities. Except for primary dealers' reports to the Fed, financial market quotes are the only printed evidence that a Treasury market exists, for everything else is electronic. Media reports are an imprecise record of the market, for their quotations are based upon "representative" trades, but they are useful as general information. Later chapters tell you how to read financial market quotations.

BOOK ENTRY SECURITIES

The market is electronic in more than its method of transactions. Your securities are electronic also. Except for savings bonds and issues of decade-old Treasury notes and bonds, Treasury and agency securities exist only in book entry form. **Book entry** means your investment resides as a blip on computer tape along with millions of other investors. You receive no physical certificate when you buy and return none when you sell Treasury and agency securities. You will, of course, receive a confirmation notice from your broker or bank and from the Fed if you buy new issues of Treasury securities.

Book entry registration discomforts investors who are used to receiving a printed certificate attesting to ownership of a security, but Treasury markets probably could not function without the advantage of book entry ownership. For one thing, some types of Treasury securities exist only for a few days or weeks, so any certificate would present more paperwork burden than investment benefit.

For another thing, the volume of buying and selling in Treasury and agency securities is tremendous. Processing certificates that represent hundreds of billions of dollars per day of trading volume would create an administrative nightmare that might impede efficient markets.

Finally, electronic book entry facilitates investors' trading and receipt of interest. The electronic network, colloquially called "the Fed wire," can credit interest payments to your bank or brokerage account within minutes of an interest payment. It eliminates the old-fashioned requirement to clip coupons, deliver them to your local bank for a cash payment, and then deposit the cash in a checking or interest-bearing account.

TERMINOLOGY OF TREASURY AND AGENCY SECURITIES

Even though the market and the securities are today electronic abstractions, the terminology of Treasuries remains delightfully bound by convention. In vocabulary of the market, you will conduct your buying and trading as if the centuries-old context still applied to a physically present security and a face-to-face transaction. Following are a few basic terms that pertain to Treasury and agency securities.

Issue Date: The date on which the security is formally issued. Treasury and agency securities are originally brought to market in a series of auctions, discussed in subsequent chapters. Once the auction is concluded, the security is issued—enters the computer bank—on a specific date.

Issuer: The organization, whether the Treasury Department or government agency, that borrows money by issuing bills, notes, and bonds.

Par Value: (also called face value, denomination, and principal) Strictly speaking, par value represents the number of dollars you will receive when a security matures. A single Treasury bond, for example, has a par value of $1,000, and that sum was at one time physically printed on the face, hence the term "face value," of the security.

Purchase Price: The amount you actually pay for a security when it is originally issued (also called subscription price) or purchased in secondary markets (also called market price). Purchase price can be greater, equal to, or less than par value.

Maturity Date: The specific date on which a security repays its par value and no longer pays interest.

Call Date: A date prior to maturity when the Treasury or issuing agency can "call" a security back from investors, repay its par value, and cease paying interest. Many Treasury bonds, for example, are **callable**

five years before maturity, but much Treasury and agency debt is **noncallable.** Once purchased, the investment pays interest until maturity.

Interest: The dollar payment you receive as an investor in Treasury and agency securities. Treasury notes and bonds and some agency paper pay coupon interest, a term that dates from the days when those securities featured actual coupons that investors detached from the security and presented physically for payment. Treasury bills, EE savings bonds, and zero coupon securities pay **accreted interest** as the difference between purchase price and par value.

Interest Date: The actual date on which interest is paid. Coupon paying securities like notes or bonds pay interest semiannually, with interest declaration dates determined by the issue date; a bond issued on May 15, for example, will have an interest date of May 15 and November 15 each year until call or maturity. Securities featuring accreted interest make only one payment of interest, at maturity.

This basic vocabulary will suffice for starting to learn more about securities in the chapters that follow. Each chapter will expand upon these terms and add new vocabulary important to understanding each type of security and how its markets operate.

TRANSACTION MECHANICS

As an investor buying and selling Treasury and agency securities in secondary markets, you can specify prices at which you want transactions to take place. You also may specify a period of time in which your order to buy or sell will remain in effect. We will discuss prices and price quotations for each type of security in chapters pertaining to each. For now, however, let's look at the kinds of orders you can place based upon prices.

If a quoted price to buy or sell is acceptable to you, you may place a **market order** for the security. You simply tell the broker, "I'll take ten (or some specified number) bonds at the market." Likewise, you may instruct the broker to sell at the market. This communication informs the broker that you are willing to buy or sell securities at the prevailing market price. The broker will execute the transaction, and you will pay or receive the market price at the moment of transaction.

However, prices change, and in placing a market order you acknowledge willingness to pay whatever price the market establishes. It may be, therefore, that your order will be executed at a higher or lower price because the market price changed during your conversation with the broker. You did not specify the exact price; you said the market price would be fine with you, and if the market price increased, so be it.

If price uncertainties disturb you, you may issue instructions for a **limit order.** Limit orders specify the price at which you are willing to purchase or sell a security. Your order will not be executed unless your security trades at that price or better.

Say you place a limit order of ten Treasury notes at $900. You inform the broker, "I'll take ten bonds at $900 or better." The broker will process your order, but it will not be executed until your price of $900 is struck. The annotation "or better" is customary but unnecessary. All you're saying is that it is all right to buy the bonds at less than $900 or sell at more than $900 if possible.

Market orders are executed immediately by the broker's Treasury desk or by the broker's trade with another dealer. In most cases, your order can be placed while you wait, and before you hang up the phone your trade will be executed. In contrast, limit orders for prices must be accompanied by a time limit.

One type of limit order is the **fill or kill,** although more frequently this limit order is used in commodity trading. A fill or kill is a one-time shot. In issuing a fill or kill order, you are saying to a broker, "Place the order at this price, and if it isn't executed immediately, forget it."

A **day order** expires at the end of the trading day. If the specified price you wish to pay or receive is not achieved by the end of the trading day, your limit order expires, and the trade isn't executed. By the same token, week orders and month orders are good for the periods stated. If your indicated price is reached during the trading week or month, the trade is executed. If the price isn't reached before the end of the week or month, the limit order expires.

One type of limit order that has no expiration is the **good 'til cancelled** order, also called an open order or GTC. A GTC order informs your broker that your willingness to purchase or sell a bond at your specified price is in force until the order is executed or until you cancel it. Thus, the time period is indefinite, and in practice GTC orders have waited years before being executed.

A special type of limit order applying to sale of securities is the stop loss order or **stop order.** The purpose of stops is to protect sellers against declines in price by placing an order to sell a security if its price falls to a certain level. Say, for example, that you own ten Treasury notes selling at $1,000. You can place a stop loss order to sell if the price falls to, say, $980, thereby preventing further losses.

RISKS OF TREASURY AND AGENCY SECURITIES

Treasury and agency securities are customarily broadcast as "risk-free investments." That term requires some clarification, for there is no such thing as a risk-free investment.

Treasury bills, notes, and bonds are full faith and credit obligations of the U.S. government, for which reason they are considered immune to business risk and default risk. Business risk refers to the possibility of capital losses or failure to receive other payments because the issuer—usually a corporation—doesn't earn sufficient revenues to support its obligations. Default risk refers to two events: the possibility that an investment will pay no return because its issuer is out of business, and the possibility that an investment will pay less than expected returns because business has been awful.

Treasury securities avoid business risk and default risk for obvious reasons: The issuer isn't a business subject to the revenue vagaries of business; the prospect of the U.S. government, and therefore its debt, ceasing to exist is remote; the entire federal tax base of the U.S. economy supports interest and principal payments of Treasury securities; and finally, Uncle Sam controls the printing press and has an endless supply of dollars with which to pay its debt.

Default risk as it applies to agency securities is another matter. Some agency securities carry federal government pledges to pay interest and principal. Other agencies have access to lines of credit sponsored by the Treasury. These agency securities are essentially Treasury securities and deserve their default-free reputation. However, other agencies have no direct claim upon the Treasury. Nonetheless, financial markets assert that these and similar agencies have a moral claim upon federal backing for interest and principal. These assertions are based upon these agencies being congressionally recognized and upon their political and economic significance. For the time being, agency securities are commonly regarded as immune to default.

These facts, however, assure only a risk-free *return* from Treasury and agency securities. That is, you are guaranteed to receive interest payments throughout the time you hold Treasury securities and to receive repayment of principal when your security matures. Treasury and agency securities are traded in public markets, so their prices rise and fall while you own them. They are, therefore, vulnerable to market risk. **Market risk** refers to all circumstances that cause publicly traded investments to decline in price.

One circumstance that causes market prices to change is interest rate risk. **Interest rate risk** refers to the relationship between interest paid by a

10

particular investment and overall interest rates in the economy. Economywide interest rates may rise and fall, but interest on Treasury and agency securities is fixed. Accordingly, economywide changes in interest rates cause fixed-income investments to decline in price when rates rise and to rise in price when rates fall. Interest rate risk is the chief cause of changes in market price of Treasury and agency securities.

From the income investor's perspective, a potent aspect of interest rate risk is **reinvestment risk**—the opportunity, or lack of it, to retain a constant yield by reinvesting interest payments. Suppose interest rates in the economy rise. If you hold fixed-income investments like most bonds, interest they receive does not increase with the economy. Not only will the price of old, publicly traded income investments fall, but you are losing income because old investments do not provide the higher returns of a higher interest environment. Suppose economywide interest rates fall. Although publicly traded fixed-income investments will increase in price, falling rates also represent loss to investors because you cannot reinvest at previously higher rates.

Inflation risk, also called purchasing power risk, is another risk of Treasury and agency securities, and it refers to changes in the buying power of interest income. Inflation is a sustained increase in the general level of prices. Because Treasury and agency investments pay fixed interest, they don't retain purchasing power as prices rise. They are vulnerable to inflation risk.

Interest rate risk, reinvestment risk, and inflation risk are key considerations for investors in Treasury and agency securities. However, these risks can be managed to reduce their effects, as you will see later in the book.

SUMMARY

Markets for Treasury and agency securities are among the largest, most efficient, and arguably most important of financial markets. Treasury and agency securities are initially issued through primary markets, the participants in which are also active in secondary market trading of existing securities. Therefore, it is customary to refer to the Treasury market as a single, seamless market.

Personal investors can buy newly issued Treasury securities directly from the Federal Reserve, can buy and sell through retail affiliates of primary dealers, or can buy and sell through institutions that work with primary dealers. In all cases, securities are traded through an over-the-counter network of electronic terminals rather than a physical exchange. The electronic nature of the market, which generally dispenses with cumbersome paperwork, facilitates transactions among issuers, buyers, and sellers. Investors receive a confirmation notice of their transactions, but the securities themselves are recorded in book entry form without a certificate.

The vocabulary of features pertaining to Treasury securities has remained unchanged despite the advent of contemporary methods of trading. Securities still are commonly discussed with respect to their issuer and issue date, interest payments, maturity, and other provisions.

Direct obligations of the U.S. government—Treasury bills, notes, and bonds—are exempt from default risk, and agency securities carry direct or implied backing by Uncle Sam. All income securities, Treasury and agency securities included, are vulnerable to other risks that can be reduced by astute management.

2

Treasury Bills

Treasury bills, commonly called T-bills, are patterned after one of history's oldest financial receipts, the bill of lading, which was used to finance goods during shipment. When a manufacturer would load his goods aboard a steamer or rail car, he received a bill of lading showing the amount and dollar value owed him. The manufacturer could take the bill to a banker, who would buy it for an amount slightly less than its dollar value. The manufacturer received immediate cash, and the banker received the full payment when the goods were paid. If the banker did not wish to hold the bill until payment, he, too, could sell it, also at a discount, to another person. Ultimately, of course, the purchaser of the goods made payment, and whoever owned the bill at that time received it.

Today's Treasury bills function according to the same principle. When originally issued by Uncle Sam, T-bills have maturities of three months (13 weeks or 91 days), six months (26 weeks or 181 days), and one year. If you buy T-bills in secondary markets after they have been issued, you can select bills maturing within a few hours, days, weeks, or months. You buy T-bills at a discount—a reduced price—below their par value of $10,000. The difference between purchase price and par is accreted interest that is paid when the bond matures. Therefore, you might pay, for instance, $9,500 for a one-year bill and receive $10,000 when it matures.

ADVANTAGES AND DISADVANTAGES OF TREASURY BILLS

T-bills offer all the customary advantages of Treasury securities, exemption from state and local income tax and immunity from default being foremost. Most any financial institution that requires you to post a good

13

faith deposit for a purchase, a compensating balance for a loan, collateral for any purpose, or a cash position for any reason will accept T-bills as an alternative to cash.

One of their greatest advantages is their accessibility. The Treasury issues more T-bills than any other security. Weekly auctions—see the announcement in Figure 2-1—bring billions of dollars of bills to market each week. In addition, billions of dollars worth of existing T-bills are traded each day on secondary markets. There is no problem finding, buying, or selling them.

For the most part, brevity of maturity is T-bills' greatest advantage. Having brief maturities, T-bills are "near to cash"—never far from producing a cash payment. And because of brief maturities, T-bills don't fluctuate dramatically in price. Finally, the brief maturities and continuous auction of T-bills assure that they provide market level rates of interest. In fact, rates of interest paid by T-bills are the definition of market level returns for short-term instruments.

For many investors, the cost of T-bills—always close to $10,000 par value—is their greatest disadvantage. If this ante is too high for you, you can invest indirectly in T-bills through money market funds and government securities mutual funds, discussed in Chapter 8.

USES OF T-BILLS

If you're holding more than $10,000 in a passbook account with a bank or S&L or a share draft account at a credit union, there's little doubt you'd be better off investing in T-bills. Like a savings account, T-bills are highly stable investments and are easily converted to cash. They are backed by the full faith and credit of the U.S. government, a superior pledge of assurance to what FDIC offers. What's more, T-bills' accreted interest is exempt from state and local tax, whereas interest from savings accounts is fully taxable. T-bills nearly always (but not always) pay higher interest than savings accounts, even before considering their tax break. In short, T-bills are safer, lesser taxed, and higher paying than a savings account.

You also should consider T-bills as alternatives to any investment that is not paying market-level interest rates and providing immediate liquidity. Curiously, one of the most popular financial products today is the short-term certificate of deposit with maturities of six months and one year. How odd it is that investors keep throwing money into short-term certificates, accepting modest rates banks or S&Ls offer, paying state and local taxes on interest income, and agreeing to pay an interest rate penalty if they cash the certificate before it matures. They could

---

Figure 2-1: ANNOUNCEMENT OF T-BILL AUCTION

Treasury Plans Sale
Of $14.4 Billion of Bills

By a WALL STREET JOURNAL *Staff Reporter*

WASHINGTON—The Treasury plans to pay down about $3.8 billion on the federal debt with the sale Monday of about $14.4 billion in short-term bills. Maturing bills outstanding total $18.19 billion.

The offering will be divided evenly between 13-week and 26-week bills, which will be dated Sept. 14 and mature on Dec. 14, 1989, and March 15, 1990, respectively.

Tenders for the bills, available in minimum $10,000 denominations, must be received by 1 p.m. EDT Monday at the Treasury or at Federal Reserve banks or branches.

---

earn the higher, tax-favored returns of T-bills and be able to sell them at any time without a penalty.

Apart from their use as a permanent savings account or as a substitute for other types of deposits, T-bills are excellent parking lots for interim funds you may be waiting to invest elsewhere. Many times you will sell a stock or discover that a certificate of deposit has expired, or perhaps you are holding a sum of money earmarked for an upcoming expense, or you have other money you are not ready to invest elsewhere. Instead of letting it stagnate in a checking account, put it into a T-bill. You will have stability, liquidity, and tax-advantaged interest.

Owners of small businesses should remember T-bills for ways to enhance cash management. For example, many business owners face recurring quarterly payments for mortgage or bank loans and single year-end payments for pension funding or bonuses. They might buy a T-bill with maturity coinciding with dates they need funds. Interest earned would help with the payment. Similarly, business owners might receive a substantial payment before they, in turn, need to pay their own suppliers.

15

They could earn interest on that payment from a T-bill with a week or two until maturity.

Finally, T-bills are one of the best investments to select for a hedge against inflation. As you will see in Chapter 10, interest paid by T-bills parallels changes in inflationary price and interest rate increases. Being short-term securities, bills produce their higher interest rates without capital losses associated with many other income investments. Therefore, they preserve capital and provide higher interest payments, commendable qualities during inflationary cycles.

BUYING NEW T-BILLS FROM THE FEDERAL RESERVE

One of the easiest and least expensive ways to buy newly issued T-bills is straight from the government—or more precisely, from the Federal Reserve, which is the Treasury's agent for placing government debt. Every week, the Treasury refinances billions of dollars worth of existing T-bills and floats new ones. Every Tuesday at 4 P.M., the Federal Reserve, as agent for the Treasury, announces a public auction of new 13-week and 26-week T-bills that will take place Monday of the following week. Every fourth Friday the Treasury announces auctions of one-year bills to take place the following Thursday. The Fed will sell you T-bills through a program called **Treasury Direct** if you follow a simple procedure.

Figure 2-2 shows Form PD 5176-1, the tender you can submit to bid on a 13-week T-bill (Use 5176-2 and 5176-3 to buy 26-week and 52-week bills, respectively). Free by request from any Federal Reserve Bank or branch, the form is largely self-explanatory. Individuals or business owners complete the investor information section according to how they wish the bill to be registered, also providing the appropriate taxpayer ID and telephone numbers.

Major national and international financial institutions, depositories of all sizes, businesses, and some private investors submit **competitive tenders** for these securities. That is, they study markets and interest rate trends and attempt to achieve the highest returns by specifying the yield at which they will purchase T-bills during weekly auctions. As you become astute in following Treasury markets, you might wish to submit competitive tenders for the purchase of your own new bills. However, there is one problem: If your competitive tender is too high—that is, if you require an interest rate too much above the average at the auction—you will not get your T-bill.

To assure you obtain your bill, submit a **noncompetitive tender.** This informs the Federal Reserve that you will accept the average interest rate and pay the average price at which the T-bills are auctioned. Although

Figure 2-2: TENDER FORM FOR DIRECT PURCHASE OF T-BILLS

FORM PD 5176-1
(January 1988)

OMB No. 1535-0069
Expires: 01-31-89

TREASURY DIRECT

TENDER FOR 13-WEEK TREASURY BILL

TENDER INFORMATION

AMOUNT OF TENDER: $ _____

BID TYPE (Check One) ☐ NONCOMPETITIVE ☐ COMPETITIVE AT ▢ . ▢ %

ACCOUNT NUMBER ▢ - ▢ - ▢

INVESTOR INFORMATION

ACCOUNT NAME

ADDRESS

CITY   STATE   ZIP CODE

TAXPAYER IDENTIFICATION NUMBER

1ST NAMED OWNER ▢ - ▢ - ▢ OR ▢ - ▢

SOCIAL SECURITY NUMBER   EMPLOYER IDENTIFICATION NUMBER

TELEPHONE NUMBERS

WORK (▢) ▢ - ▢   HOME (▢) ▢ - ▢

PAYMENT ATTACHED

TOTAL PAYMENT: $ _____

CASH (01): $ _____   CHECKS (02/03): $ _____

SECURITIES (05): $ _____ $ _____

OTHER (06): $ _____ $ _____

DIRECT DEPOSIT INFORMATION

ROUTING NUMBER

FINANCIAL INSTITUTION NAME

ACCOUNT NUMBER   ACCOUNT TYPE ☐ CHECKING
(Check One)

ACCOUNT NAME   ☐ SAVINGS

AUTOMATIC REINVESTMENT

1 2 3 4 5 6 7 8   Circle the number of sequential 13-week reinvestments you want to schedule at this time

AUTHORIZATION

For the notice required under the Privacy and Paperwork Reduction Acts, see the accompanying instructions.

I submit this tender pursuant to the provisions of Department of the Treasury Circulars, Public Debt Series Nos. 1-86 and 2-86 and the public announcement issued by the Department of the Treasury.

Under penalties of perjury, I certify that the number shown on this form is my correct taxpayer identification number and that I am not subject to backup withholding because (1) I have not been notified that I am subject to backup withholding as a result of a failure to report all interest or dividends, or (2) the Internal Revenue Service has notified me that I am no longer subject to backup withholding. I further certify that all other information provided on this form is true, correct and complete.

_____   _____
SIGNATURE   DATE

FOR DEPARTMENT USE

TENDER NUMBER
912794

CUSIP

ISSUE DATE

RECEIVED BY

DATE RECEIVED

EXT REG ☐

FOREIGN ☐

BACKUP ☐

REVIEW ☐

CLASS ☐

NUMBERS

17

you may receive a decimal lower interest than buyers who study T-bill markets full-time, you are assured of receiving a T-bill because the Federal Reserve fills noncompetitive tenders first. Often an entire auction is taken up by noncompetitive tenders.

Call or write the nearest Federal Reserve Bank or branch, and representatives will mail you complete information about buying T-bills, including preprinted forms for executing the transaction. The forms aren't absolutely necessary. The Federal Reserve will accept a letter from you if it contains all the information indicated on the form.

Mail or hand-deliver your letter or form to the Fed with a cashier's check for at least $10,000, the minimum purchase price for one bill. At the Fed's auction, T-bills are also available in increments of $5,000 beyond the minimum, so you can purchase bills for $10,000, $15,000, and so on. The amount also can be withdrawn by wire from your bank, broker, mutual fund, or other depository institution if you complete the direct deposit block on the tender form.

If you pay by cash or certified check, you pay the full par value when you submit your tender even though the bill will cost less. When your tender is accepted, the Federal Reserve will credit your checking or savings account for the difference between par value and purchase price. If, for example, 13-week bills sell for $9,900, you will receive a wire credit for $100. The credit is a return of principal and is untaxed. Your T-bill will be registered in book entry form on computer tape. You will then receive a confirmation notice indicating the registration number of your bill and its maturity.

The most convenient way to buy subsequent T-bills is to roll them over at the end of each maturity period, automatically buying a new bill of the same maturity when the old one matures. If you intend to roll bills over, so indicate in the block for automatic reinvestment when you buy bills initially. The Federal Reserve will execute your rollover as another noncompetitive tender when the bill matures. You pay no commissions or fees on rollovers.

When you purchase the subsequent bill, you will, once again, receive a credit for the difference between par value and average purchase price. However, in this case, the amount represents interest paid on the preceding T-bill. The amount may be more or less than actual interest received, depending upon the average price of T-bills at the second auction.

For example, at the first noncompetitive tender you paid $9,900 for a $10,000 T-bill, and you got back $100, which was a return of capital. When that bill matures, you are entitled to $10,000. However, perhaps at the second auction T-bills sell for $9,950—$50 more. When you roll the first T-bill over and use it to buy a second bill, you will receive a check

Figure 2-3: T-BILL QUOTATIONS

TREASURY NOTES, BONDS & BILLS

U.S. Treas. Bills Mat. date	Bid	Asked	Yield Discount		Mat. date	Bid	Asked	Yield Discount
-1989-					8-24	8.52	8.48	8.83
					8-31	8.50	8.46	8.82
5- 4	8.84	8.77	8.89		9- 7	8.45	8.41	8.79
5-11	8.63	8.57	8.70		9-14	8.49	8.45	8.84
5-18	8.56	8.49	8.64		9-21	8.51	8.47	8.88
5-25	8.39	8.33	8.49		9-28	8.48	8.44	8.86
6- 1	8.34	8.30	8.47		10- 5	8.45	8.41	8.85
6- 8	8.46	8.39	8.58		10-12	8.46	8.42	8.87
6-15	8.43	8.36	8.56		10-19	8.46	8.42	8.89
6-22	8.44	8.37	8.58		10-26	8.52	8.48	8.97
6-29	8.43	8.36	8.59		11- 2	8.50	8.46	8.96
7- 6	8.51	8.47	8.72		11-24	8.49	8.45	8.96
7-13	8.50	8.46	8.72		12-21	8.49	8.45	8.97
7-20	8.49	8.46	8.74		-1990-			
7-27	8.51	8.47	8.76		1-18	8.43	8.37	8.91
8- 3	8.54	8.50	8.81		2-15	8.51	8.48	9.07
8-10	8.44	8.37	8.68		3-15	8.50	8.46	9.09
8-17	8.51	8.45	8.78		4-12	8.48	8.45	9.12

for $50, but you will still have received $100 in federally taxable interest. Like any other borrower to whom you loan money, the Treasury will apprise you of interest earned, which makes your record keeping easier.

BUYING AND SELLING T-BILLS AFTER ISSUE

As Figure 2-3 shows, existing T-bills are traded in an active market from the moment they are issued until the day they mature, so you aren't confined to buying them when they're originally issued and holding them to maturity. In fact, you can buy and sell T-bills a week before they are issued through a system called the "when-issued" market. But if you participate in public markets, you won't be dealing through the Fed. The Fed sells only *newly issued* T-bills and only at its weekly auctions. Also, the Fed won't buy your bills back if you want to sell before they mature (for a fee the Fed will transfer your T-bills to a bank or broker who can sell them, but this is prohibitively time consuming). These disadvantages may compel you to work with a broker when buying bills.

One key to buying, selling, and managing T-bills of all maturities is to work with brokerage houses that carry their own inventories of bills. As a practical matter, that means working with full-service brokerage firms, a firm that specializes in Treasury securities, or perhaps a large bank or S&L. These institutions will carry large inventories of new and existing bills, and they likely will have greater expertise in advising you about them. Their chief advantage, however, is that they make a market from their inventories—you can buy T-bills from and sell to these houses without commissions.

Discount brokerages, smaller banks or S&Ls, and other financial institutions that don't hold inventories of T-bills will charge you a commission for your transactions. Not holding bills nor making a market from inventories, they have to execute your order in public markets. You pay them a commission to place your order, and you pay the commissions they are charged by their broker. It doesn't make much sense to buy or sell any security from an organization that doesn't have its own brokerage access.

THE BID-ASKED SPREAD

If you buy T-bills from a broker-dealer, you will be quoted a dollar price as a bid and asked spread. The bid is the dollar price at which the organization will buy your T-bill if you are selling; the asked is the dollar price at which it will sell if you want to buy. The difference is the spread, and it is the organization's profit.

For example, your broker might say, "We'll sell you the bill maturing June 2 for $9,951.86." That is the brokerage's asked price, the price it asks you to pay for the bill. If you are selling, your broker might say, "We'll pay $9,900 for the June 2 bill." That is the brokerage's bid price, the price it bids for your bill. The difference of $51.86 is the spread, income to the brokerage from a transaction for a $10,000 T-bill. Brokerages also typically transact bills in multiples of $5,000 beyond the $10,000 minimum—$15,000, $20,000, and so on.

DETERMINING A PRICE

T-bill quotations in the financial pages don't specify a price. Instead, you see in Figure 2-3 that dealers buy and sell at a specified discount from par. A discount quotation is a slightly complicated quotation for personal investors to get used to. It encodes several pieces of information—your purchase price for the bill, the dollar amount of interest paid at maturity, and the yield resulting from price and interest. In sorting out quotations, you need to remember two characteristics of T-bills: Their par value is $10,000 and their prices are less than par value. Knowing prices are quoted as a discount from par expressed in percentage terms, you can find the dollar price mathematically.

In Figure 2-3, note the bill maturing August 3. This T-bill was 91 days from maturity on the date of the reported quotation. The bid discount is 8.54 percent below par value and the asked discount is 8.50 percent of par value. The dealer will buy this bill at a 8.54 percent discount from par and sell this bill at a 8.50 percent discount from par. Let's assume you want to buy this bill at the asked price (count the day of purchase in your calculation). To determine market price for one bill of $10,000, use this formula:

$$\text{Price} = \$10,000 - \frac{(\$10,000 \times \text{asked discount} \times \text{days to maturity})}{360}$$

Enter the figures into the formula, using the financial year of 360 days rather than the customary calendar of 365 days:

$$\text{Price} = \$10,000 - \frac{(\$10,000 \times .085 \times 91)}{360}$$

$$\text{Price} = \$10,000 - (\$214.8611) = \$9,785.14$$

You will pay $9,785.14 to buy this bill. The interest you will receive upon maturity equals the dollar discount from purchase price, or $214.86. On August 3, you will receive $10,000, or $214.86 more than you paid.

CALCULATING ANNUALIZED YIELD

Here's the tricky part: The bid discount is not the yield. It is merely a price differential specified by the dealer. To determine your yield, you need to relate your purchase price—the asked price from the dealer—to the $10,000 par of bills purchased in secondary markets.

At the purchase (asked) price, the yield to maturity on this publicly traded bill is 8.81 percent, as specified in the sample quotation. Although financial quotations will give the yield, you can calculate it yourself. To perform this calculation, use this formula, which features the customary calendar year of 365 days.

$$\text{Annualized Yield} = \frac{(\$10,000 - \text{ASKED PRICE}) \times 365}{\text{number of days to maturity} \times \text{asked discount}}$$

For the bill maturing June 2, the figures are:

$$\frac{(\$10,000 - \$9,785.14) \times 365}{91 \times \$9,785.14}$$

Figure 2-4: PRICE BEHAVIOR OF T-BILLS

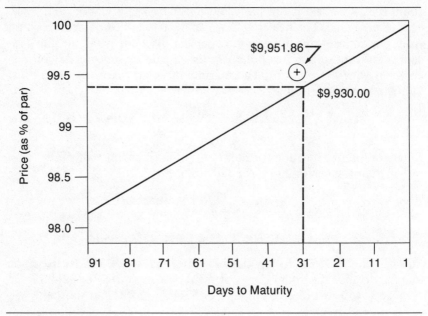

Which reduces to:

$$\frac{78423.90}{890447.74} = .08807 = 8.81 \text{ percent annualized yield}$$

THE MARKET BEHAVIOR OF T-BILLS

Most personal investors buy T-bills from the Fed or a broker when they are originally auctioned. They hold them until maturity in three months, six months, or one year, and they receive the expected interest payment on the maturity date. If they buy bills after issue, investors typically hold them until the specified maturity date. Their financial life is very straightforward and, for the most part, so is the price behavior of their T-bills. Given a steady economy and their brief maturities, T-bill prices will march predictably toward par each day until maturity, as Figure 2-4 indicates.

Figure 2-4 represents a three-month (91-day) T-bill. The horizontal axis indicates days to maturity, and the vertical axis represents price as a percent of par. For example, 98.2 represents 98.2 percent of $10,000, or

$9,820. The solid line connects purchase price and par. If there were no economic or market influences on T-bills, their prices would fall exactly upon the solid line each day. If such were the case, T-bills would have only one component of price—the interest component.

However, economies, financial markets, and interest rates change between the time a T-bill is issued and the time it matures. New bills coming to market every week incorporate these changes in their prices and yields, and so do prices of existing T-bills. In short, prices of existing T-bills have a rate change component as well as an interest component. As a result of the rate change component, prices of existing bills might be higher or lower than predicted by the normal course of events.

Let's plug in the example of a 91-day bill bought 31 days from maturity. As Figure 2-4 shows, the original price of the 91-day bill was $9,820. You bought it 31 days from maturity at $9,951.86. As determined by the interest rate component, the price for this bill should have been about $9,930, as the dotted intersection indicates. Clearly, some force in the marketplace caused this bill to increase above the expected price, reflecting the effect of the rate change component on price.

The effect of the rate change component is called **volatility.** Volatility is a characteristic of all Treasury securities, but it is greater with longer maturities. The shorter the maturity, the less volatile are prices and the effect of the rate change component. All T-bills have less than one year to maturity, so they generally are not volatile. Nonetheless, you should be aware that market forces influence the market price of T-bills, just as they influence the prices and yields of newly issued bills.

TAX CONSEQUENCES OF T-BILLS

Figure 2-4 is a useful grid to follow in managing T-bills. Easily constructed, it enables you to compare effects of the interest component and the rate change component on the market price of your bills. As noted, most investors hold bills to maturity. However, some investors sell T-bills before maturity because they wish to reinvest in another vehicle or because the rate change component has produced unexpected price gains. If you are considering selling bills before maturity, or if you simply want to keep track of your investment, you can draw your own grid.

If you hold a T-bill until maturity, your payment will be interest (subject to federal tax but exempt from state and local taxes). Interest isn't taxable until the bill matures. But if you sell your T-bill prior to maturity, the difference between your purchase price and sale price is federally and municipally taxed as a capital gain. Capital gains are taxed and capital losses declared for the year in which you sold the bill.

SUMMARY

Treasury bills are direct Treasury obligations sold at a discount from par value with original maturities of three months, six months, and one year. They exist in book entry form. You can buy them without fee directly from the Federal Reserve when they are initially issued, or you can buy and sell existing T-bills from brokerage and banking institutions. Most investors prefer to work with institutions that carry their own inventories of bills, as commissions don't apply to buy and sell transactions.

T-bills provide liquidity, capital stability, and market-level rates of interest. Accordingly, they are knowledgeable alternatives to savings accounts and other investments that don't offer those three advantages. In addition, they are excellent parking lots for personal or business capital that can earn interest while awaiting a near-term use. T-bills also are one of the best investments during periods of inflation or any time of economic uncertainty.

Price and interest rate calculations are different from other Treasury securities because bills are sold at a discount from their $10,000 par (and $5,000 increments). However, the two relatively simple formulas presented here will aid you in determining return. Your broker can calculate prices and yields for you.

3

Treasury Notes and Bonds

Unlike Treasury bills, Treasury notes and bonds are coupon-paying instruments with maturities longer than one year when they are originally issued. Often called conventional Treasury debt, or, colloquially, "vanilla Treasuries," notes and bonds are alike in that par value of both is $1,000 and both make semiannual payments of interest. That is, they pay half of their yearly coupon payment every six months—one payment during the month of issue and the second six months distant. Although some presently existing notes and bonds are represented by physical certificates, most are book entry form only.

The chief difference between notes and bonds is length of maturity. When originally issued, Treasury notes have maturities of two to ten years, whereas Treasury bonds carry maturities of ten to thirty years at original issue. In secondary markets, notes and bonds trade alongside each other and are largely indistinguishable. A ten-year note issued five years ago and a 20-year note issued 15 years ago will have a current maturity of five years, and they will trade as if both were five-year securities.

ADVANTAGES AND DISADVANTAGES OF NOTES AND BONDS

As you have seen, immunity from default and exemption from state and local income tax make notes and bonds advantaged over other types of income investments. For many investors, regular, semiannual income is a strong advantage of notes and bonds, one that you will learn more about in Section II. Similarly, broad public markets for Treasuries enable you to buy and sell with ease, a great advantage over less liquid investments.

25

Treasury notes and bonds have no particular disadvantages except for two that attend all bond investments. One of those disadvantages is capital fluctuation. As you will see, the market price of Treasury notes and bonds rises and falls with changes in economywide interest rates. If you need to sell your Treasuries when prices are depressed, you will suffer a capital loss. A second disadvantage is that the coupon income of Treasuries is fixed. Coupon payments won't increase as your personal circumstances or cost of living increase call for higher income. However, both of these disadvantages can be reduced by techniques explained in Section II.

USES OF TREASURY NOTES AND BONDS

Negligible default risk is a particular advantage if you are considering a long-term investment, as, for example, in an individual retirement account, self-employment retirement account, or a company pension. Generally, such accounts strive for long-term compounding of interest, and you can be assured that the government will pay semiannual interest. It shouldn't be surprising that personal investors and pension managers favor Treasuries, and you certainly should consider them for that use. Section II discusses how to make the most of them for this purpose.

In addition, immunity to default is important if you depend upon coupon income for living expenses or as supplements to business income. Treasuries have long been favorites for retirees and other investors who need dependable current income. Section II also discusses this subject.

Exemption from municipal taxation is a particular advantage for those who live in states and cities with onerous tax rates, and it is becoming more significant as many states pass new tax rates and legislation. If such is the case where you live, you could improve after-tax investment return by switching out of fully taxable corporate bonds or certificates of deposit into Treasuries. Take a look at your portfolio, or reconsider when it is time to renew a maturing certificate of deposit. When you can buy a top-quality Treasury that's also free of state and local taxes, don't gravitate by habit to fully taxable investments of lesser quality.

BUYING NOTES AND BONDS FROM
THE FEDERAL RESERVE

As with T-bills, you can buy new issues of notes and bonds directly from the Federal Reserve. The procedure is the same as that discussed in Chapter 2, and a sample form is illustrated in Figure 3-1. Each maturity

Figure 3-1: TENDER FORM FOR DIRECT PURCHASE OF TREASURY BONDS

FORM PD 5174-4
(January 1986)

OMB No. 1535-0068
Expires: 01-31-89

TREASURY DIRECT

TENDER FOR TREASURY BOND

TENDER INFORMATION

FOR DEPARTMENT USE

AMOUNT OF TENDER: $ _____

TERM _____

BID TYPE (Check One) ☐ NONCOMPETITIVE ☐ COMPETITIVE AT ___ . ___ %

TENDER NUMBER
912810

ACCOUNT NUMBER _____ - _____ - _____

CUSIP

INVESTOR INFORMATION

ISSUE DATE

ACCOUNT NAME

RECEIVED BY

DATE RECEIVED

EXT REG ☐

FOREIGN ☐

BACKUP ☐

REVIEW ☐

CITY   STATE   ZIP CODE

TAXPAYER IDENTIFICATION NUMBER

1ST NAMED OWNER ___ - ___ - ___ OR ___ - ___

SOCIAL SECURITY NUMBER   EMPLOYER IDENTIFICATION NUMBER

CLASS ☐

TELEPHONE NUMBERS

WORK (___) ___ - ___   HOME (___) ___ - ___

PAYMENT ATTACHED

TOTAL PAYMENT: $ _____

CASH (01): $ _____   CHECKS (02/03): $ _____

SECURITIES (05): $ _____ $ _____

OTHER (06): $ _____ $ _____

NUMBERS

DIRECT DEPOSIT INFORMATION

ROUTING NUMBER

FINANCIAL INSTITUTION NAME

ACCOUNT NUMBER

ACCOUNT NAME

ACCOUNT TYPE
(Check One) ☐ CHECKING
☐ SAVINGS

AUTHORIZATION

For the notice required under the Privacy and Paperwork Reduction Acts, see the accompanying instructions.

I submit this tender pursuant to the provisions of Department of the Treasury Circulars, Public Debt Series Nos. 1-86 and 2-86 and the public announcement issued by the Department of the Treasury.

Under penalties of perjury, I certify that the number shown on this form is my correct taxpayer identification number and that I am not subject to backup withholding because (1) I have not been notified that I am subject to backup withholding as a result of a failure to report all interest or dividends, or (2) the Internal Revenue Service has notified me that I am no longer subject to backup withholding. I further certify that all other information provided on this form is true, correct and complete.

_____   _____
SIGNATURE   DATE

of note and bond has its own paperwork. As was the case with T-bills, your personal letter will suffice in place of the form if it contains all the required information. You must buy five notes or bonds for a minimum investment of $5,000 when shopping at the Fed's auctions, and your additional purchases have to be in groups of five bonds. You may submit a competitive or noncompetitive tender for your purchases.

The same advantages and disadvantages of buying T-bills apply to direct purchases of notes and bonds. No commissions or basis pricing pertain to your purchase, as there is no broker or middleman. You can roll the notes and bonds over, again without commission or fee, when the securities mature. The Fed credits semiannual interest to your specified bank, brokerage, or mutual fund account and mails yearly financial records. The disadvantage is, again, the difficulty of selling securities before they mature. As with buying T-bills from the Fed, buying notes and bonds through the Treasury Direct program works best when you intend to hold your securities to maturity.

No coupon is announced for notes and bonds brought to auction. That is, you don't know beforehand how much your security will pay yearly. Instead, the Treasury assembles all the bids and usually sets the coupon at the highest rate to the nearest one-eighth ($1.25) below the average bid at the auction. As a result, auctioned notes and bonds often will have prices slightly below $1,000. You pay the full par, of course, and the Fed remands the difference.

One significant point to remember is that coupons on new issues are, in effect, set by the market at the time of auction. In other words, coupon payments will reflect the general level of interest rates, investors' expectations about interest rates, and investors' demands for an income return. Two forces come into play. First, investors will expect new notes and bonds to pay coupon income that is competitive with the current level of interest rates. Second, investors will usually expect coupons to increase with maturity. As a result, coupons on new Treasury issues will be competitive with the expectations of the market and will reflect forces at work.

THE AUCTION CYCLE

As agent for the Treasury, the Fed auctions new Treasury notes and bonds in a series of recurring cycles. The **quarterly refunding**, which takes place during the first weeks of February, May, August, and November, auctions two sets of notes and one bond. During each of these months, three-year notes are auctioned on Tuesday, ten-year notes on Wednesday, and a thirty-year bond on Thursday. The regular weekly of-

Figure 3-2: ANNOUNCEMENT OF TREASURY AUCTION

Treasury to Sell $28.75 Billion Of Notes, Bonds

By HILARY STOUT
Staff Reporter of THE WALL STREET JOURNAL

WASHINGTON—The Treasury said it plans to sell $28.75 billion of notes and bonds next week to raise about $11.5 billion cash and redeem about $17.3 billion of maturing government securities.

The new securities, part of the department's regular quarterly refunding operation, will consist of:

—$9.75 billion of three-year notes, to be auctioned Tuesday.

—$9.5 billion of 10-year notes, to be auctioned Wednesday.

—$9.5 billion of 29¾-year bonds, which will be auctioned next Thursday.

The three-year notes will mature May 15, 1992; the 10-year notes May 15, 1999; and the 29¾-year bonds Feb. 15, 2019.

The auctions will bring the Treasury's net borrowings this quarter to $7.5 billion. The department estimates it needs net borrowing of $2 billion for the three-month period, assuming a $30 billion cash balance when the quarter ends June 30.

At a news conference to announce the refunding, William Bremner, the Treasury's assistant deputy secretary for federal finance, said income tax receipts have held down the government's borrowing needs this quarter. He added that tax revenue so far this year has been exceeding the government's projections. "Receipts have·

fering of T-bills also takes place on Monday, so the quarterly refunding is an important cycle of bills, notes, and bonds. You can see the auction cycle at work in the announcement from the *Wall Street Journal* shown in Figure 3-2.

The quarterly refunding is the only time the Treasury auctions bonds. However, it auctions notes in three other cycles. Two-year notes are auctioned late in every month. Four-year notes and seven-year notes are auctioned in March, June, September, and December as part of the **mini-refunding,** more formally called the consolidated financing. Five-year notes are auctioned late in February, May, August, and November, but separately from the normal quarterly refunding.

Here is a thumbnail schedule of the auction cycle:

Table 3-1: AUCTION CYCLE FOR NOTES AND BONDS

Security	Auction Dates
Two-year Notes	Last week of every month
Three-year Notes	First week of February, May, August, November
Four-year Notes	Last week of March, June, September, December
Five-year Notes	Last week of February, May, August, November
Seven-year Notes	Last week of March, June, September, December
Ten-year Notes	First week of February, May, August, November
Thirty-year Bond	First week of February, May, August, November

BUYING AND SELLING EXISTING NOTES AND BONDS

To repeat a point from Chapter 2, it is important to realize that the Fed sells only new issues of notes and bonds and that the Treasury Direct program works best if you hold notes and bonds until maturity. Should you need to sell before your securities mature, you will have to transfer them from your Fed account to a broker or dealer. Buying from a broker means selling without delays and burdensome paperwork. Advantageous as Treasury Direct can be, many investors simply prefer the flexibility of purchasing through a broker. In addition, you will have to use a broker if you want to buy existing notes and bonds.

Treasury notes and bonds are widely traded on secondary markets after they are issued. As was true with bills, full-service brokerages and specialty firms trade notes and bonds from their own inventories, charging no commission. Other firms, such as discount brokerages or depository institutions, will probably add a commission to your trade. Depending on the note or bond you buy and the source from which you

Figure 3-3:   RESULTS OF COMPLETED TREASURY AUCTION

Bond Prices Take Fall As Treasury Sales Sag

CREDIT

MARKETS

By TOM HERMAN
And KEVIN DONOVAN
Staff Reporters of THE WALL STREET JOURNAL

NEW YORK — Investors unexpectedly turned an icy shoulder toward the Treasury's sale of new three-year notes, sending bond prices into their deepest slump in nearly two months.

"The Treasury threw a party and nobody showed up," said Bruce R. Lakefield, executive vice president at Shearson Lehman Government Securities Inc.

Traders said both U.S. and Japanese institutions bought far fewer of the new notes than expected. Individual investors also cut back sharply compared with their purchases at the previous three-year note sale in February. The average annual yield was 9.12%, well above what traders had expected late Monday.

In the bond market, long-term Treasury issues tumbled by about one point, or $10 for each $1,000 face amount. Most short-term interest rates rose, especially those on Treasury bills. For example, six-month bills now yield 9.02%, up from 8.88% late Monday.

Fears are growing that recent declines in interest rates may be over. Traders worry that government reports over the next few days will show strong economic growth and higher inflation that will drive up interest rates.

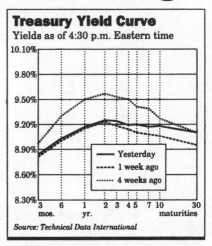

Treasury Yield Curve
Yields as of 4:30 p.m. Eastern time

Legend: Yesterday; 1 week ago; 4 weeks ago

Source: Technical Data International

Pinched profits at many securities firms also may have contributed to the slump. "Wall Street has a low tolerance for pain these days, given the fact that people haven't been making a lot of money lately," said E. Craig Coats Jr., vice chairman of Voute Coats Stuart & O'Grady L.P. in Greenwich, Conn. "So a lot of Wall Street dealers are trying to keep their positions as close to flat as possible."

The Treasury $9.79 billion note sale yesterday was the first of a huge three-part financing that will total $28.75 billion. Today, the department will sell about $9.5 billion of 10-year notes, followed by $9.5 billion of 29¾-year bonds tomorrow. Many traders had thought the have not would be

Figure 3-3: RESULTS OF COMPLETED TREASURY AUCTION (Continued)

							5⅞	MMIdx May 425	1290	1/16	·
GtNtN	40	r	¾	1⅝	r	r	r	Blkbst Jun 25	1098	1 13/16	-
GrtWF	17½	r	r	1¼	r	r	⅝	MMIdx May 475	1063	8⅝	—
Halbtn	25	r	r	4¼	r	r	r	DunBrd Aug 50	1010	1 7/16	...
29	30	⅛	½	1	r	1⅜	1¾	MMIdx May 470	974	5½	—
29	35	r	r	⅛	r	r	r	Dig Eq May 95	855	1	+

■ **Yields on 30-year** Treasury bonds rose in Thursday's auction to the highest level in a year. The average yield was 9.11 percent, up from 8.91 percent at the last comparable auction, on Feb. 9. It was the highest rate since 30-year bonds averaged 9.17 percent on May 12, 1988. The notes will carry a coupon interest rate of 8⅞ percent with each $10,000 in face value selling for $9,755.30.

									NY Close	Strike	Calls—Last			P
	47½	45	2½	3	3⅝	1/16	5/16	½						
	47½	47½	¾	1½	2	½	1⅛	1½						
	47½	50	⅛	½	1	2⅞	r	2⅝	54⅝	50	4¾	5½	6⅝	r
KerrM		45	3⅛	3¾	4¾	⅛	⅝	r	54⅝	55	¾	1⅞	3⅜	⅞
	47⅞	50	r	1⅜	2½	r	r	4⅛	54⅝	60	1/16	⅜	1⅜	r

AlldGp	58	11¼	+ ½	BobEvn	236	15½	+ ⅛	ColFst
AloyCpt	25	2⅜	......	Bogert	16	9	......	Comair
Allwast	784	17⅞	+ ⅜	Bohema	105	17¼	— ¼	Comcst
Aloette	144	11½	+ ½	BonvlP	98	9⅛	......	Cmc sp
Alpharl	3	1⅛	—1/16	BooleB	271	18¾	+ ¼	Cmdial
AlpMic	2	7⅝	+ ¼	BostAc	38	17¾	+ ½	Comeric

■ **Yields on 10-year** Treasury notes rose in Wednesday's auction to the highest level since August. The average yield was 9.18 percent, up from 8.91 percent at the last auction on Feb. 8. The notes will carry a coupon interest rate of 9⅛ percent with each $10,000 in face value selling for $9,964.50.

viACar	402	1 1/16	—1/16	Brnkmn	634	18⅜	......	CmprsL
AmCity	193	15¼	— ⅞	BritLee	1075	2 3/16	— ¼	Cmpch
AConsu	9	9¾	+ ¼	BrodN s	8	27½	......	Cmpcm
viACntl	340	⅞	......	BdwyFn	107	13¾	+ ¾	CCTC
AmEcol	6	9¾	......	BrTom s	70	6¼	+ ⅛	CptAut
				BwnTrn	35	5	......	CmpDt

■ **Yields on** 5-year Treasury notes fell in Wednesday's auction to the lowest level in 2½ years. The average yield was 8.26 percent, down from 8.72 percent at the last comparable auction, on May 25. It was the lowest rate since 5-year notes averaged 6.73 percent on Feb. 25, 1987.

Reprinted from the *Chicago Tribune,* May 11, May 12, and Aug. 24, 1989, respectively, by permission of the Associated Press.

Figure 3-4: GOVERNMENT BOND QUOTATIONS

TREASURY BONDS, NOTES & BILLS

Tuesday, September 5, 1989
Representative Over-the-Counter quotations based on transactions of $1 million or more as of 4 p.m. Eastern time.
Decimals in bid-and-asked and bid changes represent 32nds; 101,01 means 101 1/32. Treasury bill quotes in hundredths. a-Plus 1/64. b-Yield to call date. d-Minus 1/64. k-Nonresident aliens exempt from withholding taxes. n-Treasury notes. p-Treasury note; nonresident aliens exempt from withholding taxes.
Stripped Treasuries -- a-Stripped interest. b-Treasury bond; stripped principal. c-Treasury note; stripped principal.
Source: Bloomberg Financial Markets

Rate	Maturity	Bid	Asked	Bid Chg.	Yld.	Rate	Maturity	Bid	Asked	Bid Chg.	Yld.
	GOVT. BONDS & NOTES					10.50	Feb 95	109.12	109.16	−.03	8.29
8.50	Sep 89p	99.29	100.00	−.01	8.20	11.25	Feb 95p	112.21	112.25	−.03	8.28
9.37	Sep 89p	99.31	100.02	...	8.09	8.37	Apr 95p	100.12	100.16	−.02	8.26
11.87	Oct 89n	100.08	100.11	−.01	8.24	10.37	May 95	109.04	109.08	−.03	8.30
7.87	Oct 89p	99.28	99.31	...	7.87	11.25	May 95p	112.29	113.03	−.03	8.31
6.37	Nov 89p	99.17	99.21	...	8.05	12.62	May 95	119.30	120.03	−.03	8.14
10	Nov	100	.15		7.9	8.87	ul 95p	102.2	.26		8.26
11.62	Ja 92p	106.21	106.26	−.03	8.37	7.25	May 16k	89.17	89.21	−.02	8.21
6.62	Feb 92p	96.06	96.10	...	8.32	7.50	Nov 16k	92.04	92.08	−.02	8.22
9.12	Feb 92p	101.19	101.23	−.03	8.33	8.75	May 17k	105.19	105.23	−.03	8.22
14.62	Feb 92n	114.18	114.22	−.03	7.88	8.87	Aug 17k	107.01	107.05	−.03	8.22
7.87	Mar 92p	98.27	98.31	−.03	8.33	9.12	May 18k	110.01	110.05	−.03	8.20
11.75	Apr 92k	107.20	107.25	−.03	8.36	9.00	Nov 18k	108.25	108.29	−.04	8.19
6.62	May 92p	95.25	95.29	−.03	8.35	8.87	Feb 19k	107.17	107.21	−.03	8.18
9.00	May 92p	101.14	101.18	−.03	8.33	12	A 19k	28	100	−.02	12
.75	92p	18		−	37						

buy it, minimum bond lots differ. That is, some issues of bonds are available in single-bond lots, whereas you will have to buy at least five or ten of other issues. Your broker will tell you what the minimum lot is for the note or bond you are considering.

READING QUOTATIONS FOR NOTES AND BONDS

Your broker will quote you a price in plain English, but in tracking your bonds you will need to understand how to read and speak the singular language of price quotations. Figure 3-4 is a quotation of Treasury notes and bonds from the *Wall Street Journal*. This presentation is standard, although quotations in other sources, such as your local newspaper's financial pages, might differ slightly.

Treasuries are commonly named by their coupon and maturity date. For example, "the nine and one-eighths of May 18" is the name of the final bond on the page shown in Figure 3-4. Other bonds might representatively be called "the eights of November 90" or "the nines of May 98."

Accordingly, the first three items of information in the quote specify the coupon rate, year of maturity, and month of maturity.

Coupon Rate: The coupon rate is the amount of yearly cash payments that a note or bond provides. The coupon rate is quoted in decimals that must be multiplied by 10. For example, the first entry for an indicated note or bond might be "10.75." Multiplied by 10, the quote becomes 107.5, or $107.50. Owners of this bond receive $107.50 yearly in semiannual interest payments, or $53.75 every six months. A quotation of 9.5 translates into 95, or $95 in yearly interest—$47.50 every six months. You may occasionally see coupon rates expressed as fractions—$10^3/8$, for example, instead of 10.37. The fraction must be converted to a decimal and multiplied by 10 to derive the coupon payment.

Month of Maturity: An entry such as "Nov" means November and reveals two pieces of information about its note or bond: It matures in November of the indicated year, and it makes one semiannual interest payment each November. You an deduce that this bond also pays interest in May—six months from November. A quotation of "Aug" reveals a final maturity in August, an interest payment date each August, and another interest payment in February. Treasury notes and bonds pay interest on the 15th of the indicated month or on the final day of the indicated month, depending on whether they were issued at the quarterly refunding, mini-refunding, or monthly note auction.

Year of Maturity: This particular quotation abbreviates the year of maturity—"95" means 1995, "15" means 2015, and so on.

Year of Call: An entry such as "1993–98" or "2007–12" indicates that the bond is callable before it matures. That is, taking the first example, the government can pay off the par value of this bond in 1993, and "call it back" from owners without paying further interest. The "–98" and "–12" represent the years 1998 and 2012, when the securities mature.

Price Quotations: Treasury notes and bonds are quoted in points representing percentages of par. Par ($1,000) equals 100 points. Therefore, each quoted point equals $10. A quoted price of 98, for example, equals 98 percent of par or $980. A price of 101 equates to 101 percent of par ($1,000 par plus one point for a total of $1,010). A price of 123 equals $1,230.

Market prices are subdivided in decimals that actually represent 32nds of one point ($10), or 31.25 cents. Occasionally, a specific issue of

Figure 3-5: DECIMAL EQUIVALENTS

8ths	16ths	32nds	64ths	Decimal equivalent	8ths	16ths	32nds	64ths	Decimal equivalent
			1	.015625				33	.515625
		1	2	.031250			17	34	.531250
			3	.046875				35	.546875
	1	2	4	.062500		9	18	36	.562500
			5	.078125				37	.578125
		3	6	.093750			19	38	.593750
			7	.109375				39	.609375
1	2	4	8	.125000	5	10	20	40	.625000
			9	.140625				41	.640625
		5	10	.156250			21	42	.656250
			11	.171875				43	.671875
	3	6	12	.187500		11	22	44	.687500
			13	.203125				45	.703125
		7	14	.218750			23	46	.718750
			15	.234375				47	.734375
2	4	8	16	.250000	6	12	24	48	.750000
			17	.265625				49	.765625
		9	18	.281250			25	50	.781250
			19	.296875				51	.796875
	5	10	20	.312500		13	26	52	.812500
			21	.328125				53	.828125
		11	22	.343750			27	54	.843750
			23	.359375				55	.859375
3	6	12	24	.375000	7	14	28	56	.875000
			25	.390625				57	.890625
		13	26	.406250			29	58	.906250
			27	.421875				59	.921875
	7	14	28	.437500		15	30	60	.937500
			29	.453125				61	.953125
		15	30	.468750			31	62	.968750
			31	.484375				63	.984375
4	8	16	32	.500000	8	16	32	64	1.000000

SOURCE: Marcia Stigum, *Money Market Calculations: Yields, Break-Evens, and Arbitrage* (Homewood, Ill.: Dow Jones-Irwin, 1981). © Dow Jones-Irwin, 1981.

government notes and bonds will be quoted in 64ths, or 15.63 cents, if it is near to maturity or heavily traded on a particular day. Figure 3-5 displays various decimal equivalents.

Bid and Asked Spread: The next two items are the **bid price** and **asked price** specified by dealers in Treasury securities. Dealers will buy Treasuries from you at their bid price and will sell to you at their asked price.

The difference between the bid price and the asked price is profit for the dealer.

In reading bid-asked, remember that seeming decimals actually mean 32nds, or 31.25 cents. So a bid of 109.19 is 109 points plus $19/32$ of one point. Each point is worth $10, so the 109 points mean a price of $1,090. Each 32nd is 31.25 cents, and there are 19 of them in the quote, meaning $5.94. Added, $1,090 plus $5.94 is $1,095.94. Try deciphering an asked price of 109.25. You should be able to figure out that the bond's asking price is $1,097.81.

Fully rendered into English, the bid and asked means dealers in these Treasuries are willing to buy at $1,095.94 and sell for $1,097.81. You pay the dealer's asking price—$1,097.81—to buy and accept the bid price—$1,095.94—to sell. The difference of $1.87 is profit to the dealer.

Price at Close: The next entry shows the daily change in the day's final bid price. An entry of "–26," for instance, says that the security's closing bid price decreased $26/32$nds over the previous day's closing bid. Considering that $1/32$ equals 31.25 cents, you know this dealer was willing to pay $8.13 less for this bond than yesterday (31.25 cents × 26 = 812.5 cents or $8.13). An entry of " + 1.16," for example, indicates the closing bid price increased by one point ($10) and $16/32$nds of one point ($5). The dealer was willing to pay $15 more than the day before to buy this note or bond.

Yield to Maturity: The final item is the security's yield to maturity expressed in percent. An entry such as "9.28" means 9.28 percent— straight out, no hidden $1/32$nds or $1/8$ths. We will discuss yield to maturity in a moment.

Special Annotations: Lettered annotations reveal bits of information peculiar to each note or bond quoted, and they will be explained in the legend accompanying the quotations. For instance, the annotation "n" means the security is a Treasury note rather than a bond.

The quoted market for Treasuries is for lots of $1 million, and transactions involving lesser amounts mean lower bid and higher asked prices. In addition, Treasury markets are active markets, with prices and yields changing each day. Accordingly, remember that quotations in the financial pages might not reflect actual prices at the moment you are speaking with a broker or dealer.

ACCRUED INTEREST AND SETTLEMENT DATE

Although Treasuries pay interest on the 15th or last day of the month, they accrue interest each day. For example, suppose a Treasury pays $120 in yearly coupon interest with payment dates on the 15th of May and November. Each May 15th and November 15th you will receive $60. Unlike a corporate stock dividend, however, bond interest accrues regularly and predictably each day between interest declaration dates. In other words, this security accrues $10 per month in interest, or about 33 cents per day, all of which is paid on the 15th.

If you buy a Treasury between interest declaration dates, you must pay the previous owner for that accrued interest. Conversely, if you sell a Treasury between interest declaration dates, the purchaser must pay you accrued interest. To continue this example, suppose you buy this Treasury bond on June 15th, which is 30 days after the interest declaration date. You would have to pay the seller $10 in accrued interest in addition to the purchase price and commission, if any. If you were the seller, of course, you would receive the $10 from the new purchaser. Accrued interest isn't reflected in price quotations, and sometimes brokers will forget to mention it. Make sure you don't forget it, especially if you are buying multiple bonds. Accrued interest can add several hundred dollars to your payment if you buy 10 to 20 bonds.

Typically, you have to pay for Treasuries within one business day of purchase, a custom called next day settlement. If you buy from a broker's inventory, however, you might be able to negotiate a settlement of five business days. For some investors, delayed settlement is an inducement to work with a broker when buying Treasuries.

MARKET BEHAVIOR OF NOTES AND BONDS

Treasury notes and bonds look like simple propositions. They are issued at or near par of $1,000, pay a stated coupon at stated intervals, and mature on a known date at which they repay par. Between their birth and maturity, however, a great deal happens to notes and bonds. More specifically, their market prices change, and sometimes dramatically.

Unlike corporate or municipal securities, market price of Treasuries does not change because the issuer's credit rating changes. Uncle Sam's backing removes the possibility of default. However, market price changes with effects from one of the economy's most impressive forces— the general level of interest rates. Economywide interest rates rise and fall for many reasons, and for a fuller discussion of that subject pick up a copy of *Investing in Uncertain Times* by your author and Longman Financial Services. For now, you must understand that market prices of notes and bonds move inversely to economywide interest rates. As interest rates rise, bond prices fall; as interest rates fall, bond prices rise. Treasury prices change because their coupon income doesn't. With payments fixed, only adjustments in price can reflect changes in economywide interest rates.

Take the case of a 10-year Treasury note issued to pay $70 per year. That payment represents a 7 percent nominal interest rate ($70 divided by $1,000). It was competitive for the time and economy during which the note was issued, as is the nominal interest rate of all newly issued Treasury debt. Five years after the bond was issued, however, general interest rates had increased to 10 percent. At that time, investors with $1,000 could invest at 10 percent, receiving $100 yearly ($100 divided by $1,000).

Investors who own the $70 note want to sell it in order to invest at new, higher rates of interest. However, buyers won't pay $1,000 to receive the $70 offered by the old note. For that note to attract buyers in an environment of higher interest rates, its price will fall until the coupon payment of $70 matches the 10 percent opportunity generally available. That price would be $700.

The investor who paid $1,000 for the note now holds a security that markets have reduced to $700 because of increases in economywide interest rates. He or she has been victimized by increases in interest rates. The investor who profits from the change in interest rates is the new buyer who receives $70 a year but paid only $700 for that income.

Understanding that market prices fall when interest rates rise, you now see why some of the notes and bonds quoted in Figure 3-4 have prices below par. Read the quotations carefully, and you'll see that securities with bonds below $90 generally have prices less than par. Those bonds are said to be selling at a discount from par. At the time represented for that particular day of trading, April 1989, the economy had established 9 percent as its general level of interest rates. Prices of notes and bonds that didn't provide $90 in payments fell until their coupon payments reached a level of 9 percent.

If you continue reading the price quotations, you will observe that many notes and bonds, particularly those with coupons of $110 to $150, were selling far above par. At the time those notes and bonds were issued—from the late 1970s through mid-1980s—economywide interest rates demanded those hefty coupons. However, as the general level of interest rates declined, coupons of $100 and more provided substantially above-market payments. Investors who owned high-coupon Treasuries wouldn't sell them because their coupon payments substantially exceeded current rates. Buyers had to pay substantially more than par to induce owners to part with those notes and bonds. In an environment of 9 percent general interest rates, these securities could command prices of $1,100 to $1,500. They were trading at a premium above par.

PRINCIPLES OF PRICE BEHAVIORS

For any note or bond, the amplitude of price changes, known as capital fluctuation and volatility, depends upon change in economywide interest rates. More specifically, volatility depends upon the degree to which changed interest rates vary from coupon income. That degree of effect increases with the maturity of the note or bond. Section II discusses how to manage Treasuries to minimize or take advantage of capital fluctuation. To round out your understanding of this chapter, however, let's itemize the general relationships that dictate potential for price increases and decreases.

- For a given coupon, longer maturities are more volatile than shorter maturities.
- For a given maturity, lower coupons are more volatile than higher coupon bonds. (Figure 3-4 includes a bond that seems to defy this rule—a $3^1/_2$ percent coupon issue with a price of $96^{14}/_{32}$. This is a flower bond. It has a special feature that holds its price near par despite its low coupon. You will see why flower bonds sell near par in Chapter 9.)
- For a given maturity, higher coupon bonds are less volatile than lower coupon bonds

Bear in mind that capital fluctuation and volatility are relative to changes in economywide rates. Although the general principles above will hold true, the actual degree of price change depends largely upon the difference between the new rate, higher or lower, and the fixed coupon of the note or bond. Volatility is the proverbial two-edged sword. Without risk of capital loss when rates rise, there would be no possibility of capital gain when rates fall.

COMPARING BOND YIELDS—NOMINAL YIELD, CURRENT YIELD, YIELD TO MATURITY

Some investors buy Treasuries exclusively for capital gain. However, investors interested in the income from Treasury securities center attention upon the yield of a note or bond. A bond's yield is the relationship between its price and its payments. Because prices change in public trading, Treasury notes and bonds provide multiple yields.

Coupon yield (also called nominal yield) is the percentage relationship of the coupon rate to par value. Notes and bonds are nearly always $1,000 par, so a bond that pays a $50 coupon carries a 5 percent coupon yield ($50 divided by $1,000). A note that pays a $60 or $100 coupon will have a coupon yield of 6 percent or 10 percent, respectively.

In the practical sense of making investment decisions, coupon yield is important for buyers of newly issued bonds or for buyers of bonds selling at par in secondary markets, and for investors who need maximum coupon income. For other investors, coupon yield merely relates two static figures—coupon and par—and they will find it more important to assess yields in the dynamic market context of changing prices for notes and bonds.

Current yield is coupon divided by purchase price, not par. If the bond is selling at par, current yield is also coupon yield ($50 divided by $1,000, in our example). If increases in interest rates have beaten the bond's price below par, say to $500, current yield becomes 10 percent ($50 divided by $500). If declines in interest rates elevate the bond's price above par, say to $1,100, current yield is 4.55 percent ($50 divided by $1,100).

Current yield is significant, for this calculation relates the security's continuing payments to you (coupon) and your one-time payment for it (market price). If you buy a note or bond at a discount, you pay less to obtain continuing payments of interest. On the other hand, securities selling at a premium cause you to pay a higher price for coupon payments. As you can see, current yield is the result of a security's keeping pace with current economywide rates of interest after it has been issued.

Current yields are one measure of an attractive note or bond, but investors who buy a Treasury and intend to hold it until maturity are concerned with **yield to maturity**—the total return for owning the security. Yield to maturity consists of the yearly coupon and payment of principal when the bond matures. If you buy a discount Treasury, you pay less than par, but you will receive full par when it matures. That means your total return comprises coupon payments plus capital growth, which is computed as yield to maturity from this formula:

Yield to Maturity for a Discount Bond

$$C + \frac{D}{YTM} \div \frac{MP + PV}{2}$$

The C is the yearly coupon payment. D is the bond's discount from par. YTM is years to maturity. MP is market price, and PV is the bond's par value. The 2 is necessary for an average. The numerator reveals average annual gain of interest payments plus average yearly capital growth. The denominator is average annual investment, the midpoint between market price and par value. The resulting figure is the yield to maturity, the total yield produced by the bond.

Let's compute yield to maturity for a Treasury selling at $500 five years before maturity. The coupon is $50 yearly. Therefore:

$$\$50 + \frac{\$500}{5} \div \frac{\$500 + \$1,000}{2} = (\$50 + \$100) \div \$750 = \frac{\$150}{\$750} = .20 = 20\%$$

Whoever invests in these bonds for $500 and holds them until maturity receives a yield to maturity of 20 percent.

As you've also seen, decreases in interest rates cause increases in bond prices. The Treasury is obligated to repay only par, usually $1,000, so buying premium bonds adds another dimension to yield to maturity: subtracting the premium from the total return. For premium bonds, total return is interest payments minus the premium.

Yield to Maturity for a Premium Bond

$$C - \frac{P}{YTM} \div \frac{MP + PV}{2}$$

C remains the yearly coupon. *P* is the bond's premium above par. Dividing by YTM (years to maturity) reveals the average/reduction/of the premium each year. The denominator is the same as for discount bonds.

Let's compute yield to maturity for the $50 bond selling at a premium of $100.

$$\$50 - \frac{\$100}{5} \div \frac{\$1,100 + \$1,000}{2} = \$50 - \$20 \div \$1,050 = .0286 = 2.86\%$$

Whoever buys this premium bond and holds it to maturity receives a yield to maturity of 2.86 percent because the bond does not repay its purchase price of $1,100. Two years of interest payments, $100, are lost in five years because of the premium of $100 above par.

Holding period yield (HPY) is the percentage of interest income plus capital appreciation earned during the time a security is owned. You can use HPY in two ways: to measure yield you have already received on a Treasury you own, and to assess yield you expect to earn on a Treasury you purchase. In both cases, you use HPY when intending to sell a security before maturity. It is useful when calculating yields on Treasuries that have appreciated in price. For example, the high-coupon bonds with long maturities in Figure 3-3 are selling at substantial premiums. Investors who bought those bonds at par are sitting on capital gains. They might be considering selling in order to receive their capital gains as cash. They use HPY in helping with their decision.

Formula for Holding Period Yield

$$\frac{\text{Interest} + (\text{Sales Price} - \text{Purchase Price})}{\text{Purchase Price}}$$

Let's say that you bought one 15³/₄ bond of November 2001 at par in 1979. You considered selling it at a price of $1,500. For the sake of convenience with the arithmetic, we'll assume you received an even 10 years of interest payments, or a total of $1,575. Therefore:

$$\frac{\$1,575 + (\$1,500 - \$1,000)}{\$1,000} = 2.075 = 207.5\%$$

One chief advantage of notes and bonds—namely, their continuing income payments—is evident in reinvestment yield. This is the income you earn from reinvesting coupon payments instead of spending them. Reinvestment yield is a concern for all investors who plan to let coupon payments compound in a savings account, money market fund, T-bill, or other vehicle that pays continuing interest. Personal investors typically center attention upon reinvestment yield when holding Treasuries in tax-deferred accounts like IRAs, and it is also important for pension managers and small business owners who need current returns to compound for future results.

You have no doubt seen reinvestment yield advertised as "the miracle of compounding" in brokerage literature, usually replete with sweeping graphics that show how a small regular deposit, such as that provided by Treasury coupons, grows to magnificent sums when reinvested at a sustained rate of such-and-such a percent. In fact, the advertisements are entirely accurate, and reinvested coupons do truly produce astonishing results. The trouble is in achieving a consistent interest rate with which to compound coupon payments.

The results of reinvestment depend upon short-term interest rates available when you reinvest your Treasury coupons. Those rates change constantly, as noted in Chapter 1 under the subject of reinvestment risk. Therefore, achieving a consistent 7 percent or 10 percent is next to impossible. Nonetheless, the rewards can be surprising, as Figure 3-6 shows. A disciplined program of reinvesting coupon payments, is well worth noting. Those returns are the attraction of Treasuries for retirement growth, children's tuition, or other future purpose.

Figure 3-6: $50 MONTHLY REINVESTED AT VARYING RATES OF INTEREST

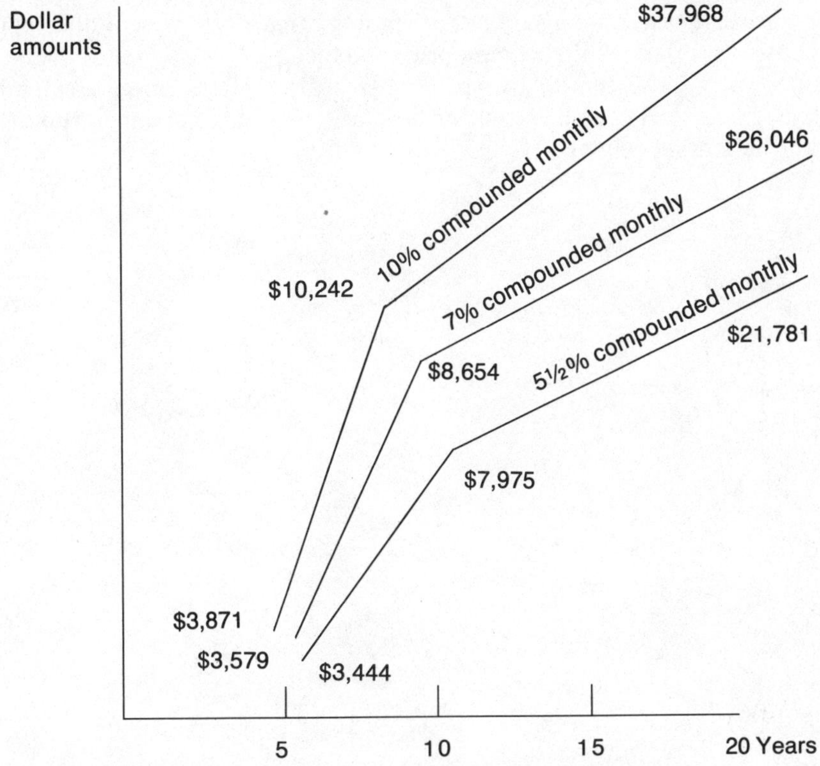

Dollar amounts

$37,968

$26,046

10% compounded monthly

$10,242

7% compounded monthly

$8,654

5½% compounded monthly

$21,781

$7,975

$3,871

$3,579

$3,444

5   10   15   20 Years

SOURCE: Donald R. Nichols, *The Income Investor* (Chicago: Longman, 1988), 18.

SUMMARY

Treasury notes and bonds are coupon-paying securities that give you a stated cash flow every six months until they mature, at which time they repay their $1,000 par value. New issues of notes and bonds are auctioned by the Federal Reserve at regular intervals, and broad public markets trade Treasuries from the day of issue to day of maturity.

Featuring maturities of two to thirty years, notes and bonds provide a longer income stream than T-bills, but they also have greater price fluctuation. If you sell a Treasury before maturity, you might suffer a capital loss or enjoy a capital gain as the result of price fluctuations. The degree to which prices fluctuate depends upon the coupon payment and length until maturity of specific securities and general changes in economywide rates of interest. As a useful rule of assessment, you should expect Treasuries with longer maturities and lower coupons to fluctuate more in price than Treasuries with short maturities and higher coupons.

Because prices change in public trading, Treasuries present different yields—the relationship between price and income—throughout the time you own them. Accordingly, specific Treasuries offer you greater and lesser inducements to buy, sell, or hold as your financial circumstances and the markets change.

4

Government Agency Securities

The term "government agency" has come to include a variety of enterprises affiliated directly or indirectly as instrumentalities of the U.S. government. Agencies come into being as expressions of national policy—that is, they are chartered to undertake operations that Congress deems in the national welfare. Accordingly, their debt securities carry a direct or implied warranty by the federal government.

If you read a list of governmental agencies that issue debt, you'd see that governmental agencies fall into several broad categories. First, agencies that support agriculture and farm lending comprise a large percentage of government agencies. Another substantial number are involved with mortgage lending (not including securities discussed in the next chapter). Agencies dealing with student loans and educational construction have evolved since the 1970s, and the very recent past has brought new agencies to support those already in existence.

ISSUANCE OF AGENCY SECURITIES

Excluding mortgage-backed securities discussed in the next chapter, federal agencies issue bills, notes, and bonds that are similar to conventional Treasury securities. Agency paper typically features short and intermediate maturities, often no longer than ten years, although a few distant maturities are available. Beyond these similarities, however, the only thing agency securities have in common with one another is that they differ.

The larger federal agencies normally raise capital through debt securities once a month. Unlike Treasury debt, however, agencies do not auction securities. Instead, they issue securities through selling groups consisting of primary dealers and other intermediaries that have demonstrated their ability to facilitate placement of agency securities through their own or customers' accounts.

Larger agencies usually publish each January a yearly calendar of monthly placements, and the agency's fiscal agent—who functions somewhat like a corporate treasurer—announces each month what amount and maturity of notes or bonds will be sold. The selling group spreads word among its customers and reports interest in the issue back to the fiscal agent. This must require quite a sales job, for the fiscal agent doesn't announce the coupon rates and price of the securities until after he or she has an indication of customer interest.

Agencies that are less frequent issuers of securities issue debt of varying maturities and coupon payments at intermittent schedules. Issuance procedures are substantially the same as for the major agencies. As a personal investor, you have two sources of information about new issues of agency debt: You can contact the agency's fiscal agent directly, or you can contact your broker. Again, full-service brokerage firms, which often are also primary dealers, and brokerages specializing in government securities provide your most comprehensive access to agency securities.

SECONDARY MARKETS FOR AGENCY SECURITIES

Securities of major federal agencies are broadly traded on secondary markets, and in many cases those markets are as fully liquid as markets for Treasury securities. In other cases, some specific issues may have fewer securities outstanding. Those specific issues may have more volatile markets as a result of their relatively small volume outstanding. When investigating agency securities for your portfolio, ask your broker about the relative size of the issue you're considering. He or she will be able to advise you if there is a specific reason why you should consider another issue.

Figure 4-1 indicates a few of the issuers, maturities, coupon payments, and other features from which to choose. Quotations for agency securities are presented in the same form as Treasury notes and bonds. In published quotations, "Rate" refers to coupon payments, which, as discussed in Chapter 3, are decimals you multiply by ten to determine a dollar amount. "Mat," representing the month and year of maturity, is quoted in calendar month and year. The varying issue schedules of agency securities dictate the specific day of maturity; ask your broker for the specific date. "Bid" and "Asked" refer to prices at which a dealer will buy and sell, respectively, the issue in question. Prices are, like Treasur-

Figure 4-1: QUOTATIONS OF AGENCY SECURITIES

GOVERNMENT & AGENCY ISSUES

Tuesday, September 5, 1989

Mid-afternoon Over-the-Counter quotations usually based on large transactions, sometimes $1 million or more. Hyphens in bid-and-asked represent 32nds; 101-01 means 101 1/32. a-Plus 1/64. b-Yield to call date. d-Minus 1/64.
Source: Bloomberg Financial Markets

FNMA Issues

Rate	Mat	Bid	Asked	Yld
12.10	10-89	100-09	100-12	7.72
12.75	10-89	100-08	100-13	8.00
9.85	11-89	100-05	100-09	7.99
11.80	11-89	100-18	100-22	7.59
16.00	11-89	101-23	101-27	6.83
11.30	12-89	100-21	100-23	8.30
6.50	12-89	99-11	99-14	8.55
11.45	1-90	100-28	100-31	8.41
11.05	2-90	100-31	101-02	8.46
17.00	2-90	103-27	103-31	8.28
8.65	3-90	99-26	100-02	8.52
9.55	3-90	106-02	106-12	8.56
7.35	4-90	99-07	99-11	8.48
10.30	5-90	101	101-04	8.52
11.15	5-90	101-19	101-23	8.45
9.85	7-90	100-31	101-02	8.49
10.00	9-90	101-07	101-13	8.52
10.1?	9-90	1?7	101-?	8.52

Rate	Mat	Bid	Asked	Yld
10.85	2-90	100-26	100-29	8.43
9.60	3-90	100-14	100-17	8.45
8.65	3-90	99-31	100-02	8.51
10.25	4-90	100-28	100-31	8.46
11.35	4-90	101-20	101-23	8.42
9.75	5-90	100-21	100-24	8.51
14.10	6-90	103-26	103-29	8.46
9.20	6-90	100-11	100-15	8.50
8.30	7-90	99-22	99-26	8.52
8.63	7-90	100	100-03	8.48
9.55	7-90	100-25	100-28	8.48
10.40	7-90	101-15	101-18	8.50
8.13	8-90	99-18	99-21	8.51
12.50	9-90	103-19	103-23	8.52
8.63	9-90	100	100-03	8.52
8.80	10-90	100-06	100-09	8.51
10.60	10-90	102-03	102-06	8.50
7.65	3-91	98-16	98-26	8.52
8.55		98	98-18	

Rate	Mat	Bid	Asked	Yld
8.45	12-90	99-24	99-28	8.54
7.63	2-91	98-21	98-26	8.52
9.90	3-91	100-20	100-30	8.07
8.55	5-91	99-19	99-29	8.59
7.75	6-91	98-19	98-25	8.51
7.60	6-91	98-06	98-16	8.52
5.60	8-91	94-19	94-29	8.55
8.00	8-91	98-25	99-03	8.52
9.45	2-92	100-13	100-23	8.61
9.50	2-92	100-17	100-27	8.53
?38		101	?1-28	

Rate	Mat	Bid	Asked	Yld
11.10	8-91	104-10	104-20	8.50
7.40	9-91	97-23	97-29	8.53
8.80	9-91	100-14	100-18	8.49
11.75	9-91	105-22	106	8.50
8.70	10-91	100-01	100-07	8.58
9.95	10-91	102-11	102-21	8.55
7.15	11-91	96-23	97-01	8.64
7.00	12-91	96-11	96-21	8.62
11.40	12-91	105-19	105-29	8.51
7.00	1-92	96-07	96-17	8.63
	2-9?		?05	8.5

Rate	Mat	Bid	Asked	Yld
?.55	12-9?	104-3?	?05-05	8.?0
8.65	2-98	99-27	100-05	8.62
9.15	4-98	103-06	103-12	8.58
8.70	6-99	100-24	100-30	8.55
8.45	7-99	99-08	99-14	8.53
8.55	8-99	99-23	99-29	8.56
12.35	12-13	114-08	114-18	8.22
12.65	3-14	115-08	115-18	8.43
0.00	7-14	12-19	12-29	8.42
10.35	12-15	118-28	119-06	8.51
8.20	3-16	96-16	96-26	8.50
8.95	2-18	104-03	104-09	8.55
8.10	8-19	95-09	95-15	8.52
0.00	10-19	8-19	8-28	8.21

Student Loan Marketing

Rate	Mat	Bid	Asked	Yld
12.85	9-89	100-01	100-04	5.04
13.15	9-89	100-01	100-04	5.31
10.90	2-90	101	101-03	8.50
9.45	6-90	100-16	100-23	8.53
6.95	8-90	98-16	98-19	8.51
7.90	9-90	99-09	99-13	8.51

Rate	Mat	Bid	Asked	Yld
9.35	12-90	100-28	101	8.51
10.90	12-90	102-21	102-27	8.53
8.30	1-91	99-15	99-21	8.56
9.10	1-91	100-14	100-24	8.50
9.30	1-91	100-28	101	8.51
9.60	1-91	101-08	101-13	8.49
7.10	2-91	97-29	98-03	8.50
7.65	2-91	98-17	98-27	8.50
11.88	2-91	104-12	104-18	8.50
7.75	3-91	98-19	98-29	8.51
10.00	3-91	101-30	102-04	8.50
7.35	4-91	98-02	98-08	8.51
9.65	4-91	101-17	101-23	8.49
7.88	5-91	98-23	98-29	8.56
8.50	5-91	99-25	99-31	8.51
9.25	5-91	100-31	101-05	8.50
8.30	6-91	99-14	99-20	8.52
8.60	6-91	99-30	100-04	8.51
7.50	7-91	97-30	98-08	8.52
8.15	7-91	99-08	99-12	8.51
7.20	8-91	97-11	97-21	8.51
8.60	8-91	100-01	100-05	8.51

Rate	Mat	Bid	Asked	Yld
9.60		99	100-02	?05
9.35	9-89	99-29	100-01	3.64
7.75	9-89	99-30	100-01	4.76
8.75	9-89	99-29	100-01	2.99
9.50	9-89	99-20	100-01	3.70
8.65	10-89	99-29	100	8.34
8.95	10-89	99-31	100-02	7.96
10.25	10-89	100-01	100-04	8.15
10.60	10-89	100-05	100-11	7.64
15.65	10-89	100-27	101-05	6.35
12.45	10-89	100-12	100-16	8.20
8.45	11-89	99-28	99-31	8.41
8.60	11-89	99-31	100-02	8.12
9.80	11-89	100-04	100-07	8.08
9.30	12-89	100-04	100-07	8.16
8.95	12-89	100-01	100-04	8.22
8.60	12-89	99-31	100-02	8.32
9.30	1-90	100-05	100-08	8.36
10.95	1-90	100-22	100-29	8.36
8.80	1-90	99-31	100-02	8.47
11.15	1-90	100-27	100-31	8.39
8.35	2-90	99-27	99-30	8.44
9.15	2-90	100-05	100-08	8.43

Rate	Mat	Bid	Asked	Yld
9.20	10-97	105-09	105-17	8.58
9.00	2-01	100-06	100-30	8.97
8.38	6-02	96-20	97-02	8.82
9.63	1-04	102-02	102-18	9.36
12.25	12-08	132-20	133-28	8.72
8.50	3-11	97-10	97-25	8.78

GNMA Issues

Rate	Mat	Bid	Asked	Bond Yld
8.00		92-17	92-21	9.18
8.50		94-23	94-27	9.37
9.00		97-03	97-07	9.53
9.50		99-05	99-09	9.74
10.00		101-09	101-13	9.93
10.50		103-07	103-11	10.15
11.00		105	105-04	10.39
11.50		106-24	106-28	10.63
12.00		108-19	108-23	10.85
12.50		109-17	109-23	11.19
13.00		110-30	111-04	11.46
13.50		111-08	111-14	11.90
14.00		111-18	111-24	12.33
15.00		111-22	111-26	13.29

ies, quoted in 32nds. "Yld" represents yield to maturity, the total dollar return, expressed in percent, that you receive from buying today and holding the security until it matures.

ADVANTAGES OF AGENCY SECURITIES

In general, the advantage of agency securities is that they customarily yield slightly more than Treasuries while offering high assurances against default. Carrying direct or implied backing by the U.S. government, agency paper is often regarded as a preferable investment because of generally higher yield. Agency securities of all types are widely held by financial institutions, for they meet "prudent man rules" that govern the portfolio selections of banks, pensions, and insurance companies.

Personal investors haven't traditionally been widespread holders of agency securities. One reason why is that institutional appetite for these securities is extensive, and financial institutions have substantial capital to purchase in quantity. As a result, it has been more efficient for primary dealers to concentrate on institutional buyers rather than on personal investors. For another reason, direct obligations of the Treasury have overshadowed agency securities. A third reason why personal investors traditionally haven't held agencies is the minimum purchase requirement. You can buy individual Treasury notes and bonds in minimums of one or five bonds, for an investment approximating $1,000 to $5,000; agency securities typically require $5,000 to $25,000 minimum investments.

On all three counts, however, circumstances are changing. Agency securities are among the fastest growing segments of government debt. Not only are existing agencies issuing more notes and bonds, but newly chartered agencies are offering billions of dollars in new securities. With higher numbers available, personal investors have more opportunity for access. In addition, brokerage firms have become more aware of advantages of agencies for personal investors and are making greater effort to inform them, with resulting increase in personal ownership. A larger number of full-service brokerages now make their own markets in agency securities from their inventories, which reduces minimum purchase requirements to more manageable sums for personal investors.

USES FOR AGENCY SECURITIES

Among personal investors, agency securities find a home in individual retirement accounts and other personal retirement plans. Higher yields and Treasury-grade quality make agencies suitable for long-term investment, which often is the strategy personal investors follow for their IRAs. Owners of small businesses and their pension managers are selecting agency securities for these same reasons. With broadened investor awareness and access, many parents gravitate to agency securities for **Uniform Gifts to Minors Accounts** (UGMA) opened on behalf of children.

More recently, though, astute personal investors, particularly those who normally buy Treasury securities, have been selecting agency paper for personal portfolios outside IRAs and UGMAs. Like direct obligations of Uncle Sam, agencies offer predictable, assured coupon income and an ample selection of maturities. That combination of features makes them suitable for investors in all stages of life and investment circumstances. Investors' heightened familiarity with agencies and newly widened market access to them also have helped to promote their place in personal portfolios, which Section II will cover more thoroughly.

THREE MAJOR AGENCIES AND THEIR SECURITIES

As measured by the size of their debt, frequency of issuance, and general presence in financial media and markets, three federal agencies provide the most commonly traded securities.

The Federal National Mortgage Association: **Fannie Mae,** as it's commonly called, is a government sponsored corporation founded in 1938 to support the secondary market for residential mortgages. During the 1960s Fannie became a publicly held corporation with stock traded on the New York Stock Exchange, where it now ranks as the nation's third largest corporation.

For purposes of this chapter, Fannie's chief securities are its notes and bonds, issued monthly through fiscal agents. Fannie typically offers one, two, or three new issues each month. Maturities have ranged between one and ten years, varying as Fannie seeks to match the maturities of its securities with the maturities of mortgages it purchases. More recently, Fannie has concentrated on maturities of four, five, and eight years. Its securities mature on the tenth day of the month during the indicated year, and interest is fully taxable.

As a review of Figure 4-1 indicates, maturities, coupons, and other features of Fannie Mae securities on secondary markets vary considerably. Maturities range from June of 1989 through October of 2019. Coupon payments range from $170 to zero coupon issues, which pay no semiannual interest. These will be discussed in a later chapter.

Federal Home Loan Bank Board: Congress established the FHLB in 1932 after massive bank and S&L failures during the Great Depression. The FHLB acts somewhat like the Federal Reserve in that it fulfills the central banking function for thrift institutions. There are 12 Federal Home Loan Banks, owned by their member thrifts. They borrow money by selling bonds that are the collective obligation of the FHLB. The total of FHLB's outstanding debt cannot exceed 12 times the net worth of the 12 Federal Home Loan Banks.

As was the case with Fannie Mae, the FHLB issues new notes and bonds monthly, typically two to four separate issues with maturities ranging from two to ten years, although longer maturities are available.

Its securities mature on the 25th day of the issue month during the established year or maturity. Interest is subject to federal tax but exempted from state and local taxes.

FHLB notes and bonds in secondary markets carry a wide selection of coupon payments but a narrow set of maturities. The current dilemma confronting FHLB is, of course, the unsettled situation with the savings and loan industry. Congress and the Bush administration appear to be committed to closing the financial black hole of the thrift industry, and their commitment to do so has reinforced some investors' confidence in agency securities pertaining to that industry. Other investors feel that the deep extent of the thrift industry's problems might exceed any reasonable commitment to resolve them with federal guarantees.

Federal Farm Credit System: The FCS was established in 1971 to provide credit to farmers and farm-related businesses. The system comprises 37 member banks in 12 districts, each of which contains a Federal Land Bank, a Federal Intermediate Credit Bank, and a Bank for Cooperatives to execute the policies of the FCS. Interest and principal are the obligation of the 37 member banks. Several types of securities emerge from this consortium.

The Federal Farm Credit Banks Funding Corporation issues Consolidated Systemwide Notes and Bonds approximately monthly. The notes typically have maturities of six months, nine months, and one year and are available in increments of $50,000. The bonds carry maturities of more than one year and are issued in increments of $5,000. The date of maturity is typically the first week or third week of the month during the indicated year. Interest is federally taxable and untaxed by state and local governments.

Federal Intermediate Credit Banks and Federal Land Banks also issue debt securities. For the most part, however, their financing needs are encompassed within issues of the systemwide placements. Where securities from these issuers exist separately, maturities range from one to ten years and denominations range from $1,000 to $100,000. Interest is federally taxable and municipally untaxable.

To large extent, the debt of farm-related agencies creates suspicions similar to those plaguing the thrift-related agencies. The 37 member banks that back the interest and principal of FCBs represent a broad but uneven base of capital assurances. The implicit backing of the U.S. Treasury for these securities has not been tested, but neither, as of 1989, has Congress enacted legislation to put the power of the Treasury behind the system's debt, as it has with some of the debt of thrift-related agencies.

OTHER AGENCY SECURITIES

The "Big Three" federal agencies provide the most readily available source of agency securities for the personal or small business investor, but they are by no means the only source of agency paper. The smaller agencies likewise offer attractive securities, but bear in mind a few special considerations while you're evaluating them. First, the issue schedules for the minor agencies are less constant, meaning a steady stream of them does not come to market. Second, their dollar volume varies substantially from issue to issue, meaning their secondary markets are thinner than Treasuries or other agency paper. Third, institutional investors often soak up the minor agency paper, leaving less of it for personal investors.

The U.S. Postal Service: The Post Office Department was reorganized as an independent entity in 1971 under legislation that authorizes it to issue up to $10 billion in debt. The Postal Service can petition the Treasury to guarantee interest and principal, and the Secretary of the Treasury can agree to provide the guarantee if the Secretary deems the national interest served by the guarantee. The Postal Service's initial offering of bonds maturing in 1997 does not carry this guarantee, but financial markets widely assume the guarantee would be there if needed. Interest from this and future Postal Service issues is federally taxable and municipally untaxed.

Tennessee Valley Authority: The TVA and its peer agency, the Chattanooga Valley Authority, are authorized by Congress to promote economic development in their respective localities. Bonds issued by these agencies are backed by revenues from projects constructed with funds from the bond offering. Interest is federally taxed but exempted from state and local taxation.

Student Loan Marketing Association: Sallie Mae is a government-sponsored private corporation founded in 1972 to provide liquidity to lenders engaged in the Guaranteed Student Loan Program and the Health Education Assistance Loan Program. Those lenders own the stock of Sallie Mae. Sallie purchases student loans from the issuing institutions, often commercial banks, and provides financing to state lending agencies.

Most of Sallie's securities are floating rate notes maturing in six months. The interest rate is indexed to the average rate paid at auction of six-month T-bills, is reset each week, and is paid only at maturity. Sallie

51

also offers fixed-rate, longer-term issues at irregular intervals with a variety of coupon payments and maturities. Sallies traded on secondary markets carry maturities out to 2022 and feature a few zero coupon bonds that do not make current interest payments.

NEW FEDERAL AGENCIES

Some new agencies have come into being to assist—some might say "bail out"—existing agencies. The charter of newer agencies and the recency of their arrival upon financial markets discomfort some investors, who are awaiting legal ruling and market acceptance before they invest in securities new agencies offer. As of late 1989, some of these agencies had issued a substantial dollar volume of debt, whereas others had not. Some carried or were stated as carrying explicit Treasury assurances, and others left that question unsatisfactorily unanswered. They bear watching for their future investment possibilities and investment problems.

Financing Corporation: FICO was established in 1987 to assist the Federal Savings and Loan Insurance Corporation, the thrift industry counterpart of the Federal Deposit Insurance Corporation for commercial banks. FICO's initial debt offering was a multi-billion-dollar placement of zero coupon securities, which are traded in secondary markets maintained by their underwriters. Also, coupon-bearing FICO bonds with lengthy maturities are traded in broad public markets.

Resolution Trust Corporation: Fully operational in 1989, RTC is tasked to close bankrupt thrifts and disperse their assets and accounts. The billions of dollars needed for this purpose will come from bonds that bear the full faith and credit of Uncle Sam.

College Construction Loan Insurance Association: Connie Lee was established in 1987 to guarantee loans for the building of colleges. It is wholly owned by the Department of Education and by Sallie Mae.

Financial Assistance Corporation: FAC was established in 1988 to assist the Farm Credit System. Its debt will be explicitly guaranteed by the U.S. government, and the Treasury will make half of its interest payments.

Federal Agricultural Mortgage Corporation: Established in 1988, "Farmer Mac" is intended to provide a secondary market for farm mortgages as another part of the effort to assist the Farm Credit System.

BONDS OF NONFEDERAL AGENCIES

Investors also extend the implied umbrella of Uncle Sam to cover the debt of international lenders that are not officially U.S. government instrumentalities. Two such organizations, The World Bank and the Inter-American Development Bank (IADB), have been frequent issuers of bonds. The World Bank (formally, the International Bank of Reconstruction and Development) and the IADB finance construction, commercial, educational, and infrastructure projects of Central and South America and third world nations. The United States has been a prominent force in the development and operation of both lenders and has contributed substantial capital to their operations.

Bonds of these international lenders are introduced through underwriters in a manner more akin to corporate or municipal bonds, not through the Federal Reserve and primary dealers—although, of course, many underwriters will also be primary dealers in Treasury and agency securities. Many of their issues are traded in active secondary markets with varying coupon rates and maturities. Underwriters also maintain secondary markets.

Uncle Sam's implied or outright guarantees also extend to selected corporate and municipal bonds issued by American borrowers. For example, some shipping and transportation company debentures carry pledges from Uncle Sam to make good on interest and principal if the corporate issuer defaults. Relatedly, bonds from U.S. protectorates—notably Guam and the Virgin Islands—are said to enjoy implicit default guarantees, as are municipal bonds issued by the District of Columbia. A full-service brokerage firm or a firm specializing in bonds are your best sources of information and access for these securities.

On occasion, the Treasury Department pledges outright to back the sovereign debt of other countries. In 1988, for example, the State of Israel floated a series of U.S. dollar-denominated bonds that it called Government Trusts. Ninety percent of the issue was supported by a direct pledge of interest and principal from the U.S. Treasury. This controversial practice of the U.S. pledging the debt of foreign nations might continue. If it does, you might be able to secure the higher yields that dollar-denominated foreign bonds often provide while receiving the backing of the U.S. Treasury.

SUMMARY

Federal agency securities of many types can extend your portfolio of government bonds to include securities with implicit or outright guarantees against default from the Treasury. You should always remember, however, that default assurances are, in many respects, an assumption on the part of financial markets. Where the direct pledge is not a matter expressed in the covenant of the securities or the charter of the issuing agency, it is merely assumed.

More generally, you should remember that agency paper is not as uniform in its characteristics as direct Treasury obligations. The size of new and existing agency securities, the liquidity of their secondary markets, and related features of these securities make them singular investment studies. These circumstances aside, however, agency securities constitute a large and growing market for your investment dollars, and certainly they represent a market in which many investors eagerly participate.

5

Mortgage-Backed Securities

In 1968, the Government National Mortgage Association, abbreviated GNMA and called **Ginnie Mae,** was spun off from the Federal National Mortgage Association to become a corporate instrumentality of the Department of Housing and Urban Development. Ginnie Mae was empowered by the Housing and Urban Renewal Act of 1968 to guarantee interest and principal upon pools of mortgages that it had purchased from private lenders and to reissue its own debt based upon these mortgages. The agency lent its name to the resulting debt, and one of the nation's most popular securities was born in 1970—a mortgage-backed security called a Ginnie Mae pass-through.

Mortgage-backed pass-throughs function as their name implies. Ginnie Mae purchases mortgages insured or guaranteed by other governmental agencies, normally the Federal Housing Administration or the Veterans Administration but occasionally the Farmers Home Loan Administration. Ginnie bundles these mortgages together and resells them to public investors. The original borrowers make monthly payments to their original lenders, who forward those payments, minus a processing fee, to the agency. Ginnie passes those payments through to investors who purchased the securities.

Interest and principal paid by Ginnie pass-throughs are the obligation of homeowners who originally took out mortgages contained within the pass-throughs. However, the agency pledges to make good on interest and principal if the mortgage holder defaults. This pledge places Ginnie Mae pass-throughs on a plane with obligations of the U.S. government. Interest payments are taxed federally and by most states. Ginnie's pass-throughs typically yield more than Treasury notes or bonds of similar maturities. They also provide monthly cash flow rather than semiannual payments. The result is essentially a U.S. government security that customarily outyields Treasuries and pays you monthly.

USES OF GINNIE MAES

Savings and loan associations have been the largest buyers of Ginnie Maes, for the underlying mortgages are a supplement to mortgage income from local lending. Insurance companies and small business pension funds also hold them for their constant income. Even so, personal investors represent a growing number of purchasers, buying Ginnies through full-service brokerage firms and investment companies that specialize in government or mortgage securities. (Most personal investors invest in Ginnie Mae funds offered by brokerages and mutual funds that buy Ginnie Maes and reoffer them to the public for an investment of $2,000 to $5,000. These are discussed in a later chapter.)

Personal investors customarily have held them in tax-deferred accounts such as IRAs and Keoghs. Their often higher yields relative to Treasuries and accompanying federal guarantees have made them ideal for this use. Their monthly payments also produce more frequent income for compounding, a primary advantage for retirement anticipation accounts. Retired persons who need current income from their portfolios and investors whose strategies involve reinvestment of income also hold Ginnie Maes outside tax-deferred accounts. These investors are attracted by Ginnie's monthly payments.

TYPES OF GINNIE MAE POOLS

Ginnie Mae pass-throughs are customarily called pools, a term that derives from the practice of pooling mortgages with similar characteristics for resale. Each pool is of a specified size (original face amount), bears a coupon slightly below the interest rate of mortgages it contains, and achieves a stated—albeit undependable—maturity coincident with mortgage maturities in the pool. Each pool is identified by a number established by GNMA when it is issued. Ginnie's pools are, to use the term loosely, "bonds" with characteristics formed by their mortgages. Ginnie Mae sponsors five types of pools.

GNMA I—30-Year: The original pass-through security is still the most prevalent, with some $200 billion outstanding. "Ginnie Ones" are comprised of at least twelve 30-year mortgages totaling at least $1 million in face value.

56

GNMA II—30-Year: "Ginnie Twos" are similar to Ginnie Ones, except that not all mortgages in the pool have the same interest rate. All mortgages in Ginnie Twos had 30-year maturities when originally issued.

GNMA—15-Year: "Midgets," as these pools are known, contain mortgages with an original maturity of 15, rather than 30, years.

Graduated Payment Mortgage Pools: GPMs are mortgages with interest rates that are lower during the early years of repayment and increase over time. This arrangement permits homeowners to start mortgage indebtedness with a lower interest rate, with later increases to be met from increases in personal income. As home mortgage rates fell below double digits, graduated payment mortgages became less popular, and the number of GPM pools diminished.

Mobile Home Pools: Mortgages within this type of pool are loans to owners of mobile homes, and they carry maturities of 12 to 20 years. Interest rates on these mortgages, hence on their pools, often are higher than mortgages on conventional residences.

SPECIAL CHARACTERISTICS OF GINNIE MAES

As an investor considering Ginnies, you have to be aware of two special characteristics of these securities.

First, monthly checks from Ginnies include payments of interest and principal. Other bond-type securities pay semiannual interest but repay principal only at maturity. Ginnies simply pass through to you the payments from mortgage holders, and mortgage payments include an amortization of loan principal as well as interest. In short, Ginnies are self-liquidating securities, just like the mortgages they contain. Further, as mortgages within the pool are paid off, a greater portion of the pool's monthly income will include payments of principal.

Second, maturity is an approximate concept with Ginnies, not a covenant as pertains to Treasury and agency securities. A 30-year Treasury bond produces its final interest payment and repays principal on a specific date. Not so with Ginnies, again, because mortgages underlie them. Homeowners often pay off a mortgage before it comes due, perhaps because they move or because they refinance when interest rates fall. When this happens, Ginnies lose that mortgage from the pool.

It's important to reemphasize these twin characteristics and their relation to one another. Under normal circumstances—that is, given relatively steady levels of mortgage interest rates—Ginnies' monthly payments include interest and principal, not just interest. There is no absolute way to determine beforehand how much of your monthly income will be interest and how much will be principal. You do know, however, that as homeowners prepay their mortgages, a greater portion of your monthly payments will be return of principal. Additionally, accelerated prepayments result in your pool "maturing" before its stated date.

MORTGAGE PREPAYMENTS: FHA, PSA, AND CPR

Investors who buy Treasury and agency paper generally prefer predictability and dependability in their investments. To an absolute degree, Ginnie Mae pass-throughs provide neither. Every investor faces the possibility that mortgages will be retired early and that principal payments will merely give them their own money back. However, mortgage lenders, federal agencies, and brokerage institutions have monitored payment histories for mortgages and codified them into tools for estimating the life of mortgage-backed securities. They can be useful to you.

One formerly popular set of mortgage data that you may still encounter is FHA experience—Federal Housing Administration averages showing percentages of insured mortgages outstanding each year of the 30-year conventional term. Mortgages with prepayments paralleling FHA data are said to be "paying off at 100 percent of FHA experience" or "at FHA speed." Mortgages estimated to pay off at "zero FHA experience" or "zero speed" should make only scheduled payments of interest and principal without prepayments. Mortgages paying off principal slower than FHA experience might, for example, be said to pay "at 85 percent of speed," and mortgages being rapidly prepaid might be announced as paying "at 200 percent of FHA experience."

Although you might still see FHA experience referred to in brokerage literature or advertisements for Ginnie Mae funds, it is no longer a widely used standard. FHA speed falls short as a measure of mortgage prepayments, because it is based on lengthy historical information, does not distinguish among varying coupon rates, and changes each year over the life of a mortgage. The need for a more accurate and contemporary standard became obvious, and the mortgage-backed securities industry developed PSAs and CPRs in response.

PSA stands for Public Securities Association, which evaluated characteristics of mortgage prepayments and developed a set of simplified assumptions based on its research. The model it developed is defined by a monthly series of annual prepayment rates, simply called PSAs. The PSA standard is a straight-line method of assessing mortgage prepayments. The PSA standard specifies that .2 percent (or 2.4 percent on an

Figure 5-1: HOW GINNIES PAY DOWN

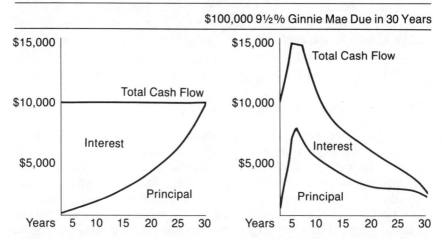

$100,000 9½% Ginnie Mae Due in 30 Years

At 0% FHA Speed. . . .Slight increase in total cash flow occurs as the .50% mortgage servicing fee declines. Notice how share of total cash flow represented by principal increases over time.

At 100% FHA Speed. . . .Principal payments, including unscheduled prepayments are a larger share of cash flow but total cash flow declines as mortgage balance shrinks.

Courtesy Gabriele, Hueglin & Cashman.

annualized basis) of outstanding mortgages are retired in their first month. The PSA measure increases by .2 percent per month until the 30th month of the mortgage, at which time PSA rises to 6 percent for the remaining life of the mortgage.

Accordingly, mortgages prepaying "at PSA speed" parallel the Public Securities Association findings. Mortgages "at 200 percent PSA" demonstrate a prepayment rate of twice the PSA standard—.4 percent for the first month, increasing in a straight line up to 12 percent in the 30th month, and remaining at 12 percent thereafter. Mortgages paying "below PSA"—say, "50 percent of PSA"—are not being retired as fast as PSA averages, half the rate in this case.

PSA has become one of the most widely used measures of estimating mortgage prepayments, but CPR, the Constant Prepayment Rate, is one of the most accurate. CPRs annualize monthly mortgage prepayments and express them as a percentage of outstanding balances of mortgages. For example, if you started the month with a mortgage pool of $1 million and received $5,000 in prepayments the first month, you would have a CPR of 6 percent ($5,000 ÷ $1 million × 12 = .06 or 6 percent).

A conscientious brokerage firm will prepare estimates of a pool's likely relationship to PSA or CPR experience to guide your investment decision. However, mortgage experience can be erratic even with stable economic circumstances, and it will change with economic conditions. FHA's historical averages and a brokerage's good faith estimate based upon them are not and cannot be ironclad assurances about your specific investment.

HALF LIFE AND FACTORS

In a further effort to quantify the uncertain longevity of Ginnie Maes, mortgage markets developed the concept of "half life." Half life is the estimated time it will take for a pool to repay half of its principal. Half life shortens as estimated speed accelerates. This relationship and its converse—half life extending as speed decelerates—are logical results, given the logic of mortgage prepayments. If a mortgage pool is expected to pay principal in excess of experience, it will return a greater portion of principal earlier in its stream of payments. The reverse applies if prepayment experience is expected to be less than norms.

You can trace the principal amount outstanding after in a Ginnie Mae pool. Each month, The American Banker-Bond Buyer publishes a *Factor Book,* a page of which is reproduced in Figure 5-2 for a Ginnie I pool. The information in Figure 5-2 includes such items as pool number, mortgage banker who issued and services this pool, and type of pool (single family or multi-family housing project). The columns of attraction are "Factor," "Original Balance," and "7/89 Balance" (outstanding balance reported August 1989).

Factor measures the percentage of a pool's original principal balance still outstanding. Factors range between zero (no original outstanding) and 1 (all original principal outstanding). Note the final pool in the figure, Pool Number 009281X. This pool has a factor of .54363891, indicating 54.36 + percent of the original face amount of mortgages in this pool was outstanding during the period the *Factor Book* covers. If you multiply the original face amount of this pool by its current factor, you derive its present principal balance. Figure 5-2 shows this to be the case ($1,004,829.41 × .54363891 = $546,264.37). If you had purchased a $25,000 denomination in Pool 009281X, its principal amount would have been $13,590.97 on the last day of August ($25,000 × .54363891 = $13,590.97).

As the pool ages, factors decrease, reflecting normal, scheduled payments of principal. As mortgage holders make unscheduled payments of principal, factors also decrease. By following the *Factor Book* you can

Figure 5-2: PAGE FROM GINNIE MAE FACTOR BOOK

GNMA MORTGAGE-BACKED SECURITIES–GNMA I PROGRAM

PAGE 90   AUG /89

POOL NO	FACTOR	ISSUER NO	ISSUER	POOL TYPE	ORIGINAL BALANCE	7/89 BALANCE	INTEREST RATE	ISSUE DATE	MATURITY DATE
009188X	.33776743	1418	BANC ONE MORTGAGE CORPORATION, AN INDI	SF	2,365,025.08	798,828.45	8.500	03/01/76	02/15/06
009189X	.38657066	1595	LOMAS MORTGAGE USA,INC	SF	2,011,976.15	777,770.94	8.250	06/01/76	05/15/06
009190X	.28953529	1595	LOMAS MORTGAGE USA,INC	SF	3,021,444.22	874,814.72	8.250	04/01/76	03/15/06
009191X	.19714970	1595	LOMAS MORTGAGE USA,INC	SF	2,017,468.04	397,743.21	8.500	04/01/76	03/15/06
009192X	.29061537	1595	LOMAS MORTGAGE USA,INC	SF	1,613,899.55	469,024.01	8.250	07/01/76	06/15/06
009193X	.46544129	3052	NCNB MORTGAGE CORPORATION	SF	1,044,404.38	486,108.92	8.500	03/01/76	03/15/06
009194X	.28118144	1446	CALIFORNIA MORTGAGE SERVICE	SF	3,010,231.84	846,421.31	8.250	04/01/76	04/15/06
009195X	.28460550	1446	CALIFORNIA MORTGAGE SERVICE	SF	3,017,523.82	858,803.89	8.250	05/01/76	04/15/06
009196X	.21120047	1446	CALIFORNIA MORTGAGE SERVICE	SF	3,011,304.84	635,989.00	8.250	04/01/76	04/15/06
009197X	.01059860	1933	EQUITABLE CREDIT & DISCOUNT CO	MH	503,339.99	5,334.70	9.500	04/01/76	03/15/91
009__X	.0940?	1645	...NATION MORT...E COMP...	SF	1,5__,969.	453,8__.49	9.250	04/01/__	03/1__
009260X	.1725?56	...	STAN...D FE...AL ...INGS ...NK	SF	__001.37	__845.16	8.__	04/__	__15/__
009261X	.25072989	1697	BRIGHT MORTGAGE COMPANY	SF	1,494,070.28	374,608.07	8.500	05/01/76	02/15/06
009262X	.32250920	3277	CHARTER BANK FOR SAVINGS	SF	1,123,772.64	362,427.01	8.250	04/01/76	04/15/06
009263X	.38670356	1615	MIDLAND MORTGAGE CO	SF	4,014,220.95	1,480,057.54	8.250	04/01/76	03/15/06
009264X	.28674439	1742	WEYERHAEUSER MORTGAGE COMPANY	SF	8,015,466.59	2,298,390.04	8.250	06/01/76	05/15/06
009265X	.20806423	1742	WEYERHAEUSER MORTGAGE COMPANY	SF	1,014,214.96	623,821.30	8.000	04/01/76	05/15/06
009266X	.27311822	1737	WATERFIELD MORTGAGE COMPANY, INC	SF	1,014,985.45	277,211.02	8.250	04/01/76	02/15/06
009267X	.25571556	1422	BANK OF AMERICA NT & SA, REAL ESTATE L	SF	4,257,130.62	1,088,614.56	8.250	04/01/76	04/15/06
009268X	.30641627	1739	WESTERN MORTGAGE LOAN CORPORATION	SF	1,021,682.99	313,060.29	8.250	04/01/76	04/15/06
009269X	.40804860	2538	INDEPENDENCE ONE MORTGAGE CORPORATION	SF	1,519,824.42	620,162.22	8.500	03/01/76	03/15/06
009270X	.48355255	2538	INDEPENDENCE ONE MORTGAGE CORPORATION	SF	3,507,711.38	1,696,162.79	8.250	04/01/76	03/15/06
009271X	.28539548	9035	GMNA/THE NEW YORK GUARDIAN MTGE CORP 1	SF	10,019,150.85	2,859,420.41	8.250	04/01/76	03/15/06
009272X	.32771198	9035	GMNA/THE NEW YORK GUARDIAN MTGE CORP 1	SF	8,014,240.92	2,626,362.77	8.250	05/01/76	02/15/06
009273X	.30906631	1985	STANDARD FEDERAL SAVINGS BANK	SF	2,031,492.41	627,865.87	8.250	04/01/76	02/15/06
009274X	.39474286	1985	STANDARD FEDERAL SAVINGS BANK	SF	2,006,001.12	791,854.62	8.250	04/01/76	03/15/06
009275X	.58715252	2180	CHEVY CHASE SAVINGS BANK	SF	1,027,352.69	603,212.72	7.500	03/01/76	06/15/05
009276X	.57928396	2036	BANNER BANC SAVINGS ASSOCIATION	SF	1,532,484.13	887,743.47	8.250	05/01/76	05/15/06
009277X	.38678495	2813	CENLAR FEDERAL SAVINGS BANK	SF	15,152,560.32	5,860,782.24	8.250	05/01/76	05/15/06
009278X	.38581885	1628	FLEET MORTGAGE CORPORATION	SF	1,037,302.79	400,210.97	8.000	03/01/76	02/15/06
009279X	.51449374	1460	COLONIAL MORTGAGE COMPANY	SF	1,104,191.28	568,099.50	8.250	04/01/76	04/15/06
009280X	.38486280	2813	CENLAR FEDERAL SAVINGS BANK	SF	1,061,557.79	408,554.10	8.500	04/01/76	04/15/06
009281X	.54363891	1403	FLEET REAL ESTATE FUNDING CORP	SF	1,004,829.41	546,264.37	8.250	04/01/76	03/15/06

Figure 5-3:   PRICE QUOTATION FOR GINNIE MAES

GOVERNMENT AGENCY ISSUES

GNMA Issues

Rate	Mat	Bid	Asked	Yld
8.00		87-08	87-12	10.04
8.50		89-31	90-03	10.13
9.00		92-22	92-26	10.23
9.50		95-06	95-10	10.36
10.00		97-26	97-30	10.47
10.50		100-11	100-15	10.59
11.00		102-17	102-21	10.76
11.50		104-13	104-17	10.98
12.00		106	106-04	11.24
12.50		107-18	107-24	11.48
13.00		108-30	109-04	11.77
13.50		109-30	110-04	12.10
14.00		110-12	110-16	12.53
15.00		111	111-04	12.02

monitor principal, half life, and the relationship of your pool to FHA experience. (You can subscribe to the *Factor Book* by contacting The American Banker-Bond Buyer at (800) 322-0047. The cost is $245 per month for Ginnie I pools and $85 per month for Ginnie II pools. Factor books for other mortgage-backed securities are also available.)

PRICING A GINNIE MAE POOL

Figure 5-3, quoted from the *Wall Street Journal,* suggests that Ginnie Maes are priced as other Treasury and agency securities. This suggestion is misleading. Suppose you want to invest in a $100,000 denomination of Ginnie Maes. When you read a quotation of 87^{12}/$_{32}$, you mistakenly expect to pay $87,375. If the quote reads 111^{4}/$_{32}$, you mistakenly conclude price to be $111,125. The quotations have misled you because a $100,000 denomination of Ginnie Maes may not have $100,000 in outstanding mortgages. To determine purchase price, you first must determine the outstanding balance of the mortgages in the pool. That balance is the loose equivalent of par value for Ginnie Maes, and you find it by multiplying the face amount of your intended purchase by the pool's factor.

Let's illustrate this point by starting with a pool that does contain its full outstanding balance in mortgages. Suppose you were considering investing in a Ginnie Mae pool that was one month old. As you would expect, given its newness, the full amount of principal was still outstanding, and the pool had a factor of 1. The pool was priced at 100 percent of par, the outstanding mortgage balance. The following illustration is based on denominations of $100,000, although you can derive smaller investments as well.

The first step is to determine how much mortgage principal underlies that denomination of $100,000 by multiplying denomination by factor. In this case, the factor is 1, so what you see is what you get: $100,000 × 1 = $100,000. You buy $100,000 outstanding balance of mortgages for your investment. The second step is to multiply the outstanding balance by price. Again, your price is 100, or 100 percent of par. One hundred percent of $100,000 is $100,000. That is your investment cost.

Suppose the pool had a factor of .8, indicating 80 percent of the original balance was outstanding. The price remains 100 percent of par. Again, determine the outstanding balance of mortgages in the pool. In this case, $100,000 × .8 = $80,000 in mortgages outstanding. Price is 100 percent of that amount, so the investment cost is $80,000.

Let's alter the example further. Suppose the factor remains .8, but the price is 90 percent of par, or 90 percent of the value of the outstanding mortgages. Cost would be $72,000. The calculation is $100,000 × .8 × .90 = $72,000.

Finally, consider pools with prices above 100. Suppose the factor remains .8, but price is 105 percent of par. Actual cost for denominations of $100,000 is $100,000 × .8 × 1.05 = $84,000.

WHAT HAVE YOU BOUGHT?

Repayment of Principal

When you paid 100 percent of par, your actual cost was $100,000 or $80,000, respectively. You purchased $100,000 or $80,000, respectively, worth of mortgages. If you hold this pool for its entire life, you will receive all your principal back.

When the price was 90 and the factor was .8, you paid $72,000. You purchased $80,000 worth of mortgages for $72,000. Your price was less than the balance of mortgages in the pool. You bought this Ginnie at a discount. If you hold this pool its entire life, you will receive $8,000 in payments of principal beyond your purchase price.

When the price was 105 and the factor was .8, you paid $84,000 for a pool with an outstanding mortgage balance of $80,000. Your price was more than the balance of mortgages in the pool. You bought this Ginnie at a premium. If you hold this pool its entire life, you will receive $4,000 less in principal than you paid.

We will see why these pools were priced at discounts and premiums in a moment. For now, let's test your knowledge of Ginnie Maes with a question: When will you receive these payments of principal? Answer: Along with payments of interest as mortgage owners make their payments.

A second question to test your understanding of FHA experience: At what years during the time you hold the pool will you receive the largest payments of principal? Answer: You don't know for certain, as interest payments can be irregular.

However, you can estimate relative payments of principal by comparing the pool to its expected relationship to PSA or CPR speed. If the pool is paying ahead of speed, you will receive a greater portion of principal early; if it is paying less than speed, greater portions of principal will be returned to you in later years. However, it is important to remember that payments of principal vary. A pool may continue for many years with small payments of scheduled or unscheduled payments of principal and then deliver a single or a series of larger principal payments.

Interest Payments

The income stream from a Ginnie Mae includes payments of interest. Let's assume that the pool we have been examining has a coupon rate of 9.5 percent, or interest payments of $95 per $1,000 of par value. Again, par refers to the pool's outstanding mortgage balance. Therefore, if you buy a pool at par of $100,000, you cannot expect to receive a consistent $9,500 per year in interest payments. The amount of interest you receive among your monthly payments will vary as mortgages are repaid, both scheduled and unscheduled payments. Interest may constitute a large percentage of monthly payments for a time, and then decrease as mortgages are retired on schedule or paid ahead of schedule.

Prepayment experience has a bearing on interest payments, too. With relatively less principal being paid, interest will constitute a larger portion of your monthly income stream. As prepayments of principal are accelerated, interest payments decline as a relative percentage of monthly income.

Cash Flow

Because of irregular payments of principal and interest and the uncertain life of mortgage pools, normal yield calculations don't always apply to

Ginnie Maes. That is, you can't calculate current yield and yield to maturity as if they were dependable, predictable values, as they will be with conventional bonds. Instead, Ginnie Mae investors generally look at the estimated cash flow.

Estimated cash flow is a computation of the pool's monthly interest and principal payments that takes prepayment speed into account. It gives you an approximate idea of the dollar amount of your monthly income at varying estimates of speed. The faster the estimated speed, the faster the principal will be repaid and the higher the cash flow will be. The converse is true of lower estimated speeds.

Cash flow is a significant concept with Ginnie Maes because it enables you to make investment decisions based upon an estimated basis of payments. Although admittedly only an estimate that can change with the pool's prepayments of principal, cash flow enables you to gauge the capital you will have available for an immediate purpose.

To understand the advantage of cash flow that includes a return of principal, you need to step aside from a conventional mentality of fixed-income investing. Suppose you were a business manager who faces a series of near-term pension payments or a retired investor who needs income for current expenses. You would have immediate needs for a return of principal as well as interest. The return of principal that Ginnie Maes provide enables you to meet your own payment obligations with principal. Were you to depend upon conventional income securities, you would have to sell them or wait until they mature before you could use principal to meet your obligations.

Further, suppose you want to reinvest an income stream rather than consume it. Even though a Ginnie Mae's cash flow is not assured or consistent, it does give you the opportunity to make subsequent investments monthly rather than quarterly or semiannually. When monthly payments include a return of principal, you can reinvest principal as well as interest. With conventional securities, you can reinvest only interest until the security is sold or matures, at which time you can reinvest principal.

VARIABLES AFFECTING PRICE, FACTOR, MATURITY, AND CASH FLOW

Overall, the single greatest variable affecting the features and performance of your pool will be changes in mortgage interest rates or changes in the general level of economywide interest rates. A newly issued pool will contain new mortgages with nearly identical interest rates. Its price will probably be at par, and its coupon payments will reflect the current interest rates on mortgages and general economywide rates of interest.

Its factor likely will be 1, indicating a full balance of outstanding mortgages. Now let's apply interest rate scenarios to this situation.

Stable Interest Rate Scenario

If interest rates remain relatively constant, a newly issued pool will perform predictably. Price will remain relatively constant. The factor will hover around 1 until normal principal payments and unscheduled—but not unexpected—prepayments reduce the factor. Cash flow will parallel the estimated amortization of interest and principal. The half life and maturity of your pool likewise will replicate initial estimates. In short, stable interest rates mean that nothing substantial happens to alter the characteristics and performance of your pool.

Rising Interest Rate Scenario

In secondary markets, market price varies inversely with changes in mortgage rates and general interest rates. If mortgage rates or the general level of interest rates rise, the price of your pool will fall, reflecting the lower interest rate your pool pays in relation to other rates. A capital loss will be likely. However, rising interest rates discourage mortgage owners from refinancing. Therefore, factor likely will remain constant, falling only with normal, scheduled payments of principal—falling as the pool ages, in other words. Cash flow will parallel your original estimates of interest and principal payments. Half life and maturity will again replicate initial estimates. In sum, rising rates produce lower market prices, but they do not materially alter the income or other features of your pool.

Falling Interest Rate Scenario

If rates fall, the price of your pool will rise, reflecting the higher interest it pays relative to other rates. If rates do not decline enough to encourage mortgage refinancing, you enjoy a capital gain without material alteration in other aspects of your pool.

However, if interest rates fall far enough, homeowners will refinance mortgages. The pool will lose its mortgages. Factor will decline with unscheduled prepayments of principal. Cash flow will increase, stimulated by accelerated principal payments. The amount of interest included in cash flow will decrease as retired mortgages no longer generate interest income. Half life and maturity will fall.

Now you see why Ginnie Mae pools in earlier examples could sell at par, discount, or premium. As with other bond investments, their prices will vary as their payments become more or less attractive in a changing environment of interest rates. Other things being equal, the age of a pool is less significant than its coupon payments in determining whether the pool sells at par, discount, or premium.

With this understanding of price, factor, and maturity, you can see what might result from your investment in a newly issued pool. However, new pools aren't your only alternative, for you can also invest in pools that are already on the market. When you buy these pools, you have to weigh the merits of investing at par, discount, or premium. So let's look at the advantages, disadvantages, and differing purposes of investing in Ginnies already on the market.

THE PAR POOL

One advantage of pools selling at par is their simplicity. Par pools are likely to be new or relatively recent pools with coupon rates closer to current market conditions. Par pools are the most like bonds in the sense of buying an ordinary bond at par. Your purchase price equals the amount of outstanding mortgages in the pool, and your monthly income stream will likely consist of interest rather than principal, at least during your initial years of ownership.

Pools selling at par are best for the investor who doesn't follow mortgage markets extensively, who is not experienced at evaluating Ginnie Maes, and who essentially wants to buy interest income with eventual return of principal assured. If you want higher cash flow and faster return of principal, par pools, especially newly issued pools, probably won't serve you well unless interest rates fall and their prepayment speed increases in the future.

Older pools selling at par are likely to have shorter half lives than newer pools selling at par. If you buy an older pool at par, its factor probably will be less than a newer pool, reflecting scheduled payments of principal that have already occurred. An older par pool with a lower factor can be especially attractive, for it will cost less than a new pool with a higher factor. As a result, you will receive cash flow competitive with a new pool, but your investment cost will be less even though both pools sell at par.

THE DISCOUNT POOL

Discount pools are older Ginnies with coupons lower than current rates. They sell at discounts because mortgage rates or the general level of interest rates rose and their coupon payments became less attractive. Your purchase price will be less than the amount of outstanding mortgages in the pool. Their half life tends to be shorter than par pools, assuming stable mortgage market conditions.

Obviously, discount pools pay less interest than par or premium pools, but they offer one immediate advantage: Being older pools, they often have low factors, thereby giving them some of the most attractive prices in the Ginnie Mae market. At a factor of .5, for example, a $25,000 denomination of Ginnies contains $12,500 worth of mortgages. If a discount pool is priced at, say, 80 percent of par, you pay an affordable $10,000.

Discount pools are most productive when interest rates fall. Lower rates make their coupon more attractive, producing a capital gain as with any bond investment. Also, falling interest rates accelerate prepayments of principal as homeowners refinance mortgages. Cash flow is improved and you receive principal payments more quickly when mortgages are prepaid sooner.

Of course, what goes up can come down. If rates rise, a discount pool's coupon income becomes less attractive, and its prepayments of principal slow. Volatility of market price is a concern with discount pools.

THE PREMIUM POOL

Ginnies sell at premiums because their coupon payments exceed current mortgage market or overall interest rates. On the surface, this would seem to make premium pools unquestionably attractive, for they provide the highest interest income. However, premium pools require the most studied analysis to determine whether they will deliver on their first impression.

The high coupons of premium pools are especially attractive for investors who seek maximum current receipts and are willing to pay above par to receive them. If interest rates remain stable, premium pools continue to deliver those fetching interest payments. Even if interest rates rise, premium pools remain attractive. Enjoying high coupons, you can reinvest proportionately more capital than is provided by discount or par pools, maximizing your return as rates rise.

Higher coupons create a second advantage of premium pools: somewhat more stable prices than discount or par pools. Prices tend to be more stable because the higher coupon supports the market price of premium Ginnies. If rates rise, market price does not fall as dramatically because the high coupon can be reinvested to take advantage of high rates. If rates fall, market price does not rise as rapidly for the reverse reason. Accordingly, premium pools can appeal to investors who are intolerant of excessive capital fluctuations, especially those who expect interest rates to rise.

However, having read this far, you can anticipate the presiding problem of premium pools: substantially declining rates. Homeowners are more likely to refinance high-rate mortgages if rates decline, thereby curtailing your attractive coupon income as mortgages disappear from the pool. Further, falling rates and faster prepayments will accelerate the built-in capital loss inherent with premiums. For instance, the pool selling at 105 will eventually return only $1 of principal for every $1.05 you paid. If prepayments accelerate, you lose that premium more quickly.

Reasonably accurate estimations of future interest rates, mortgage prepayments, and relationship to prepayment experience are needed to assure that premium pools provide their optimum results. Any investment in a Ginnie Mae requires analysis, but the need is greater with premiums because you have a built-in loss of principal. Par and discount pools do not share this trait.

OTHER MORTGAGE-BACKED SECURITIES

Ginnie Maes aren't the only pass-through securities based upon pools of mortgages. Two other agencies issue pass-throughs in forms similar to Ginnies, but they do not equal the volume of Ginnie Maes presently traded.

The Federal Home Loan Mortgage Corporation (Freddie Mac) performs many of the same functions as GNMA, but for conventional mortgages rather than FHA and VA mortgages. Freddie Mac participation certificates do not carry the same assured backing as Ginnie Maes. Freddie issues two types of pass-throughs—30-year certificates similar to a Ginnie Mae I, and 15-year certificates called "Gnomes" that are similar to Ginnie Mae midgets.

The Federal National Mortgage Association (Fannie Mae) creates pass-throughs from pools of mortgages originating from its own portfolio. Fannie Mae pass-throughs contain both conventional and FHA/VA mortgages. Fannie Mae, as you will recall from Chapter 4, is a publicly owned corporation. Although it is presumed to be able to call upon the

U.S. Treasury, you should regard its pass-throughs as corporate securities.

SUMMARY

Pass-through securities earn their name from the practice of assembling pools of mortgages and conveying their interest and principal payments to investors who hold them. The availability and wide markets for these securities give you access to securities originating in the multi-trillion-dollar mortgage market, but their complexity makes them a special study.

Mortgage-backed pass-through securities differ significantly from other types of Treasury and agency paper. Being self-liquidating, they provide monthly, not semiannual, payments that include interest and principal. They do not feature a consistent maturity. Par value of these securities depends upon the dollar amount of mortgages remaining in the pool, which can be all or a fractional amount of the original issue.

In addition, the singularities of pass-through securities present a challenge in calculating price and yield. Although pass-throughs sell at discount, premium, and par, you have to derive their price by computing the factor of mortgages remaining in the pool. Conventional yield calculations do not always apply to pass-throughs; instead, investors concentrate on cash flow of anticipated interest and principal.

Market prices vary inversely with interest rates, but there is a catch on the upside: If interest rates fall substantially, mortgages leave the pool, so pools pay proportionately higher principal and "mature" ahead of schedule. The chief determinants of market behavior and investment suitability are the expected course of interest rates and the extent to which a mortgage pool parallels standard experience regarding payments of interest and prepayments of principal.

6

Zero Coupon Bonds

Zero coupon bonds are one of today's most popular financial instruments, but they are not new. Dozens of securities have been zero coupon investments for decades. In fact, you've met one already—Treasury bills—and a second—EE savings bonds—is surely well known to you. What is a relatively recent development, however, dating from the early 1980s, is the creation of zero coupon securities from conventional, coupon-paying bonds. This chapter will discuss the many types of directly issued and "stripped" zeros available to investors in Treasury and agency securities.

Many varieties of zeros are now available, and they all have one similarity. Instead of paying semiannual coupon interest, they pay accreted interest as the difference between purchase price and par value. Which is to say, you purchase them at a price below par value. When they mature at par, whether in a few days or decades, the difference between your purchase price and their par value is your interest payment. During the interim between purchase and maturity, you receive no payments.

We will start our discussion with zeros that are created by brokerage firms. After fleshing out the basics of those, we will examine zero coupon securities that are directly issued by the Treasury and government agencies.

DERIVATIVE ZEROS

In the early 1980s several investment bankers hit upon an idea that made as much money for investors as it did for brokers. They purchased millions of dollars worth of U.S. Treasury bonds and reconfigured them into a new type of security that paid no immediate or semiannual interest.

To fix a mental image of how this process works, let's step back to when Treasury notes and bonds were represented by physical certificates. Before computerized, book entry records, a Treasury bond was an ornate certificate about the size of a standard 8½-by-11 page perforated into two sections. Let's say you bought a 10-year Treasury that paid $40 every May and November. The first section of the bond declared the Treasury's obligation to pay you $1,000 par at maturity, and the second half contained 20 coupons that you could present to any bank to claim $40 interest payments.

Now imagine a stack of 100 bonds. When the investment bankers looked at their bonds, they noticed that the pile of coupons, all identical and all paying interest on the same day each May and November, resembled one single bond. The same was true of the half of the bonds representing entitlement to principal. All of those were, in effect, like one bond. When it came down to cases, the government's $4,000 interest payment every May and November was no different from repaying $4,000 worth of principal every six months. So they asked themselves, Why not sell all of those coupons and the principal as if they were one bond?

However, there was one consideration. If they resold all the coupons, how would they pay interest to lenders? Their answer: Sell them for less than their terminal value. Investors would receive interest as the difference between what they paid and what the "bonds" were worth when they matured. Investors make one investment, and at maturity they receive one payment. For convenience, the investment bankers structured their "bonds" in customary par values of $1,000. Out of this discovery came the **derivative zero** coupon bond that paid accreted rather than coupon interest by stripping the coupon half of the bond from the par value half and selling them separately.

These now-familiar zero coupon bonds represent a bestiary of financial felines. To differentiate their product from competing houses, the issuer gives its derivative zeros clever names. **CATS,** which stands for Certificates of Accrual on Treasury Securities, are created by Salomon Bros. **TIGRs,** Treasury Investment Growth Receipts, are from Merrill Lynch. There are also **RATS** and **COUGRS** and **TINTS,** but all are created by stripping interest and principal from existing Treasury bonds and reselling parts of the bond as separate investments.

These financial instruments are advertised as "government-backed." That claim isn't false, but it is not precisely true either. When an investment bank creates derivative zeros, it purchases bonds from which zeros are created. After stripping them, the brokerage places the Treasury bonds in permanent escrow. The Treasury backs the escrowed bonds from which the zeros are created, but not the zeros themselves. However, derivative zeros will default only if the U.S. Treasury repudiates its debt, if the escrow agent does something dishonest, or if the brokerage refuses to make payment when the zeros are due. None of that is likely to happen, so you can regard derivative zeros with all of the security due a Treasury obligation.

ADVANTAGES AND DISADVANTAGES OF DERIVATIVE ZEROS

Investors accepted derivative zeros enthusiastically. As of mid-1989, about $62 billion of them were outstanding in financial markets. Their acceptance is justified, for they provide an exceptional array of advantages.

- Highly predictable returns. If you hold a zero coupon security until maturity, you will receive its stated par. This gives you extreme predictability in setting an investment strategy.

- Continual reinvestment. Total return from coupon bonds depends upon the interest rate you receive by reinvesting semiannual coupons. In contrast, zeros continually compound at the rate of interest established when you buy them.

- Impressive returns, especially over longer maturities. For example, a long-term zero maturing at $1,000 can be purchased for about $200 as of mid-1989. You can double, triple, or quadruple your capital with lesser maturities.

- Multiple maturities. You can buy a zero maturing tomorrow morning or in the next century. Whatever your investment horizon, you can find a zero that will mature when you need the money.

- High quality. Treasury zeros and zeros created from Treasury bonds offer excellent assurance against default.

  However, zeros as a category also have some disadvantages.

- Accreted interest from zeros is usually taxable each year even though it is not paid until maturity. This disadvantage is called taxation on **phantom interest,** a subject that we will come back to. Many investors minimize the disadvantage by holding zeros in lesser taxed or tax deferred accounts.

- Zeros are more volatile than other types of bonds, although this is not true of all zeros. In addition, the volatility of zeros offers a greater possibility for more capital gains than other types of Treasury or agency securities.

- Prices for zeros, even for years of identical maturity, vary widely, so you have to shop carefully.

- Commissions are somewhat higher as a percentage of initial investment than are commissions for other investments. However, you minimize commissions when you buy derivative zeros from the inventory of the brokerage that creates them.

UNDERSTANDING PRICE QUOTATIONS

Most investors buy derivative zeros directly from the inventory of a full-service broker or specialty bond house whose firm has stripped the bonds. Buying from inventory is a particular advantage because the broker acts as a principal rather than an agent and cannot charge a commission for the trade; instead, the broker will charge a small basis price representing his or her firm's markup. It is important to save on commissions when buying zeros. Having no coupon to offset commissions, zeros' transaction costs are, in effect, a direct addition to purchase price and a reduction in their yield. Besides saving you transaction costs, the firm will likely have a full range of zeros, giving you a selection of prices, yields, and maturities to choose from.

As Figure 6-1 reveals, zeros are customarily quoted in percent of par, just like coupon-paying bonds. Therefore, a price of, say, 20 represents 20 percent of $1,000, or $200. It might help to think of prices as dollars per hundred even though you buy zeros in increments of $1,000. If your broker, for instance, quotes a price of 17.59, you multiply by 10 to derive the zeros' price of $175.90.

A few derivative zeros are traded on listed exchanges, and the financial press likewise quotes prices per hundred. Normally found under the section for corporate bonds, a representative quotation for derivative zeros might read:

Issuer	Yld	Volume	Close	Net Change
CATS zr09	...	220	$12^3/_4$	$- ^1/_4$

These zeros are Certificates of Accrual on Treasury Securities created by Salomon Bros. The "zr" identifies the issue as a zero, and "09" is the maturity date of 2009. There is no current yield because there is no cou-

Figure 6-1: QUOTATIONS FOR STRIPPED TREASURIES

STRIPPED TREASURIES

Rate	Maturity	Bid	Asked	Bid Chg.	Yld.
.00	Aug 89a	99.21	99.22	...	7.94
.00	Nov 89a	98.15	98.16	+ .01	8.09
.00	Feb 90a	96.14	96.16	...	8.24
.00	May 90a	94.16	94.18	+ .01	8.26
.00	Aug 90a	92.17	92.20	...	8.30
.00	Nov 90a	90.21	90.25	...	8.30
.00	Feb 91	88.26	88.30	...	8.30
.00	May 91a	86.31	87.05	...	8.31
.00	Aug 91	85.11	85.17	...	8.22
.00	Nov 91a	83.15	83.21	...	8.31
.00	Feb 92a	81.24	81.31	- .01	8.31
.00	May 92a	80.03	80.11	- .01	8.30
.00	Aug 92a	78.15	78.23	- .01	8.30
.00	Nov 92a	76.28	77.06	- .02	8.29
.00	Feb 93a	75.11	75.21	- .03	8.28
.00	May 93a	73.28	74.06	- .02	8.26
.00	Aug 93a	72.15	72.26	- .03	8.22
.00	Nov 93a	71.00	71.11	- .03	8.22
.00	Feb 94a	69.18	69.30	- .02	8.22
.00	May 94a	68.07	68.19	- .02	8.20
.00	Aug 94a	67.02	67.15	- .02	8.13
.00	Nov 94a	65.16	65.29	- .02	8.20
.00	Feb 95a	64.04	64.17	- .01	8.22
.00	May 95a	62.26	63.07	- .02	8.22
.00	Aug 95a	61.19	62.00	- .01	8.21
.00	Nov 95a	60.11	60.25	- .02	8.21
.00	Feb 96a	59.03	59.17	- .02	8.22
.00	May 96a	57.28	58.11	- .02	8.22
.00	Aug 96a	56.23	57.06	- .02	8.22
.00	Nov 96a	55.18	56.01	- .02	8.22
.00	Feb 97a	54.13	54.28	- .02	8.23
.00	May 97a	53.10	53.25	- .02	8.23
.00	Aug 97a	52.07	52.23	- .02	8.23
.00	Nov 97a	51.05	51.21	- .02	8.23

Rate	Maturity	Bid	Asked	Bid Chg.	Yld.
.00	Aug 01a	37.17	38.01	- .02	8.26
.00	Nov 01a	36.24	37.09	- .03	8.26
.00	Feb 02a	35.31	36.16	- .03	8.27
.00	May 02a	35.08	35.24	- .02	8.27
.00	Aug 02a	34.17	35.01	- .02	8.27
.00	Nov 02a	33.26	34.11	- .03	8.27
.00	Feb 03a	33.04	33.21	- .03	8.27
.00	May 03a	32.15	32.31	- .02	8.27
.00	Aug 03a	31.26	32.10	- .02	8.27
.00	Nov 03a	31.05	31.21	- .02	8.27
.00	Feb 04a	30.17	31.01	- .02	8.27
.00	May 04a	29.29	30.13	- .02	8.27
.00	Aug 04a	29.09	29.26	- .03	8.27
.00	Nov 04a	28.22	29.06	- .03	8.27
.00	Feb 05a	28.04	28.20	- .02	8.27
.00	May 05a	27.17	28.01	- .03	8.27
.00	Aug 05a	26.31	27.15	- .03	8.27
.00	Nov 05a	26.14	26.30	- .02	8.27
.00	Feb 06a	25.30	26.14	- .01	8.26
.00	May 06a	25.13	25.29	- .01	8.26
.00	Aug 06a	24.29	25.12	- .01	8.26
.00	Nov 06a	24.12	24.28	- .01	8.26
.00	Feb 07a	23.28	24.12	- .02	8.26
.00	May 07a	23.13	23.28	- .01	8.26
.00	Aug 07a	22.30	23.13	- .01	8.26
.00	Nov 07a	22.15	22.30	- .01	8.26
.00	Feb 08a	22.01	22.17	- .02	8.25
.00	May 08a	21.19	22.02	- .01	8.25
.00	Aug 08a	21.06	21.21	- .01	8.24
.00	Nov 08a	20.25	21.07	- .01	8.24
.00	Feb 09a	20.12	20.27	- .01	8.23
.00	May 09a	19.31	20.14	- .01	8.23

pon payment. The "220" is trading volume—220 bonds or $220,000 in par value changed hands. To translate quotations into a price, convert fractions to decimals and multiply by 10. In this case, 12³/₄ becomes 12.75. The closing price of this zero on the New York Bond Exchange was $127.50. At that price, the bond was selling for $2.50 less than the previous day.

UNDERSTANDING YIELDS

No current yield or coupon yield is possible because zeros make no coupon payments. A zero has only yield to maturity, and that yield is the same as the interest rate created by the difference between purchase price and par value. Another advantage to buying zeros from the inventory of a broker is that he or she can quote the yield to you, usually to four decimal places. However, with a little effort, you can calculate it yourself, and it's worthwhile to understand how zeros achieve their yield.

Take the example of a zero quoted at a price of $360 for maturity in approximately 11 years. In establishing a price of $360, the market says that $1,000 to be received in 11 years from this zero is worth $360 today. In other words, the present value of $1,000 is $360. Your question is, $1,000 is worth $360 today according to what rate of interest? That interest rate will be the same as yield to maturity.

Sophisticated pocket calculators have compound interest keys that enable you to calculate interest rates without knowing what you are calculating. For a personal calculation, turn to a present value table in a book of compound interest figures, and through trial and error, under columns of figures for 11-year maturities, find these entries:

Years	9% Nominal Annual Rate	9.5% Nominal Annual Rate
11	0.3797 008	0.3602560

These numbers declare the present value of $1 to be received 11 years from now. To find the present value of $1,000, multiply by 1,000. Accordingly, at a 9.5 percent nominal rate of interest, $1,000 to be received 11 years from now is worth $379.70. At 9 percent nominal interest, $1,000 to be received 11 years from now is worth $360.26.

The price of $360 falls approximately at the 360.26 that indicates a 9.5 yield. Reasoning with given information about price and years to maturity, we see that today's price of $360 represents a yield closer to 9.5 percent than 9 percent. This figure is the approximate yield to maturity of the zero—the yield you would receive if you held the zero for its full term of maturity.

Use the present value schedule for semiannual compounding. Even though zeros are presumed to pay phantom annual interest, their yields and sometimes tax consequences are calculated using semiannual compounding tables, as they would be for coupon-paying bonds.

CHARACTERISTICS OF ZEROS— PRICE, YIELD, AND MATURITY

As you see from the discussion of how to estimate interest rate, zeros' price and yield are interrelated: Price determines yield; yield determines price. Yet price and yield are also related to maturity. Let's outline this series of relationships.

For all zeros, the difference between purchase price and par value is the *amount* of accreted interest you receive if you hold the zero to maturity. For example, a zero priced at $600 pays $400 in accreted interest at maturity.

The *rate* of interest is the mathematical relationship of price and par value to maturity—the time value rate of interest we have just discussed. In general, price and rate are inversely related. The higher the price, the lower the rate, and vice versa.

Interest rate is usually positively related to maturity. The longer the maturity, the higher the interest rate. However, this is not always the case. At times, zeros of different maturities can offer the same rate of interest. For example, a zero priced at $414.64 to mature in 10 years and a zero priced at $171.94 to mature in 20 years both carry a 9 percent interest rate. We will discuss this phenomenon, called an undifferentiated yield curve, in Section II.

As the example above illustrates, price is inversely related to maturity. A zero of longer maturity will have a lower price than a shorter zero even if their interest rates are the same.

If we were also discussing corporate and municipal zeros, we would add that quality—assurance against default—is also a major determinant of price and yield. However, as we're covering Treasury and agency zeros, quality is presumed to be unimpeachable. Therefore, concerns about default don't adversely affect price and yield. For a full discussion of other types of zero coupon products, pick up copies of *The Personal Investor's Complete Book of Bonds* and *The Income Investor* also by your author and Longman Financial Services.

COMPUTING TAXABLE INTEREST

It is important to know the yield on your zeros because that is the basis upon which you must calculate annual tax liability if you hold zeros outside tax-deferred accounts. Remember: Zeros don't produce actual payments until maturity, but the IRS usually expects you to calculate and declare a portion of accreted interest as if it actually were paid.

Unfortunately, there are a thousand qualifications in computing your yearly tax liability from zeros held outside tax-deferred accounts. Your actual tax owed on phantom interest depends on whether you bought the zero when it was originally issued or in a secondary market, when the zero was issued regardless of when you purchased it, whether you inherited it, and the type of zero. Within these ranges, you pay phantom interest tax either yearly or when you dispose of the bond. You will calculate that interest on a straight-line constant interest method, or you will use a compound interest calculation as if the zero were a conventional coupon-paying bond.

If you are going to buy a derivative zero for other than a tax-deferred account, you must request copies of IRS Publication 1212 (*List of Original Issue Discount Obligations*). It indicates the tax liability on zero coupon investments of many types and provides an exhaustive—but by no means definitive—list of derivative zeros and computed yearly interest liability per $1,000 par value. It is indispensable if you are going to invest in zeros, so be sure to request an updated issue from the IRS each year.

For all derivative zeros issued after December 31, 1984, phantom interest is taxable yearly according to the semiannual compound interest formula used on conventional bonds. First multiply the zeros' yield to maturity times the cost of the zeros; then multiply that figure times one-half. The result is the amount of taxable phantom interest for the first half-year you owned the zeros.

To determine phantom taxable interest for the second half-year, add the result of the calculation above to the purchase price of the bond and repeat the two steps above. This gives you the total phantom taxable interest for one full year of ownership for derivative zeros issued after December 31, 1984.

For example, say that you paid $10,000 for an issue of zeros yielding 10.5 percent. To determine phantom taxable interest for a six-month period:

$$\$10,000 \times 10.5\% \times .5 = \$525$$

For the second six-month period, add $525 to the purchase price and recalculate:

$$\$10,525 \times 10.5\% \times .5 = \$552.56$$

For a full year of phantom taxable interest, add the two sums:

$$\$525 + \$552.56 = \$1,077.56$$

When figuring phantom taxable interest for the next six-month period, your basis for calculation becomes $11,077.56 ($10,000 + 1,077.56).

TAX ON PHANTOM INTEREST RECONSIDERED

The most frequently cited disadvantage of zeros is that they don't pay current income but they do generate a current tax liability from phantom interest. This is one reason why most investors hold Treasury and corporate zeros only in tax-deferred accounts like IRAs, where their phantom interest compounds without taxes. In fact, some advisors argue that tax on phantom interest is so serious a disadvantage that derivative zeros don't belong outside IRAs and Keoghs. This point of view bears reconsideration.

For one thing, many recommended investments like real estate, precious metals, collectables, and growth stocks pay no current income yet often involve taxes, carrying charges, insurance fees, safe-deposit rentals, appraisal costs, and other current costs without current income. In this comparative sense, taxation on interest you don't receive until maturity is no more onerous than circumstances you face with other investments.

Moreover, let's be honest about what really happens with bond coupons. Too often, we spend them instead of reinvesting them and wind up only with par value to show for the investment. Even if you have to pay taxes on phantom interest yearly, at least you will have capital accumulations when your zeros mature.

ORIGINAL ISSUE TREASURY ZEROS

Derivative zeros are created by stripping Treasury bonds of coupon and interest payments. However, the Treasury and many federal agencies are direct issuers of zero coupon securities. Called **original issue** Treasury and agency zeros, these securities are not derived from an existing bond. They are originally issued as zeros. They present a variety of maturities and other considerations that make them as attractive or more attractive than derivative zeros. For the most part they are similar to derivative zeros, but each has distinguishing features.

Treasury Bills

By this time you should realize that Treasury bills are, in fact, zero coupon bonds. As you will recall from Chapter 2, they are sold at discounts from their $10,000 par to mature in 13, 26, or 52 weeks. T-bill prices and yields are calculated differently from other zeros, as explained in Chapter 2. Interest is exempt from state and local taxation, and federal tax need not be declared until the year in which the bills mature.

EE Savings Bonds

At bottom, zero coupon bonds are progeny of the Series E (now **Series EE) savings bond.** What's more, the original zero is still the most accessible and convenient, for you can buy them at any savings institution, through payroll plans at work, and directly from a Federal Reserve Bank or branch. The EE bond works like all the zeros we've discussed—sold at

Figure 6-2: SAVINGS BOND ANNOUNCEMENT

U.S. Savings Bonds To Carry 7.81% Rate, The Highest in 3 Years

By a WALL STREET JOURNAL Staff Reporter

WASHINGTON—U.S. savings bonds will earn interest at an annual rate of 7.81% for the next six months, the highest rate of return in three years, the Treasury announced.

For the past six months, savings bonds carried an interest rate of 7.35%. The interest rate on savings bonds is adjusted on May 1 and Nov. 1 each year to reflect changes in market interest rates.

The rate is 85% of the average market interest rate on five-year Treasury bonds for the past six months. Bonds must be held at least five years to earn market-based rates.

However, holders of savings bonds are guaranteed a minimum rate regardless of what happens in financial markets. The minimum is currently 6%; for bonds purchased before Nov. 1, 1986, it is 7.5%.

a discount to pay interest as the difference between price and par. However, there are several differences between EE bonds and other zeros.

- Par values of EE bonds are $50, $75, $100, $200, $500, $1,000, $5,000, and $10,000; par for other zeros is nearly always $1,000.

- You buy EEs at half of par value. With other zeros, price decreases with maturity.

- The maturity of EE bonds is 12 years. Other zeros have longer and shorter maturities. However, EE bonds purchased after November 1965 are eligible to enter extended maturity. Even though they nominally mature in 12 years, Uncle Sam will continue to compound EE bond interest until the bond is 30 years old.

- EE bonds purchased after November 1982 pay a rate of interest that increases the longer you hold the bond. Other zeros pay a fixed rate of interest determined by price. There is another aspect to sliding EE bond interest: Held five years, EE bonds pay 85 percent of the average yield on five-year U.S. Treasury notes and are guaranteed to earn no less than 6 percent. Whenever average yields on five-year Treasuries exceed 6 percent, a EE bond matures to more than stated par value. Therefore, par value is an approximation with EE bonds, not a fixed figure.

- EE bonds will never be worth less than purchase price even if cashed before maturity, nor will they ever be worth more than their scheduled value as determined by how long you have owned them. Because EE bond prices don't vary inversely with interest rates, they don't offer dramatic short-term gains, but they never suffer capital losses.

- You may declare accreted interest from EE bonds as it accrues yearly, or you may postpone declaring interest until the bond matures or is cashed. Thus, EE bonds are an exception to tax on phantom interest. Also, accreted interest from EE savings bonds is exempt from state, city, regional, and local taxes.

- EE bonds paying accreted interest may be exchanged for HH bonds paying coupon interest. The convertibility of EE bonds is an advantage for some investors and will be discussed in Chapter 11.

All things considered, you should not dismiss EE savings bonds as stodgy and unappealing investments. They have a number of very attractive features.

STRIPS

In August 1984, the Treasury Department undertook administrative actions that make it easier for financial institutions to create derivative zeros. It created **STRIPS,** which stands for Separate Trading of Registered Interest and Principal of Securities. Under the STRIPS program, certain government bonds have multiple identification numbers. The whole bond—principal and interest—has one number, and each component of the bond—principal and each coupon—has its own number. This makes it easier for financial institutions to resell severed interest and principal payments because each has preestablished identification.

STRIPS are direct issues of the Treasury, but they are sold only to financial institutions that have book entry securities accounts with the Federal Reserve. However, financial institutions resell STRIPS to investors under their trade names. For instance, Shearson Lehman sells STRIPS under its trade name TINTS. You can regard STRIPS exactly as any other derivative zero, because that's the way you will end up with them. STRIPS produce phantom taxable interest yearly, so if you hold them outside IRAs and Keogh Plans you will declare accreted interest each year. However, phantom interest on STRIPS is exempt from state and local tax. IRS Publication 1212 reveals phantom interest due on STRIPS held outside IRAs and Keoghs.

Federal Agency Securities

In late 1984, the Federal National Mortgage Association issued several billion dollars worth of Zero Coupon Subordinated Capital Debentures maturing in 2019. Since then, Fannie Mae has issued other series of **Capital Debentures,** which is its trade name for its zero coupon debt.

These are original issue zeros from a private corporation that is presumed to be able to call upon the backing of the U.S. government. Consequently, they are regarded as a close proxy for CATS and TIGRs and other derivative zeros even though they are not, strictly speaking, backed by the government. Like all zeros they are sold at discounts from par, with a minimum face value of $5,000. Capital Debentures can be purchased without commission from the underwriters and are listed on the New York Bond Exchange.

Among other agency zeros are those of the Student Loan Marketing Association (Sallie Mae), the Federal Intermediate Credit Bank, and the Federal Farm Credit System. Some of their zeros are short-term and range from five-day to 30-day discounted notes similar to T-bills. Others are more conventional, carrying maturities of many years. They, too, are available without commission from their underwriters and are listed on public exchanges.

MARKET BEHAVIOR OF ZEROS

The market price of bonds moves inversely to economywide interest rates, but the market price of zeros fluctuates more severely than coupon bonds. That's because zeros pay interest only at maturity and only that rate of interest produced by their price. They also lack a coupon to provide intermediate payments. So when economywide rates rise, the market is severe in beating zeros' prices.

Conversely, prices of zeros increase more sharply when economywide interest rates fall. With coupon bonds, your rate of compounding declines when economywide rates decline. Zeros continually compound at the same interest. When economywide rates are falling, investors want to lock in zeros' constant yield. They buy zeros, and market demand increases their price.

The negative aspect of capital fluctuation (capital losses) and the positive aspect (capital gains) are most dramatic with long-term zeros. In the early 1980s, long-term Treasury zeros were priced to yield upwards of 14 percent to maturity. When interest rates fell sharply a few years later, zeros produced such extraordinary capital gains that many investors sold their zeros at four to six times their original purchase price after owning them only a few years.

Short-term zeros, typically those maturing inside five years, will fluctuate less in price and will also march more predictably toward par as they approach maturity. That is, their compound accreted value will be more predictably and consistently expressed in changing market price.

Let's say that you pay $800 for a zero maturing in four years. This zero owes you $200 in accreted interest and will pay it relatively soon. Being short-term, its price will generally increase steadily—around $50 each year. The market recognizes the approach of par and accommodates about-to-be paid interest in market price—that is, in compound accreted value.

A long-term zero will be very erratic in market price, and the market will not anticipate forthcoming interest through steady compound accreted value. Other things being equal, such as no dramatic change in economywide interest rates, a 20-year zero may not start to increase in market price for several years.

Some investors welcome zeros' capital fluctuation for potential gains and trade them actively as capital gains investments. Others are indifferent to capital fluctuation because they buy zeros for their terminal value. Still other investors can't stand it. You can reduce capital fluctuation if you buy zeros of shorter maturities, but you can't avoid it altogether, except for buying EE savings bonds. If you buy zeros, you must understand that your investment has a distinctive behavior that usually is more volatile than conventional coupon bonds.

USES FOR ZEROS—TAX-DEFERRED ACCUMULATIONS

Except for EE savings bonds, zeros reach their fullest use in tax-deferred individual retirement accounts and related investments like SERPs (formerly Keoghs) for the self-employed. Zeros' predictable returns, range of maturities, handsome accumulations, ease of purchase, solid default assurances, and attractive yields combine with deferral of phantom interest to make them perfect for IRAs and SERPs. EE savings bonds also find favor among investors who seek tax-deferred compounding for retirement or tuition planning or for any life purpose. Available in affordable denominations, EE bonds let you accumulate a nest egg without draining income.

Also, if you are investing long term, you need not be concerned with interim capital fluctuations. In fact, depressed prices for long-term zeros are welcome, for they present buying opportunity when economywide rates increase. We will discuss using Treasury and agency securities, including zeros, for retirement accounts in Section II.

As you will see in Section II, you can be almost endlessly innovative in using zeros' predictable returns, attractive yields, continual compounding, and ease of purchase in tax-deferred or ordinary accounts. With zeros, you can invest for reinvestment opportunity, locked-in distant yields, or maximum accumulations. You can pool maturities to produce a lump sum at a known date, and, as we see later, you can serialize maturities to produce a stream of income.

Relatedly, zeros fit well in Uniform Gifts to Minors Accounts for many of the same reasons they are at home in retirement accounts. Purchased when children are many years from college age, zeros with 15 to 20 years until maturity enable parents to salt away modest sums that grow to formidable sums. Treasury or agency backing allows great confidence in holding them for long periods. With the first $500 in accreted interest exempt from any taxes, children can enjoy many years of untaxed accumulations.

SUMMARY

Derivative zeros created from Treasury bonds and original issue zeros from the Treasury and federal agencies are sold at discounts from their par value and pay accreted interest as the difference between purchase price and par. Unlike conventional Treasury and agency bonds, zeros pay interest only at maturity, not semiannually.

Apart from their high security against default, zeros offer the advantages of predictable accumulations, handsome yields, and a wide range of maturities to facilitate many investment purposes. Their versatility also includes reasonable purchase prices, starting at $25 for savings bonds. On the negative side, they tend to be more volatile than other bonds, particularly zeros with long maturities, and their phantom interest payments are taxed each year.

7

Federally Insured Bank Deposits

Since 1933 and 1934, the federal government has been insuring deposits in S&Ls and commercial banks. That effectively makes deposits insured by the Federal Deposit Insurance Corporation government-guaranteed obligations issued by private corporations. Most investors don't think of bank deposits as government securities, but that's essentially what they are. They are also one of the most frequently purchased investments from banks, savings & loans, credit unions, and brokerages.

SAVINGS ACCOUNTS

Almost all investors started their financial life with an ordinary savings account from the local depository institution where parents banked. Most of us have outgrown this longstanding investment, but it still offers advantages. Savings accounts are constant dollar investments with no market risk, and if they are backed by federal guarantors their default risk is minimal. They are convenient and may be added to for exceptionally small sums. They are commonly liquid, except that the fine print in many passbooks permits the institution to require written notice of withdrawal and perhaps a 30-day waiting period. The overriding disadvantage to savings accounts is their typically low interest. Investors holding large sums in their savings accounts are doing themselves a disservice, for savings accounts pay a flat rate that is often lower than competing rates on other instruments.

CONVENTIONAL CERTIFICATES OF DEPOSIT

Most investors are familiar with conventional certificates of deposit (CDs) that are contractual deposits offered by commercial banks, S&Ls, and credit unions. You agree to leave funds with the institution for a specified period, and the institution agrees to pay a stated rate of interest plus compounding. At the end of that period, the institution returns the amount you initially invested plus interest. As a consequence of straightforward circumstances, these income investments have many attractions.

They are available without commissions and fees and are easily purchased from virtually any financial institution. Their constant dollar price appeals to investors concerned about capital losses and market risk. They pay predictable interest which, depending upon the size of your deposit, you can arrange to have mailed to you for current income or leave on deposit for compounding. Generally, only larger denomination certificates offer a current income payment. Interest will increase with the term of deposit, ranging from slightly more than a passbook rate for short certificates to interest akin to Treasury securities for longer maturities.

ADVANTAGES AND DISADVANTAGES OF CONVENTIONAL CDs

Conventional CDs are secure against default risk, assuming the institution issuing them is affiliated with the Federal Deposit Insurance Corporation or a related federal or state overseer. High quality makes certificates acceptable for conservative and quality-minded portfolios.

Certificates are available in varying maturities from six months to 20 years, and varying investments of $500 to $1 million, although a minimum investment of $1,000 is customary. They are available to investors of all budgets and preferences in maturity.

However, drawbacks of conventional CDs sometimes overshadow their advantages. Most institutions charge interest penalties for withdrawing deposits before maturity (although sometimes older investors or CDs held in individual retirement accounts are exempt from penalties). Escalating with maturity, common penalties are forfeiture of one, three, or six months of interest. As a first result of interest penalties, your guaranteed rate of interest may become irrelevant if you need your deposit in an emergency. As a second result, interest penalties essentially render conventional CDs suitable only for a buy-and-hold investment strategy.

Moreover, banking institutions don't maintain secondary markets for CDs, with occasional exception of Jumbo CDs in $100,000 denominations. Absence of a market means you can't escape interest penalties by selling. Further, it means you can't sell your CD to another investor who might pay more for it. The advantage of capital stability becomes the disadvantage of no potential for capital gain. Interest penalties and illiquidity present another disadvantage: They might keep you from investing in long-term maturities, which typically pay the highest rates.

In addition, conventional CDs don't necessarily give you the maturity you want because their products are standardized. If your bank or thrift offers, say, two-year and three-year maturities, you are going to have to make accommodations if you want, say, a 32-month maturity.

Most certificates pay a fixed rate of interest and compounding established on the date of issue. Therefore, they can be vulnerable to inflation risk. Interest from certificates is fully taxable. Most certificates are "locked." You can invest $550 in a $500 certificate, but you cannot invest $500 and add $50 later.

Generalities aside, you might face more disadvantages pertaining to specific rules and products of your local bank or S&L. Your local institution's rates are competitive locally, but not always nationally. Also, your local institution may not offer innovative CD products now available. Finally, a growing number of banks and thrifts are beginning to charge account fees for certificates. Fees detract from yield, and they might be imposed in addition to interest penalties.

NEW PRODUCTS FROM DEPOSITORY INSTITUTIONS

Depository institutions have created new products that counteract many of these disadvantages, although not, many observers say, in a significant manner. The "designer certificate" permits you to select a term of maturity and rate of interest that are less rigid than the customary certificate. For example, where a normal certificate may pay 8 percent for deposits of five years, you could negotiate a designer certificate of four years that pays between 7 and 8 percent.

Investors who have recently taken a retirement distribution from an employer or union pension may have $100,000 for a Jumbo. Where guarantors are involved, the Jumbo is secure against default and market fluctuations. Jumbos pay competitive rates that may be fixed or variable, thereby overcoming one disadvantage to certificates. Jumbos come in short and long maturities. Some can be sold any time, overcoming illiquidity of most certificates.

Variable rate certificates pay fluctuating interest determined by the rate of inflation or interest on competing instruments, defeating the fixed-rate disadvantage. The straight variable pays less interest when the related index declines.

Variable up-fixed down certificates are ratcheted to an index. When yields represented in the index increase, so does the certificate. When yields represented in the index decline, they revert to a base rate usually higher than the newer rate, or they continue paying the higher interest of the previous period.

Zero coupon certificates came into being when brokerages purchased Jumbos and reconfigured them into smaller, lower priced certificates—typically $250 for a 12-year zero and $500 to $750 for lesser maturities. You buy a zero certificate for less than its maturity price and the difference between purchase price and maturity value is accreted interest. Zero certificates are excellent for tax-deferred accounts.

THE BROKERED CD

Even though innovations on the conventional CD overcome some of the drawbacks of depository institutions' products, they don't stack up favorably against Wall Street's version of the CD. CDs retailed by brokerage institutions, **brokered CDs,** offer the best of conventional CDs combined with features to overcome their disadvantages. Essentially, brokered CDs are certificates originating from commercial banks or other depository institutions, but they are retailed to personal investors by a brokerage underwriter.

In concert with the brokerage underwriter, banks and thrifts decide upon the type of CD, maturity, and interest rate appropriate to market circumstances. Once type and terms are decided, the issuing bank or thrift creates a master CD certificate that is placed with a trust company. The trust company keeps transaction ledgers, identifies owners, and generally handles records.

Through its network of brokers, the underwriter retails beneficial holdings of the master certificate. Essentially, you buy clusters of the master certificate in denominations set by the brokerage, customarily $5,000 or $10,000, although sometimes the minimum may be $1,000. Each CD carries the same features, interest rate, and maturity as the master certificate. This arrangement is similar to a bond, wherein the total issue may consist of millions of dollars but you buy individual bonds in smaller denominations that carry the same features as the whole.

You buy the certificate from your broker in the same way you would purchase any investment, and interest payments go to your account. You pay no commission. Cash from your purchase ultimately flows through the depository trust to the issuer, minus payments to the underwriter and depository trust.

ADVANTAGES AND DISADVANTAGES OF BROKERED CDS

The first advantage of brokered CDs is that they are functionally like conventional CDs. In other words, you can buy them for all the reasons that you would buy a conventional CD, including FDIC insurance up to $100,000 per depositor per institution. As an added benefit, the underwriter screens issuers to assure safety against default.

Second, brokerages maintain secondary markets in brokered CDs. A secondary market allows you to sell your CD before maturity without interest penalties. You also receive all accrued interest the CD earns to the date of sale.

Secondary markets also establish the price you will receive. You might be able to sell your brokered CD at a capital gain in addition to receiving accrued interest. Of course, a capital loss is also possible. In that case, you can hold the brokered CD to maturity, or you can wait out interest rates. Either way, you have flexibility not accorded conventional CDs, opportunity to use CDs as growth investments, and greater liquidity investing in longer maturities. Constant flow of new issues and investor acceptance of the product eliminate a thin float that otherwise creates volatile prices and reduced liquidity. In addition, brokered CDs are widely traded, which reduces the spread between selling prices and purchase prices.

Secondary markets let you buy existing CDs from other investors who want to sell. That gives you a way around the cemented maturities of conventional CDs. If you are looking for a CD maturing in 32 months, your broker can locate one in the secondary markets and quote you a price. You can invest according to *your* maturity preferences, not the bank's.

Third, brokered CDs give you access to a national market and a diversified choice of products. You aren't constrained to the yield, maturity, and type offered by your local bank or thrift. Brokered CDs are available in fixed-rate, variable-rate, zero coupon, and even **Eurodollar CDs** with rates pegged to international exchange. Maturities on new issues offer the same ranges as conventional CDs, and there's always the secondary market to expand your choice of maturities.

The fourth and major incentive for many investors, competition in financial markets, helps to assure market level yields that can be substantially higher than yields available locally. Also, brokered CDs can offer higher rates because it costs less for a banking institution to raise, say,

$1,000,000 in CDs through a broker than to solicit 1,000 patrons for $1,000 CDs. In addition, brokered CDs broaden a local institution's access to capital, not only from personal investors nationwide but also institutional investors such as pensions, mutual funds, and insurance companies. Rates are important in keeping that clientele coming back. These higher rates are particularly attractive if you intend to hold your brokered CD until maturity, but they make brokered CDs more attractive in secondary markets if you do decide to sell before maturity.

The few disadvantages that do apply to brokered CDs are modest. For example, blackout rules sometimes keep a local bank or S&L from offering brokered CDs in the same geographical area as its conventional CDs. You might not be able to buy your local bank's brokered CDs through your broker, but nothing prevents your investing in brokered CDs offered by another institution.

Brokered CDs feature a market price that varies inversely with the general level of interest rates. Accordingly, brokered CDs, particularly those with lengthy maturities, are not capital stable investments. This extra dimension can work for you or against you, depending upon the progress of economywide interest rates. If you hold CDs to maturity, of course, you will receive stated interest and principal regardless of capital fluctuation before maturity.

In addition, FDIC insurance doesn't apply to capital gains. The insurance covers only principal and interest, not market growth. This hardly qualifies as a major deterrent to brokered CDs, for the insurance feature remains otherwise intact.

USES FOR CERTIFICATES OF DEPOSIT

CDs are best employed in the income component of the portfolio, where they produce consistent interest payments for current expenses or for compounding. CDs from banks and thrifts are capital stable investments, but the illiquidity of conventional CDs limits their usefulness. You want to invest in conventional CDs when economywide interest rates are falling. If you are holding a certificate paying, say, 8 percent, the bank or S&L owes you that 8 percent even if other investments have fallen to 6 percent.

Brokered CDs offer all the advantages of conventional products and of a negotiable security. You can use them in the income component as you would a conventional CD, and you can use them as capital growth investments, for their prices will rise when general interest rates fall. Of course, their prices will fall when general rates rise, a disadvantage not associated with conventional products, but brokered CDs can be held to maturity to assure full repayment of initial principal.

Variable rate CDs, both conventional and brokered products, can be used in the income component to take advantage of rising interest rates. The drawback for this use is that their payments will decline when rates fall.

Ideally, you should redeem a conventional CD prior to maturity only if an alternate investment presents an opportunity that is promising enough to compensate for the interest you will forfeit to redeem a certificate. In less than ideal situations, you should reclaim a conventional CD only if you need the money and your alternatives are going into debt or selling a profitable liquid investment. In addition, if you suspect the issuer is facing solvency problems, even an institution backed by guarantors, take your money and reinvest, preferably in direct Treasury securities.

SUMMARY

Conventional certificates of deposit from depository institutions are constant dollar investments known for reliability, easy access, assurance against default, and absence of commissions and fees. Larger certificates present the opportunity to take interest payments in cash or in compounded interest. Conventional certificates are also known for their illiquidity, penalties for premature redemption, vulnerability to inflation risk, and lessened opportunity for reinvestment.

Brokered CDs overcome many of the disadvantages of conventional CDs. In particular, they offer high interest, potential for capital gains, and full liquidity prior to maturity. These advantages added to the advantages of conventional CDs make brokered CDs one of today's most attractive investments.

8

Indirect Investment—Treasury and Agency Mutual Funds

Thus far, we have discussed direct personal ownership of Treasury and agency securities—that is, you pick the bonds, phone your broker, and buy or sell for your account on your instructions. However, direct ownership might not be the best course for some investors. Limited capital, limited patience with bond markets, and limited time to examine bonds might keep you from managing your portfolio adroitly. The simplest way to avoid these dilemmas is through indirect ownership: buying shares of companies that invest in Treasury and agency securities. Such companies are called open-end investment companies, better known as mutual funds.

GENERAL DESCRIPTION

A mutual fund is operated—investments are made—by professional managers who have access to primary dealers and bond exchanges and legions of data. Those professionals accept your capital, pool it with capital from thousands of other investors, and invest it on behalf of all subscribers to the fund. The managers receive a fee, and the investors receive returns produced by the fund.

A portion of the interest that bonds in the fund pay is credited to you according to how many shares of the fund you own, just as if you owned the bonds personally. If the bonds within the fund increase in price, the price of shares of the fund, the **net asset value,** increases in price, producing capital gains. The same situation works in reverse to produce capital losses.

You buy and sell mutual fund shares directly from the sponsoring fund at a price determined by net asset value. Although some bond funds are sponsored by your brokerage firm, the most widely available funds are sponsored by mutual **fund families** that offer dozens of different types of bond funds.

GOVERNMENT BOND FUNDS

We are concerned with a specific type of mutual fund, namely the bond fund that invests in Treasury and agency securities. Government bond funds permit you to own Treasury and agency securities in ways that can be highly advantageous. Even more, government bond funds have some advantages that direct ownership of bonds can't match.

One major advantage is a fund's low cost. The minimum for initial and subsequent investments is low—often $1,000 or less to start, with minimums of $50 to $100 for purchasing additional shares in the fund. Your ability to invest small sums means you can be fully invested in government bonds even if you can afford only $50 or $100. Accordingly, funds are ideal for beginning investors and all investors with modest budgets.

One related aspect of net asset value is that it allows investors to purchase fractional shares. That is not the case with direct ownership of bonds. If you have $1,000 and want to buy a Treasury selling at, say, $850, you can buy one only. If you send your $1,000 to a mutual fund, you can invest your whole $1,000 in a fund that may include that bond and will diversify your investment into other bonds in the fund.

Second, government bond funds compound interest monthly, not semiannually, as do directly held bonds. Obviously, funds hold millions of dollars of Treasury and agency paper with varying maturities and payments. They receive portfolio income continuously and, therefore, distribute it to subscribers. You can structure a personal portfolio of Treasuries to pay monthly income, as we will discuss in Section II, but funds do it for you in a single, consolidated investment.

The third advantage is one that direct ownership doesn't offer: ability to reinvest returns for compounding or to take interest and capital gains as current income.

If you are a long-term investor who wants to accumulate a position in Treasury and agency securities, you could instruct your fund to reinvest all payments—interest and capital gains—in more shares of the fund; this is an excellent choice for maximum compounding.

93

However, suppose you are investing a sizable sum, as retirees often do, and you need current income for living expenses. In this case, you can elect to have interest and capital gains paid directly to you. The fund also gives you another choice: You can receive interest *or* capital gains as cash payments, reinvesting the remainder in additional shares for growth and compounding. Either is a good choice for investors who need optimum cash income from their funds, and funds will agree to mail you checks monthly, quarterly, or semiannually as you require.

Special Note: The ability to take capital gains as cash without selling your shares can be very rewarding when interest rates are falling and bond prices are rising. By subscribing to a fund and electing to take capital gains as cash, you can keep your bonds and receive their capital appreciation by check. This advantage isn't available with direct investment in bonds. If you buy Treasury and agency securities directly, capital gains become income only when you sell, and selling removes the source of future interest and gains from directly held bonds.

Government bond funds do have a few disadvantages, but they don't apply to all funds on the market.

One disadvantage of some government bond funds is that their interest payments may be classified as dividends rather than interest. If so, you pay state and local tax on income from government bond funds even though you would be exempt from such taxation if you owned the bonds directly. To avoid this problem, buy government funds that are legally constituted as partnerships or have satisfied other legal arrangements that define fund's interest payments as flow-through interest. Having met these requirements, interest from the partnership will be exempt from state and local tax, and only federal tax will apply to interest income. Capital gains will be fully taxable under present law.

A few government bond funds charge front-end **loads,** which are the equivalent of a sales charge. In the recent past, sometimes loads approached 8 percent on investments in a government bond fund. If you invested $10,000, $800 went toward commissions. If you had bought $10,000 in Treasuries from your broker, commissions would have been $100 to $200, and if you had bought at Federal Reserve auction you would pay no commissions. Fortunately, most investors have caught on to this unreasonably high fee, and funds have lowered their loads. Many government bond funds have no loads. Anything above a 2 percent charge for a government bond fund is unconscionable, and you should find a fund with lower charges.

One charge you won't avoid, however, is a management fee. All mutual funds, government bond funds included, pay managers a percentage of the portfolio value. The fee ranges from seven-tenths of one percent to one percent of the portfolio value, and it applies every year. Management fees don't pertain to direct ownership of Treasury and agency securities. They are the most damaging disadvantage of government bond funds.

WEIGHTED AVERAGE MATURITY

A government bond fund will usually advertise itself as a short-term, intermediate-term, or long-term fund. The difference is in the range of maturities of bonds within the fund. The short-term fund, for example, may have an average portfolio maturity of five years, whereas intermediate-term funds carry average maturities of 10 to 12 years, and long-term funds beyond 12 years. Some government bond funds, of course, have no stated average maturity. Their managers simply populate the fund with bonds of maturities they deem attractive and lengthen or shorten maturities as conditions dictate.

Weighted average maturity is an important concept to understand if you intend to invest in funds. Unlike directly owned bonds (and target funds, discussed shortly), bond funds are perpetuities. They will be in business forever, constantly buying and selling bonds in their portfolios, and there is no date when the portfolio finally matures. Consequently, a short-term fund refers to the weighted average portfolio maturity of all bonds it contains.

Weighted average maturity is the arithmetic mean of all the fund's maturities statistically weighted to represent the heaviest concentration of maturities. That is, a long-term fund may have 10 percent of its portfolio maturing in two years, 10 percent maturing in ten years, 60 percent maturing in 20 years, and 20 percent maturing in 25 to 30 years. This long-term fund has a weighted average maturity of more than ten years, but that doesn't mean that all its bonds are long bonds. Weighted average maturity means that your investment is constantly and on the average invested at the short, intermediate, or long point of the maturity spectrum even though the fund contains bonds of shorter or longer maturities.

Weighted average maturity is important for two reasons: interest and capital fluctuation. As a general rule, funds with shorter average maturities pay less interest than funds with longer maturities. From your reading thus far, you understand why this is generally true. Shorter bonds generally pay less interest than longer bonds. Therefore, the fund holding shorter maturities will yield less than funds with longer maturities. Investors concerned with highest income from their funds generally prefer longer average maturities.

However, the longer the average maturity, the more the fund's net asset value will fluctuate, as is the case with the bonds in the portfolio.

Conversely, net asset value of short-term funds will fluctuate less than that of longer funds. As a result, investors desiring minimal capital fluctuation stay with shorter average maturities. Those who are willing to risk declining net asset value in exchange for potential of capital gains select funds with longer average maturities.

A related aspect to weighted average maturity and capital fluctuation is that all bond funds will fluctuate indefinitely in price. Remember that bond funds never mature. Managers are always investing new capital from subscribers and reinvesting interest and principal. Moreover, they stage their investments at the weighted average maturity of the fund. As a result, there is no time when the net asset value of a fund stabilizes with approaching maturity.

To illustrate, let's say you invest today in a Treasury bond maturing in 12 years. That bond's capital fluctuation will stabilize as the bond approaches par. But if you invested today in an intermediate-term bond fund, your fund will always contain bonds with intermediate-term maturities of, say, 12 years. A bond fund never matures, and its bonds are perpetually invested at an average of 12 years' maturity. The fund will not stabilize in price within a few years, as will the bond you bought directly.

TYPES OF GOVERNMENT BOND FUNDS

General

Government bond funds, sometimes called Treasury funds, are of several general types as defined by the securities they contain. Some of the older government bond funds invest only in securities backed by the full faith and credit of the United States; they do not include agency securities. If you must have the ironclad guarantee of Treasury backing, you will want a fund that invests only in direct obligations such as Treasury bills, notes, bonds, and similar obligations of Uncle Sam. Such rigorously constrained funds are relatively few in number, however.

Today, most government funds include direct obligations and securities of federal agencies such as Fannie Mae. These general purpose funds suit all the reasons why you invest in Treasury and agency securities—high assurance against default, reliable payments, liquid markets, and so on—and they are the most numerous of the government bond funds available. You can invest in them with confidence. Because they hold agency securities, their yields are often slightly higher than strict Treasury-only funds.

Some of the most recently introduced funds revert to the selectivity of their ancestors and invest only in agency securities. To date, Ginnie Mae funds, discussed later in this chapter, are the chief examples of single-source agency securities. They are not a general purpose government bond fund nor a broad Treasury and agency portfolio.

Target Funds

A **target fund** is a government bond fund that has a terminal maturity because all the bonds in its portfolio mature in the same year. Fund managers buy and hold bonds maturing in an indicated or target year. Initial and subsequent investments are used to buy bonds maturing in that year. The fund holds no bonds with other maturities, so average maturity and terminal maturity are the same.

Target funds are identified by their year of maturity and typically are offered by mutual fund families in a series of escalating maturities. Today's most common target funds have portfolios of 1990, 1995, 2000, 2005, and 2010 maturities. You buy shares in each portfolio as a separate investment. When the fund matures, its portfolio terminates, managers send distributions to subscribers, and that's that.

Target funds offer all the inducements of conventional bond funds, including opportunity to take distributions in cash or to let them compound. Yet their terminal maturities present some special advantages. One advantage is that you can invest in a target fund as you would invest in a single bond. If you are interested in intermediate-term bonds, you can subscribe to a target fund and choose the portfolio maturing in, say, 2000. In effect, each investment you make buys part of a bond portfolio centered exactly upon that year, unlike funds with weighted average maturities. In 2000 the fund closes, much like a single bond would mature, and you can reevaluate your needs, reinvest in a target portfolio with a longer maturity, or cash your holdings.

The net asset value of funds with distant maturities fluctuates more than targets with shorter maturities, the typical characteristic of longer bonds and funds. If you are striving for capital gains, longer maturities provide them. But here, again, the fund's single-bond personality has a singular effect: Net asset values don't fluctuate indefinitely, as conventional funds do, because bonds in the fund—therefore the entire fund—mature in a fixed year. As maturity approaches, net asset value stabilizes, as would the price of an individual bond.

As with all mutual funds, your purchase price is the fund's net asset value plus any loads that might apply. Most target funds have no loads, but some have yearly account fees. The minimum initial investment is

97

Figure 8-1: MONEY MARKET FUND QUOTATIONS

MONEY MARKET MUTUAL FUNDS

Wednesday, July 26, 1989

The following quotations, collected by the National Association of Securities Dealers Inc., represent the average of annualized yields and dollar-weighted portfolio maturities ending Wednesday, July 26, 1989. Yields are based on actual dividends to shareholders.

Fund	Avg. Mat.	7Day Yld.	e7Day Yld. Assets
AALMny	35	8.37	8.72	174
AARP	57	8.09	8.42	315
AMA TrP	11	7.63	7.92	17
AMA PrP	64	8.08	8.41	129
AMEV	31	8.61	8.99	82
ASO Pr	61	8.69	9.07	307
ASO US	42	8.49	8.85	134
ActAsGv	63	8.43	8.78	251
ActAsMny	63	8.87	9.27	3113
AlexBwn	32	8.68	9.06	1135
AlxBGvt	29	8.61	8.98	231
AlgerMM	20	9.30	9.74	60
AlliaCpRs	53	8.46	8.83	1633
AliaGvR	36	8.16	8.50	423
AlliMny	49	8.53	8.90	602
AlturaPr	30	8.65	9.03	249
AlturUS	26	8.49	8.85	48

Fund	Avg. Mat.	7Day Yld.	e7Day Yld. Assets
FidDom	35	8.98	9.39	1333
FIDSPM	46	9.47	9.92	3016
FidTrLP	42	7.99	8.31	102
FidUS Tr	6	8.85	9.25	315
FidelUS	45	8.59	8.97	1516
FinDIInc	8	8.52	8.89	343
FnclRsv	37	8.85	9.25	449
FstAmer	21	8.83	9.22	128
FtBost	44	8.72	9.10	120
FtInvCs f	23	8.46	8.80	282
FtPraMM	15	8.45	8.81	306
FtPraGv	5	8.20	8.54	202
FtVarG f	51	8.13	8.47	365
FlexFd	40	8.99	9.40	208
FtWash	31	8.59	8.96	80
Founders	33	8.18	8.52	58
FountSq	20	8.53	8.90	145
FrkMny a	13	8.32	8.67	1479
FrkFdl b	1	8.15	8.48	127
FrnkGvt	3	8.88	....	89
FrnkIFT	11	8.77	....	131
FreeCsh	30	8.48	8.84	968
FreeGv	30	8.36	8.71	168
FremntMM	39	8.64	9.01	41
FdSrce	29	8.53	8.90	131
FdSMony	15	8.88	9.28	125
FSWash	14	8.60	8.97	119

Fund	Avg. Mat.	7Day Yld.	e7Day Yld. Assets
MerLyIn af	45	8.86	9.26	1659
MerLyRdy	57	8.54	8.91	10234
MerLyRet a	60	8.59	8.97	4287
MerLyUSA	8	8.36	8.72	286
Metl.fStMM	43	8.54	8.91	86
MdIncTrGvt	41	8.04	8.37	106
MdInInst	26	8.81	9.20	116
Mon&ManPr	34	8.33	8.69	142
MonManGvt	18	8.10	8.44	27
MonMMgt f	44	8.53	8.90	206
MonMkTrst	44	8.94	....	1614
MonitorGov	27	8.63	9.01	104
MonitorMM	28	8.80	9.19	335
MutlOmah	40	8.40	8.76	189
MtlOmahC	37	8.17	8.50	51
NLR Cash	28	8.68	9.06	1781
NLR Gvt	27	8.27	8.61	127
NatlCash	32	8.46	8.82	49
NatwMM	38	8.65	9.04	497
NeubCsh	41	8.65	9.03	206
NeubGvt	51	7.74	8.04	164
NEMMkt	52	8.68	9.06	996
NEUSGvt	6	8.18	8.52	56
Newton	47	8.96	9.37	123
Nicholas	29	8.62	8.99	62
OppMoney	27	8.60	8.97	878
PSB Gov	15	8.43	8.79	34

$1,000 ($250 to $500 for IRAs and Keoghs), and the minimum for subsequent investments is usually $50 to $100.

Target funds are not comprehensive substitutes for conventional government bond funds. For one thing, there are considerably fewer of them than their conventional counterparts. At present, most target funds consist of zero coupon Treasuries, although targets holding conventional, coupon-paying Treasuries also are available.

Money Market Funds

Most investors are familiar with money market mutual funds, so named because they hold money market instruments, which are short-term, high-quality securities that are particularly sensitive to changes in economywide interest rates. Of the three types of money funds, the one that concerns us is often called a government reserves fund or something similar.

The government money fund differs from other money funds in that it invests only in T-bills and existing issues of Treasury notes and bonds with very brief maturities—always within one year and customarily within a few days or weeks. Mutual fund managers constantly add and delete securities as they mature, striving to produce the highest yields. Because maturities are exclusively short-term, returns from the government money fund fluctuate with market conditions, rising as short-term rates rise and falling as they fall.

However, money market funds differ from other government funds in a singular respect: They have a **constant-dollar** share price. This means the money fund's net asset value is pegged at $1. Unlike fluctuating net asset value of ordinary government bond funds, government money funds hold a constant share price of $1. Send $1,000 to the fund, and you buy 1,000 shares. Interest your $1,000 earns will vary, but your $1,000 will always be there.

Accordingly, government money funds offer three important advantages: absolute assurances against default, no possibility of capital loss, and market-level interest rates. These three advantages make government money funds useful in many ways. They are excellent parking lots for capital awaiting investment elsewhere. They are superb alternatives to ordinary savings accounts and certificates of deposit, particularly for investors whose accounts are with troubled institutions. They are an easy way to buy T-bills indirectly for modest investments, often $1,000 and hardly ever more than $5,000. Finally, as you will see in Section II, they are excellent investments for economic hard times of inflation and depression—inflation because their interest rates increase without decreases in net asset value; depression because their short maturities and high security prevent capital losses.

Further, government money funds have all the advantages of ordinary money market funds. If you hold a government money fund with a mutual fund family, you will have checking privileges that permit you to make withdrawals like an ordinary checking account. (Most funds require checks to be written in a minimum of $250 or $500 and also allow a limited number of check withdrawals without charge.) If you hold your government money fund with a broker, dividends from stocks, interest from bonds, and proceeds from sale of securities will be reinvested automatically in your fund for immediate earning of interest. Conversely, money is automatically withdrawn from your fund account to pay for securities you buy.

Interest from government money funds is paid monthly. You may have interest reinvested in shares or mailed to you by check. In general, interest from money funds is taxable as dividends even though it isn't a dividend.

UNIT INVESTMENT TRUSTS

Unit investment trusts (UITs) are similar to conventional bond funds in that they take money from many investors and purchase a portfolio of bonds in which each investor owns a part. They differ from funds in several major respects.

As an investor in a UIT, you buy units in a larger, diversified portfolio. The minimum purchase is usually five or ten units, requiring an initial investment of $5,000 to $10,000, and sometimes UITs won't permit subsequent investments. Bond funds usually require $500 to $2,000 for an initial investment and permit subsequent investments at any time.

UITs are unmanaged portfolios. Their managers select bonds with the intention of holding them to maturity—although the entire trust will not have a single maturity, as do target funds. As the bonds mature, the trust pays par value to investors. Bond mutual funds have no terminal maturity, and fund managers trade bonds often.

Few UITs consist of direct Treasury obligations, but they are widely represented by the Ginnie Mae fund. As its name implies, the Ginnie fund purchases Ginnie Mae pass-through certificates and sells shares in the portfolio to individual investors for smaller amounts, occasionally as little as $1,000. Mortgage interest and capital payments are credited to the subscriber's account—the pass-through is passed through.

Because of their lower prices compared to direct purchase, the Ginnie Mae fund is the most popular way for personal investors to hold Ginnies. Apart from lower cost, there are a few other advantages of investing indirectly in Ginnies through a fund. For one, the trust portfolio contains a diversity of Ginnies, so interest income and prepaid principal are likely to be more consistent in terms of average cash flow.

However, there are several disadvantages—besides the inherent disadvantages of Ginnies themselves—to buying Ginnies through a UIT. For one, your stated yield may not represent circumstances accurately. Remember, cash flow is the appropriate way to assess a Ginnie's payments; however, UITs are permitted to advertise current yield, which may be much higher at any given moment than cash flow. Second, sales charges for UITs often turn out to be more expensive than other forms of indirect investment.

Figure 8-2: GOVERNMENT BOND FUND QUOTATIONS

MUTUAL FUND QUOTATIONS

Tuesday, September 5, 1989

Price ranges for investment companies, as quoted by the National Association of Securities Dealers. NAV stands for net asset value per share; the offering includes net asset value plus maximum sales charge, if any.

Fund	NAV	Offer Price	NAV Chg.
AAL Mutual:			
CaGr p	11.09	11.64	− .04
Inco p	9.58	10.06	.....
MuBd p	9.89	10.38	.....
AARP Invst:			
CaGr	34.29	NL	+ .03
GiniM	15.04	NL	.....
GenBd	15.10	NL	.....
GthInc	26.20	NL	− .03
TxFBd	16.80	NL	.....
TxFSh	15.19	NL	.....
ABT Funds:			
Emrg p	10.86	11.40	− .05
GthIn p	11.64	12.22	− .03
SecIn p	11.18	11.74	.....
UtilIn p	15.69	16.47	− .02
AdsnCa p	18.50	19.07	− .01
ADTEK	10.86	NL	.....
AdvntG p	9.15	9.58	.....
AIM Funds:			
Chart p	6.99	7.40	− .02
Const p	9.85	10.42	+ .01
CvYld p	10.67	11.20	− .04
HiYld p	7.83	8.22	+ .02
LimM p	9.78	9.95	− .01
Sumit	8.48	.....	− .03
Weing p	12.38	13.10	.....
A M A Funds:			
ClaGt p	10.61	NL	− .01
EMT r	15.40	16.17	+ .10
GlbGt p	22.99	NL	− .05
GlbIn p	19.55	NL	− .03
GlST p	9.79	NL	− .01
GrPl p	22.07	NL	− .12
MdTc p	10.58	NL	+ .01
USGv p	8.53	NL	+ .01
AMEV Funds:			
AstAll	12.00	12.57	+ .01
Capitl	16.24	17.75	+ .03
CapAp	15.55	16.28	+ .03
Fidcur	25.68	26.89	+ .01
Grwth	21.53	23.53	− .08
HiYld	9.38	9.82	+ .01
Specl	26.54	26.54	− .09
TF Nat	9.93	10.40	+ .01
[illegible]Gvt	[illegible].69	10[illegible]	.01
Equit f	2.49	2.49	+ .01
Incom f	1.86	1.86	.....
ShtTr f	1.58	1.58	.....
Clipper	48.51	48.51	+ .13
Colonial Funds:			
AGold p	20.59	22.08	+ .19
CalTE p	7.00	7.35	.....
CpCsh p	47.02	47.98	− .05
CCsII p	45.00	45.92	− .02
DvsdIn	7.54	8.09	.....
Fund	21.49	23.05	− .02
GvSec p	11.17	11.98	− .01
Grwth	14.01	15.02	− .02
HiYld p	6.93	7.28	+ .01
Incom p	6.60	6.93	− .01
IncPls	9.72	10.42	.....
IntEq p	18.32	19.23	+ .04
MATx p	7.13	7.49	− .01
Mi TE p	6.58	6.91	.....
MnTE p	6.87	7.21	.....
NYTE p	6.65	6.98	.....
OhTE p	6.81	7.15	− .01
SmlIn p	14.07	14.77	.....
TXIns p	7.63	8.01	.....
TxEx p	13.03	13.68	.....
US Gv p	7.14	7.50	.....
US Id p	17.22	18.08	− .06
Colonial VIP:			
AggG t	13.06	13.06	+ .04
DvRet t	11.93	11.93	.....
HiInc t	9.78	9.78	+ .01
HYMu t	9.92	9.92	.....
Co DTE	9.98	10.39	.....
Columbia Funds:			
Fixed	12.62	12.62	− .02
Grth	27.06	NL	− .01
Muni r	11.60	NL	+ .01
Specl r	45.38	45.38	+ .05
Common Sense:			
Govt	11.34	12.16	.....
Grwth	13.60	14.86	− .04
GrInc	13.23	14.46	− .01
MunB	12.36	12.98	− .01
Cwlth AB	1.57	1.70	.....
Cwlth CD	2.20	2.38	.....
[illegible]mpsG[illegible]		unavail	
DisEq	13.65	13.65	− .02
Eq Inc	29.88	30.49	− .09
EqIdx	13.73	13.73	− .04
Europ r	15.41	15.72	− .01
Exch	84.36	84.36	− .21
Fidel	19.65	19.65	− .02
FlexB	6.88	NL	− .01
Fredm	15.58	NL	+ .01
GloBd r	10.90	10.90	− .01
GNMA	10.26	NL	− .01
GovtSc	9.52	NL	− .01
GroInc	19.01	19.40	− .03
GroCo	20.18	20.80	+ .04
HiInc	8.32	NL	.....
HiYld	12.70	NL	.....
InsMu	10.99	NL	.....
IntBd	10.05	NL	.....
IntGr r	12.95	13.08	+ .01
LtdMn	9.26	NL	.....
MagIn	63.89	65.87	+ .03
MI TF	11.06	NL	− .01
MA TF	11.13	NL	.....
MN TF	10.42	NL	− .01
MtgSc	10.09	NL	− .01
MunBd	8.10	NL	− .01
Oh TF	10.70	NL	.....
NJ HY	10.56	NL	.....
NY HY	11.79	NL	− .01
NY Ins	10.83	NL	.....
OTC	23.45	24.18	.....
Ovrse	26.33	27.14	+ .09
PcBas r	14.97	15.28	+ .01
Pa TF	9.85	NL	.....
Puritn	15.00	15.31	− .05
RealEs	10.13	10.34	− .01
ShtBd	9.31	9.31	− .01
ShtTGv	9.91	9.91	+ .01
Sht TF	9.45	NL	+ .01
SprtG	10.43	10.43	− .01
SpcSit	19.90	20.73	+ .03
TX TF	10.30	NL	.....
Trend	50.05	50.05	+ .17
UtilInc	12.32	12.57	− .02
Value	34.04	NL	− .13
Fidl Inv Instit:			
STAR r	9.20	[illegible]	− .01
Gintel Group:			
CaAp p	17.09	NL	− .02
Erisa p	44.17	NL	− .15
GintFd	85.68	NL	− .31
Gradison Funds:			
EstGr p	20.03	NL	− .02
GvIn p	12.94	13.20	+ .01
OpGr p	15.28	NL	+ .02
Grnspg	13.81	NL	− .03
GwWsh p	14.84	15.62	− .05
Grth Ind	9.92	9.92	+ .01
Guardian Funds:			
Bond	11.78	NL	+ .01
ParkA	25.76	26.97	+ .04
Stock	24.15	NL	+ .02
HTInseq	13.72	14.37	+ .01
HanColo	9.62	10.10	.....
Harbor Funds:			
Grwth	13.81	NL	− .01
Intl	16.17	NL	+ .04
US Eq	14.34	NL	− .02
Hartwell Fds:			
EmgGt	15.70	16.19	.....
Gwth	20.46	21.09	− .02
HrvstG p	11.15	11.83	− .02
HeartG p	9.16	9.59	.....
HeartId p	16.73	17.52	− .01
Helmsman Fds:			
DiscEq	11.96	11.96	− .05
GrEq	11.89	11.89	.....
Income	9.91	9.91	.....
IncEq	11.12	11.12	− .02
Heritge p	14.57	15.18	+ .02
HrtgCv p	10.53	10.97	.....
HiMark	12.20	NL	− .03
HmGvSc	9.44	9.91	+ .03
HmHYBd	9.62	10.10	− .01
Hor Man	22.49	NL	− .05
Hummer	16.78	NL	− .04
IAI Funds:			
HilBd	5.84	6.30	.....
HiInII	8.87	9.31	.....
MuBd	10.60	11.13	.....
TFCA p	5.17	5.43	.....
MMA p	10.68	11.21	.....
MMD p	10.89	11.43	+ .01
MNC p	11.25	11.81	.....
MSC p	11.36	11.93	.....
MuTN p	9.85	10.34	.....
MuVA p	11.02	11.57	.....
MWV p	10.76	11.30	.....
MuHY	9.70	10.18	.....
MFS Lifetime:			
CapG t	12.14	12.14	+ .01
Globl t	12.48	12.48	+ .05
Sectr t	11.24	11.24	+ .02
Emg t	7.92	7.92	.....
DivPl t	9.55	9.55	− .01
GvPl t	7.73	7.73	.....
HiInc t	6.77	6.77	.....
IntInc t	9.45	9.45	+ .01
MuBd t	8.39	8.39	.....
MIM Funds:			
BdInc	9.86	NL	.....
SCO Inc	11.02	NL	+ .01
SCO Gr	10.65	NL	− .01
MIMLIC Funds:			
AstAll	11.89	12.52	.....
Invl	13.27	13.97	− .02
MtgSc	10.11	10.64	− .01
MSB Fd p	21.25	21.25	− .05
MacKay Shields:			
CaAp t	12.45	12.45	− .05
Conv t	9.05	9.05	+ .01
CrpBd t	8.27	8.27	.....
Globl t	10.17	10.17	− .05
GovPl t	8.98	8.98	− .01
TxFB t	9.71	9.71	.....
TotRt t	11.77	11.77	− .02
Value	12.5[illegible]	[illegible].57	+ [illegible]

READING MUTUAL FUND QUOTATIONS

Nearly all mutual fund families offer at least one and often more government bond funds. You can locate funds for potential investment and track your fund after you have invested by reading the mutual fund pages in your local paper or national financial media. Figure 8-2 shows sample listings for government bond quotations.

- The first entry names the fund in abbreviations—"Government Securities," for example.

- The second entry identifies the net asset value of the fund. Net asset value is calculated by dividing the value of the fund's total portfolio by the number of shares outstanding. When bonds held by a mutual fund increase in price, the net asset value of the fund's shares increases. Conversely, if bonds held by your fund decrease in price, your fund's NAV decreases.

- The third entry specifies the offering price—the price you pay to purchase shares of the bond fund. When a bond fund has a front-end load, your purchase price is higher than net asset value by the amount of the load. The annotation "NL" indicates the fund is no load; you pay net asset value to subscribe to the fund.

- The final entry specifies the change in net asset value in straight dollars and cents: " + .01" means net asset value increased by a penny over the previous day's trading.

Besides following daily accounts in the newspaper, check the many financial magazines that publish monthly, quarterly, or year-end reports of mutual funds, including government bond funds, ranking their price and income performance. *Mutual Fund Profiles,* a joint publication by Standard & Poor's and Lipper Analytical Service, reports the performance of government bond funds. It is probably available from your broker.

Mutual fund quotations do not reveal two important pieces of information: the interest income per share that the fund currently pays, and the amount of fees and charges per share, no-load fund or otherwise. This information is outlined in the prospectus, which will be mailed free if you contact the sponsoring fund family. Mutual fund families advertise in major newspapers and are often listed in the phone book. The advertisements will provide a toll-free number to call for information.

USES FOR GOVERNMENT BOND FUNDS

In most respects, uses for government bond funds are as numerous as uses for Treasury and agency bonds. They are excellent for current or compounded income in your personal account. Funds are particularly appropriate for long-term accumulations in tax-deferred IRAs and Keoghs; their security against default is important for retirement planning, and your ability to make small, continuous investments is highly advantaged for IRA-type investing. Further, government bond funds can be excellent vehicles for Uniform Gifts to Minors Accounts, wherein parents can plan for children's education much as they would for their own retirement.

MANAGING MUTUAL FUNDS

Switch Privileges

If you are concerned with Treasury and agency securities, a government bond fund probably will be a permanent feature of your overall portfolio. However, a buy-and-hold strategy, whereby you make continuing investments for the sake of long-term compounding or current income just as you would invest directly in Treasuries, is only one way to make the most of a fund. It is equally possible to manage government bond funds actively.

It may seem contradictory to speak of managing an indirect portfolio when one of the chief advantages of a fund is professional management by others. Nonetheless, active management on your part is possible and, in some instances, desirable. We have noted, for example, that changes in economywide interest rates cause price fluctuations in bonds and in the net asset value of government bond funds. Although long-term investors ride out capital fluctuations, some want to avoid them, fearing capital loss, and still other investors seek them out, hoping to profit from capital gains. The aspect of mutual funds that satisfies all these investors is your ability to switch your investment into and out of your fund as conditions warrant.

By subscribing to a fund family you have **switch privileges** with other funds in the family. As your investment goals change or as another type of bond investment becomes more advisable for personal or investment reasons, you can transfer into and out of your government bond fund by switching for shares of another fund within the family.

Table 8-1: ILLUSTRATION OF DOLLAR COST AVERAGING

Month	Net Asset Value	Shares Purchased	Portfolio Value
Jan.	$10 per share	10	$100
Feb.	$ 8	12.5	$180
Mar.	$ 9	11.111	$302.50
Apr.	$10	10	$436.11
May	$11	9.091	$579.72
Jun.	$12	8.333	$732.42

Some investors use switch privileges in a limited way. As interest rates rise, they move from a bond fund to a money market fund. As rates fall, they relocate into the bond fund. Other investors follow a broader course, moving not merely between money fund and bond fund but among a government bond fund and perhaps a stock fund or other type of bond fund. Eventually, they wind up back in the Treasury portfolio and start over again.

Whatever your orientation, you can appreciate the convenience and maneuverability of switch privileges. In effect, whole new portfolios can be yours with a single phone call. We will discuss when and why you might want to manage your portfolio actively with switch privileges in Section II, but now let's look at one profitable technique for managing a government bond fund. This technique, not available with direct purchase of bonds, is called **dollar cost averaging.**

MANAGING BOND FUNDS

Dollar Cost Averaging

Dollar cost averaging is a simple procedure that requires investing a fixed amount at a fixed interval in a government bond fund. To illustrate dollar cost averaging, let's assume you buy shares of a fund in amounts of $100 each month. Six months from now, your purchase record might resemble the one shown in Table 8-1.

You ended the period with a portfolio value of $732.42 (61.035 total shares times $12 per share on the closing date) on an investment of $600. You achieved that gain because dollar cost averaging buys more shares when net asset values are lower and fewer shares when they are higher.

Dollar cost averaging is especially useful because funds permit you to buy fractional shares, whereas you can't buy part of a government bond if you purchase it directly. Once you have decided to invest regularly, dollar cost averaging eliminates timing decisions, for you automatically profit from buying more shares when net asset value is depressed. In addition, you—not the market—establish how much you invest per period through dollar cost averaging.

However, dollar cost averaging doesn't assure continual gains, because net asset values fluctuate. Notice what happens in February in Table 8-1. Two months into dollar costing, you had placed $200 into a fund valued at $180 (12.5 shares at $8 per share). Had you redeemed the shares, you would have lost 10 percent of your investment. By continuing to dollar cost, you bought more shares at net asset values of $8 and $9 and benefited when net asset values improved because you were holding more shares.

INVESTING IN GOVERNMENT BOND FUNDS

Your chief source of information about a government bond fund is the prospectus, which your broker or mutual fund family must provide before you invest. The prospectus must list the fund's goals, restrictions, advisors, fees, and portfolio. You want to examine these features in light of the advantages and disadvantages we have discussed as well as to confirm that the fund meets your maturity and cost considerations.

Examine the fund's performance record. All funds have swings in performance, but most investors look not so much for highs and lows as for consistency and returns that are generally competitive with market averages. The prospectus will disclose income performance during the past few years.

Funds constituted as partnerships and funds that offer checking privileges insist upon signature verification when you complete the application accompanying the prospectus. Mark appropriate spaces for special services like telephone withdrawal, transfer privileges, and checking. Remember to specify if earnings are to be invested or paid as cash, and which types of earnings are to be compounded or cashed.

The applications ask if you want to hold certificates as evidence of ownership. There's no reason you should. Regular communications from the fund will detail your holdings, and if you redeem shares you will have to execute the certificates and mail them back, entailing delays and paperwork. You redeem shares by calling the fund if you have so specified in your application. Otherwise, you will have to send written notice of intention to redeem. You need not sell all shares, subject to minimum withdrawals and account balances.

After completing the application, mail a check or money order to the fund, and you will be a subscriber and indirect investor in Treasury and agency securities.

SUMMARY

Government bond mutual funds bring you a whole portfolio with a single investment. Available for modest sums, these various funds let you select Treasury or agency bonds, conventional or zero coupon bonds, and portfolios of varying average maturity or potential for price fluctuation. You can use bond funds for cash-in-hand payments or reinvested interest and capital gains in personal, retirement, or children's accounts.

Immediately liquid with a phone call and maneuverable through switch privileges, government bond funds enable you to manage your portfolio with speed and versatility. Dollar cost averaging is a particularly useful technique for accumulating a position in bonds gradually and at built-in gains. So long as you are aware that fund fees may exceed commissions for directly held investments, you can select and switch mutual funds for opportune advantages while employing professional managers and record keepers.

9

Other Treasury and Agency Securities

Treasury and agency securities covered in the preceding chapters are the most widely used by personal investors. However, the Treasury Department issues other types of securities that you should be aware of. In addition, financial institutions have been busy applying the diversity and advantages of Treasury securities to create innovative investment products.

TAX ANTICIPATION BILLS

One related form of Treasury bill is the **tax anticipation bill.** A direct obligation of Uncle Sam sold at a discount from par like T-bills, TABs mature in 23 to 273 days after issue and usually come due within a week of required quarterly tax payments by corporations. Corporations are chief owners of TABs because the bills may be submitted at par value in payment of corporate taxes. If you own a business, consider TABs as one way to meet your quarterly tax filings.

CASH MANAGEMENT NOTES

Since 1975, TABs have been supplemented by cash management notes, also direct Treasury obligations. Issued in $10 million denominations, they mature in 30 days or less and are timed to come due when an existing issue of Treasury debt matures. This gives the Treasury additional flexibility in managing final principal and interest payments on existing debt. Hardly a common element in the portfolio of personal investors because of their hefty price, cash management notes are nonetheless available, and you may see occasional mention of them in the financial press.

FLOWER BONDS

Flower bonds are an ordinary Treasury bond with a special feature: They are accepted at par, regardless of market price, in payment of estate taxes if the decedent was the owner at the time of death. Flower bonds were issued as recently as 1971, and the last of them, bearing a $35 coupon, matures in 1998.

Flower bonds are not particularly attractive on their income merits—note the low coupon. However, families and executors facing the closing of an estate constitute enough of a market for flower bonds to keep their prices relatively stable at slightly below par. You should keep flower bonds in mind for their positive estate tax consequences if you face this selective investment situation.

CONVERTIBLE TREASURY ZEROS

You will recall that derivative zeros are created by stripping the interest and principal from conventional Treasury bonds and that some long-term Treasuries are callable five years before maturity. Nearly all derivative zeros are stripped from noncallable Treasuries, but a few derivatives created from callable bonds have a special feature: They convert to current income bonds when they mature.

The process works this way: Institutions buy callable Treasury bonds and strip the interest and principal. For the sake of illustration, let's say the stripped bond is callable in 2007 and matures in 2012. This bond presents a dilemma: The brokerage can't sell zeros based upon coupons after 2007, because those coupons won't be available if the Treasury calls the underlying bond. Accordingly, the brokerage strips the principal and sells it as a convertible. Derivatives based on principal mature to par of $1,000 in 2007. If the Treasury calls the underlying bond, the brokerage pays $1,000 to owners of the derivative zero. If the Treasury doesn't call the bond, it continues to pay interest. The sponsoring brokerage prorates that interest among owners of the derivative zero and pays it semiannually. In short, the zero converts to a current income bond.

In truth, most advisors do not recommend that you invest in convertible derivatives with the expectation of receiving their five years of current income. They point out that many convertibles are based upon high-coupon Treasuries that have a good chance of being called before maturity. Advisors do, however, recommend that you follow prices and markets for these products. Being somewhat eccentric additions to the concept of derivative zeros, their prices may be lower and yields higher than ordinary, nonconvertible derivative zeros maturing in the same years. When such is the case, you get a bargain—and perhaps a lucrative surprise—if they do convert to coupon instruments.

Don't confuse the convertible derivative zero with the more established convertible zero coupon municipal bond. The convertible municipal is a direct obligation of an issuing municipal government, not a derivative zero. By covenant, it starts its life as a zero and then converts. The convertible municipal zero is specifically designed to convert to a coupon-payer and usually is not callable until several years after coupon payments begin. For a full discussion of convertible municipals, buy a copy of *The Income Investor* and *The Personal Investor's Complete Book of Bonds* by your author and Longman Financial Services.

BABY ZEROS

Virtually all derivative zeros have par values of $1,000, but the **Treasury Bond Receipts (TBRs)** created by E.F. Hutton, now merged with Shearson Lehman, are an exception. TBRs are "baby zeros" with par value of $250, $275, $285, or $475. Their reduced par means that purchase prices are even smaller than for CATS or TIGRs with pars of $1,000. Accordingly, they are especially useful for investors with very modest amounts to set aside. The minimum required investment ranges from $500 upward, for which you can purchase two to five bonds. The most distant maturity of TBRs is 2006.

Apart from their unusual par values, TBRs are functionally the same as other derivative zeros. You might keep TBRs in mind if you have odd sums in your IRA or Keogh. A few hundred dollars might not be enough to purchase a required lot of CATS or TIGRs, but it will be enough to buy a few TBRs. TBRs have one disadvantage: They are few in number, so their markets are not as liquid as conventional derivative zeros. You should be aware of their comparative illiquidity if there is a chance you will sell before maturity.

SPLIT FUNDS

Since 1985, several major brokerage firms have marketed unit trusts that mate the assured maturity value of derivative zeros with other investments. Trusts that combine derivatives with common stocks are the best known and most widely advertised, but other types of **split funds** take the concept further by combining derivatives with aggressive investments in commodities and precious metals.

The concept is a simple one. Managers take about half of your investment and place the money in Treasury zeros. Zeros will grow to equal the amount of your original investment in five years (or longer, with some trusts). The remainder of your investment is placed into securities for capital growth or aggressive gains. Thus, these trusts offer the chance for capital gains and assure that if you hold them until maturity you will at least get your original investment capital back. This is particularly attractive if you want to invest in commodities, for which prospects of capital loss are high.

Apart from assurance that you will receive all of your original capital back if you stay in the trust until it terminates, you have diversification within a portfolio of other investments and the advantage of professional managers investing on your behalf. One disadvantage—if you view it as such—is the holding period: To ensure that you will receive back all your principal, you have to hold these trusts for their full maturity. You can redeem your fund prior to maturity with written notification to the sponsoring brokerage. If you do so, you aren't assured of getting all your capital back or securing an investment gain unless your fund performs well. Minimum investment is usually $5,000 ($2,000 for an IRA). Some split funding trusts permit subsequent investments, others don't.

Trusts investing in stocks and precious metals coins are available to all investors, but you usually have to meet federally mandated suitability requirements before you may invest in the aggressive trusts dealing in commodities. For example, you may have to demonstrate net worth of at least $75,000 excluding home and personal possessions or a minimum net worth of $30,000 plus an annual income of at least $30,000. Suitability standards may be higher in some states.

COMMON AND PREFERRED STOCK OF FANNIE MAE

Our final miscellaneous investments are the common and preferred stock of the Federal National Mortgage Association. They are included here precisely because they should not be. They are not securities of the federal government and should not be mistaken for them. As we have noted and as Fannie Mae states in its literature, Fannie Mae is a publicly traded corporation whose stocks are listed on the New York Stock Exchange.

Fannie's bonds may offer some assurances of Treasury backing, but its common and preferred stocks do not. As a stock investment, Fannie

Mae should be evaluated as you would evaluate any other company whose basic industry is the mortgage business. As a quick review of Fannie's stock performance indicates, that business can be a volatile as well as a profitable one.

SECTION

II

Managing Treasury and Agency Securities

10

Treasury and Agency Securities for Savings

Savings are the most neglected aspect of Americans' overall finances, not just their portfolios. Every investor, regardless of age, income, or financial sophistication, should have a savings component in his or her portfolio. Moreover, every investor should understand what the savings component is supposed to accomplish, should have a disciplined plan for meeting savings goals, and should recognize which Treasury and agency securities are suited to the savings component.

SAVING AND SAVINGS

The distinction between *saving* and *savings* is an important one. Saving is a process—or, to apply an accounting metaphor, saving is a flow of income from salary or securities scheduled toward a specific investment destination. More or less continual at every stage of life, saving is a disciplined process undertaken in addition to other financial and investment activities. Savings, by comparison, is that component of your portfolio into which flows the amount of funds you save. The savings component is the investment destination for saving. It is a reservoir, a pool of capital that preserves and multiplies the money you save.

The distinction between saving and savings may seem like an unnecessarily fine one, but it is not, for different decisions go into each. Saving money is a process of applying self-discipline in postponing consumption, for the only way you save money is by not consuming it. On the other hand, managing savings is a matter of directing money saved into appropriate savings-type investments. In short, savings decisions are actually a type of investment decision. To make the right decision you have to understand what the savings component is supposed to accomplish.

FUNCTIONS OF THE SAVINGS COMPONENT

The first function of the savings component is to prevent loss of the money you have saved. It is often said that the savings component consists of capital that is not at risk, although all investments entail some form of risk. Therefore, it is more accurate to say that the first task of the savings component is to defend capital against two specific types of risk, namely default risk and market risk.

Default risk is the possibility that an investment will not make its expected payments of interest and repayment of principal. Treasury and agency securities minimize default risk better than any other investment, so they are ideal for the savings component. However, defending against default is not sufficient in itself to justify an investment for the savings component. A 30-year Treasury bond is immune to default, but it is not appropriate for the savings component because it is vulnerable to market risk.

As you will recall from Section I, market risk is associated with changes in the market price of securities. Capital fluctuation—changes in the price of a bond or net asset value of a mutual fund—is the result of market risk. In other components of the portfolio, you accept the negative side of market risk (capital losses) in exchange for the potentially positive side (capital gains). In the savings component, however, capital losses are intolerable and capital gains are not your goal. Your goal is stability of principal, and that goal is served only by constant-dollar vehicles that protect against market loss from fluctuations in price.

Further, investments within the savings component need to generate market-level returns—that is, rates of interest competitive with prevailing economywide interest. Earning market-level returns is important for two reasons. First, you want maximum payments consistent with capital stability because you want your savings to grow through compounded interest as well as through your regular investments in the savings component. Second, you need market-level interest to ensure that increases in the general price level don't erode the purchasing power of your savings. In other words, you want your savings component to defend against purchasing power risk.

Finally, the savings component requires more than minuscule default risk, market risk, and purchasing power risk; it requires immediate

116

liquidity—unimpaired ability to convert investments to cash with minimal transaction fees and delays. Immediate liquidity is essential because savings often need to be tapped for emergencies and unexpected or planned events. The requirement for immediate liquidity further restricts the types of investments that are appropriate for the savings component, for many investments are secure and stable but not necessarily liquid.

In sum, the savings component presents a more detailed set of investment considerations than many investors realize. To meet all the requirements of the savings component, you have to center upon a selected group of investments. Treasury and agency securities offer an array of alternatives for doing so.

PASSBOOK ACCOUNTS

For most investors, the federally insured passbook account at a commercial bank or savings and loan provides a convenient first alternative for the savings component. Passbook accounts meet the requirement of capital stability, for they are constant-dollar vehicles with no capital fluctuation. And because the institution will be aided by federal guarantors if it approaches insolvency, default risk is low.

Passbook accounts also rank high in liquidity. Withdrawals are easily accomplished in person or via automated teller machines at multiple locations throughout the institution's business area. Account and withdrawal fees almost never apply. Relatedly, passbook accounts offer one advantage over other savings-type investments in that their minimum deposits are exceedingly low, permitting you to save any sum that your budget permits.

Their general suitability aside, passbook accounts come up short in paying market-level rates of interest. The standard 5 to 5½ percent rates long established for these accounts don't always compare favorably with other rates available on savings-type investments that also provide capital stability, low default risk, and liquidity. For this reason, passbook accounts should never constitute the majority of the savings component after you have accumulated enough to move into higher-paying securities. They are an excellent place to initiate the savings component, but their fixed rates should deter you from holding your savings there indefinitely.

CERTIFICATES OF DEPOSIT

Unfortunately, many investors regard certificates of deposit (CDs) as the chief investment of the savings component. Like passbook accounts, they are constant-dollar securities carrying federal guarantees of interest and principal, and they often pay higher rates than deposit accounts. They are available for relatively small sums, normally $500 to $1,000, and will accommodate larger deposits of almost any size. Apart from these points of suitability, however, CDs don't really belong in the savings component.

The drawbacks of CDs are their illiquidity and interest penalties. CDs are contract deposits in which you agree to leave your funds on account for a stated period. If you need your funds before the CD matures, you often must forfeit a portion of interest earned. On both counts, CDs detract from the basic purpose of the savings component.

One compromise, albeit a partial one, is to hold brokered CDs purchased through a brokerage firm rather than a bank or S&L. Unlike their depository counterparts, brokered CDs are liquid before maturity; you can sell them to another investor without interest penalties, and they still carry the federal default assurances of depository products.

The dilemma about using brokered CDs is that they are not constant-dollar products. Their market price rises and falls with changes in economywide interest rates. If you sell before maturity, you might enjoy a capital gain, but you might also suffer a capital loss, and that's unacceptable for the savings component. In point of sound investment practice, conventional and brokered CDs are best for the income component of your portfolio, not the savings component.

GOVERNMENT MONEY MARKET FUNDS

For most investors, money market funds concentrating in Treasury securities are the investment of choice for the savings component. Invested in T-bills and Treasuries about to mature, government money market funds certainly meet the low default criteria of savings. As constant-dollar securities with a steady $1 net asset value, they are immune to market risk.

A further point favoring the government money fund is accessibility. Widely available from mutual fund families and brokerage firms, they hardly ever entail fees, and immediate liquidity is possible by checking privileges, telephone, and personal withdrawal. If you buy Treasury and agency securities directly, having a government money fund with your broker will facilitate speedy transactions and assure continual compounding of interest. As an indirect investor in one of the many types of Treasury and agency mutual funds, you have switch privileges with the money fund that your investment company no doubt sponsors.

Where government money funds really shine for the savings component, however, is in paying market-level rates while permitting modest initial and subsequent investments. Market-level rates are assured because securities the fund holds pay them continually, and, as noted in Chapter 7, required minimums start around $1,000 for initial investment and are as low as $100 for subsequent investment. Some funds have much lower minimums, meaning you can avoid passbook accounts, start your savings component with government money funds, and hold them continuously as the mainstay of savings.

T-BILLS FOR SAVINGS

Treasury bills are well suited for the savings component, although their $10,000 price is prohibitive for many investors. They are immediately liquid, capital stable, and secure against market, default, business, and political risk. T-bill interest is exempt from state taxes and is the definition of a market-level rate of return for short-term investments. The historical record shows that T-bills have kept pace with changing price levels for 40 years, as shown in Figure 10-1.

If you are holding $10,000 in another savings-type investment, by all means consider T-bills as an alternative. You are losing liquidity, interest, or tax advantages where you are currently holding your savings. This point shouldn't have to be mentioned, yet investors will hold upwards of $20,000 or $30,000 in a fully taxed savings account, and never consider that a T-bill provides a market-level rate of interest, ultimate defense against default, and municipally untaxed interest.

Most investors prefer the three-month bill for savings, although the six-month and one-year bills are appropriate. Buy them from a broker and roll them over as they mature. Don't buy T-bills through the Treasury Direct program for your savings component, as cashing them before maturity is difficult and time consuming.

You get more from your savings with T-bills on all fronts, and T-bills remove you from the problems that the U.S. banking system faces. Especially if you are holding your savings in a savings and loan institution, the most troubled segment of the depository industry, switch to T-bills and escape the industry's problems.

SHORT-TERM BONDS FOR SAVINGS

Further, consider short-term bonds—maturities of two or three years—as another alternative for your savings. Capital stable and liquid through exchanges, short bonds may offer slightly higher rates than T-bills or other securities. Commissions will apply, however, and that will reduce

Figure 10-1:   T-BILLS AND THE GENERAL PRICE LEVEL

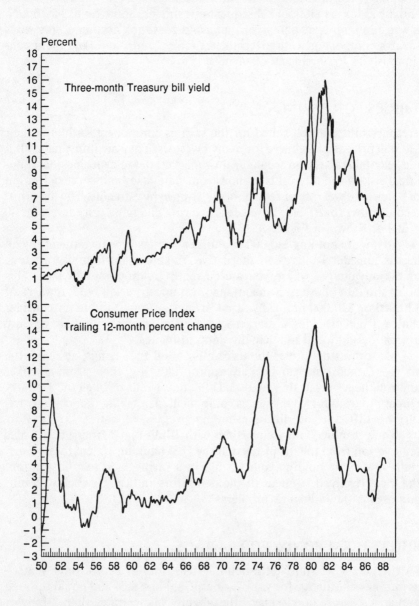

SOURCE: Bureau of Economic Analysis, U.S. Department of Commerce.

your return. For this same reason, don't rely upon short-term Treasury funds for savings. The fees will erode yields.

For the savings component, unlike other components of the portfolio, you don't want issues selling at a premium. Premium notes and bonds may be great for higher up-front income, but the premiums on short-term bonds will erode yields. Stay with short maturities at par.

SIZING THE SAVINGS COMPONENT

Even though you recognize which constant-dollar investments are appropriate for the savings component, you must also decide how large an adequate component is. Many advisors counsel you to hold between 10 and 25 percent of your total portfolio value in these vehicles, depending upon your age and life circumstances. Another common standard requires you to hold the equivalent of three to six months net salary in constant-dollar investments, regardless of your portfolio value.

With the wider availability of lines of credit, these ratios may decline, for you can draw upon other sources for short-term emergency funds—assuming you are able to repay borrowings. Nonetheless, it is necessary for you to have an accessible source of ready cash as defense against life's proverbial slings and arrows.

ACCUMULATING SAVINGS—THE SELF-TITHE

To acquire an adequate quantity of savings-type investments, most advisors are unanimous in recommending the "self-tithe"—setting aside 10 percent of net income every payday before you can get your hands on it. The advantages to the self-tithe are ease of figuring (multiply take-home pay by one-tenth) and its small dent from consumption. Also, by maintaining a constant 10 percent of regular income, saving grows with salary.

The best way to implement the self-tithe is to participate in automatic deposit programs offered by depository institutions and money market funds. These intermediaries generally will make arrangements to withdraw a specified amount from your checking account at regular intervals, often the first and/or fifteenth of the month. The funds are deposited electronically, and your checking account shows the amount withdrawn. Even those surviving on modest salaries can afford 10 percent of salary as a regular contribution.

MANAGING THE SAVINGS COMPONENT

The first key to managing the savings component is consolidation—having your savings in one vehicle. For some reason, many investors like to diversify their savings. They might hold half of their liquid financial assets in one stock, but they will have a savings account and a half dozen money market funds. This is counterproductive. Consolidate your savings in one and maybe two places—a government money fund and an issue of short bonds, for example. If you need to draw down savings, having them in one vehicle facilitates accessibility. Having your constant-dollar investments in one place also makes it easier to move them to higher-paying investments that offer capital stability.

Maneuvering the savings component from one investment to another is the second important part of managing it. Don't be afraid to move savings-type investments as the savings component grows. Many investors hold $20,000 and more in a passbook account, either because they figure they don't have enough to do anything else, or because they are afraid to move the money. Manage your savings component by moving into other investments featuring stability and liquidity as you build the capital to do so.

In its rudimentary form, the self-tithe involves placing a portion of monthly pay into a conventional savings account until you accumulate adequate sums to enter other investments. If you save 10 percent of net salary each month, you will acquire three months' salary in slightly under three years. By that time, the savings account will likely be large enough to move into a money market fund. As sums equaling three to six months' net income increase, you can shift the constant-dollar investment into Treasury bills or short-term bonds, or you can leave them in the government money fund.

SUMMARY

Wise investors are conscientious savers. Saving is a selected type of investing, and the savings component consists of investments that provide capital stability, minimal risk of default, and market-level returns. Securities with Treasury guarantees are excellent for the savings component because they fill those requirements.

You can't allow the savings component to be inert. You need to manage it by accumulating adequate savings, perhaps through the tested technique of the self-tithe, and then shifting your investments into progressively more advantaged savings-type vehicles.

11

Treasury and Agency Securities for Income

Most investors find Treasury and agency securities unparalleled for the income component of their portfolios. Whether they are investing for current income needed for consumption, as is often the case with older investors, or whether they are investing for interest and dividends that they permit to compound for the future in a personal or retirement account, investors understand the advantages of Treasury and agency securities.

The chief advantage of Treasury and agency securities in the income component is their default-free payments of interest and principal. Further, the wide availability of these securities, their abundant quantity, frequent issue schedules, assortment of maturities, and generally broad markets assure optimum selection and versatility of management for the income component.

FUNCTIONS OF THE INCOME COMPONENT

Obviously, the first function of the income component is to produce dependable interest and dividends. That function is best served by investment-grade securities, particularly Treasury and agency paper. Given that you are investing for dependable payments, investment-quality securities offer the maximum assurance of receiving payments.

Relatedly, investment-grade securities, again Treasury and agency securities in particular, have broader, more liquid markets than lower-rated investments. This facilitates management of your income portfolio, buying and when necessary selling securities to align your holdings for income performance.

(Special note: Some investors deliberately forsake investment-grade quality in the income component, preferring lower-rated securities for the sake of higher payments. This specialized strategy of managing for aggressive income entails wider risks of default and capital fluctuation than are appropriate for the income component. For a discussion of aggressive income, buy a copy of *The Income Investor* by your author and Longman Financial Services.

Second, the income component needs to produce frequent income in addition to dependable income. Whether investing for current consumption or for compounding, you need to structure the income component to produce frequent payments. Monthly or quarterly payments of interest and dividends assure the necessary stream of income to underpin consumption and to maximize frequency of compounding.

Third, investments within the income component need to balance capital stability and maximum income. As a practical matter, this function is served by managing maturities of income securities. You have seen that longer maturities typically offer higher yields, but their prices fluctuate more dramatically. By contrast, shorter maturities have more stable prices, but their returns often are less. The income component needs some stability, but it need not have rock solid capital stability; it must provide generous income, but not at the sake of undependable principal. Instead, it must reconcile income and price behaviors for an appropriate balance.

Fourth, the income component needs to balance reinvestment opportunity and reinvestment risk. You will recall from Section I that reinvestment risk pertains to changes in economywide interest rates that keep you from stabilizing income in your portfolio. If economywide interest rates rise, your existing investments may not produce a level of income competitive in the new environment. On the other hand, if rates fall, your existing securities may be producing above-market income, but you have lost the chance to maintain the previous level of payments in the lower rate environment. In meeting this function of the income component, you need to manage maturities, yields, and coupon or dividend payments for versatility in responding to changing economic circumstances.

With these four functions of the income component in mind, let's examine how individual Treasury and agency securities can be useful.

TREASURY NOTES AND BONDS

Direct obligations of the U.S. Treasury are without peer in meeting the requirements of the income component. Their quality is unchallenged, and their range of maturities (from this year into the next century) presents the widest selection of possibilities in arranging frequent payments. In addition, the range of maturities permits you to manage for capital stability and reinvestment opportunity. Treasuries also offer a diverse selection of coupon payments, ranging from $70 to $150, and their markets are among the most liquid of any securities anywhere, permitting you flexibility in buying and selling as portfolio needs dictate. In addition, new issues are brought to market at established and regularly recurring times, assuring a steady opportunity to add to your holdings.

TREASURY BILLS

T-bills are the most abundant of all Treasury securities, and they are issued weekly (in the case of three-month and six-month bills) and monthly (in the case of one-year bills). They also are capital-stable investments that defend the income component against price fluctuations.

T-bills present one overriding advantage in that their interest payments are the definition of market-level returns, assuring that the income component provides optimum available yields when economywide interest rates are rising. This advantage, of course, presents a disadvantage, for when economywide rates fall, T-bills, being of short maturity, do not sustain their yields.

The brief maturities and wide selection of T-bills enable you to schedule them to provide income between interest or dividend payments of other securities. For example, you may have two bonds that pay semiannual coupons in, say, April/October and June/December. You can mix newly issued or existing issues of T-bills having three-month or six-month maturities with these securities, and when the bills mature they will provide payments in May and/or November, filling in the missing months of income.

AGENCY SECURITIES

For the income component, agency securities offer the advantage of frequently having yields in excess of Treasuries while providing nearly the same assurances against default. In the case of the major agencies, you also have a substantial range of maturities and yields to choose from in managing the income component. The major agencies also issue new securities at regular intervals, giving you the opportunity to add to your portfolio regularly.

On the other hand, agency securities are not as uniform in their appeal, availability, and liquidity as Treasuries. You have to exercise greater selectivity when adding these securities to the income component. Properly chosen and managed, however, they are excellent additions noted for reliable payments.

The requirement to be selective also applies to the newer agencies whose securities involve troubled areas of the economy. Although the "moral" imperative of Treasury backing likely will take effect if any of these securities has difficulty, many investors prefer to sidestep any such possibility by avoiding these issues. Nonetheless, there are ample numbers of Treasury and proven agency securities to select for the income component. Your portfolio will not suffer if you choose them over less proven securities.

CERTIFICATES OF DEPOSIT

CDs have long been the mainstay of the income component for many investors. CDs purchased from FDIC-backed depository institutions are secure against default, and their payments are assured and predictable. They also have the advantage of being capital-stable investments, defending the income component against price fluctuation. They are readily available from nearly every commercial bank, S&L, and credit union, usually without fee or commissions.

The chief disadvantages of CDs from depository institutions are their relatively limited selection of maturities, their illiquidity, and their fully taxable interest. On these counts, they definitely take second place to Treasury and agency securities, which offer an exceptional range of maturities, generally have broad public markets, and may pay interest exempt from municipal taxation.

For the most part, brokered CDs provide the customary advantages of conventional CDs without the disadvantages, and you should consider them over depository products for the income component. Brokered CDs carry FDIC backing, and they have the added benefit of being liquid in **broker-maintained markets.** You can sell your brokered CD prior to maturity without interest penalties, but you must remember that their prices are not constant. Selling may generate a capital gain or loss. Also, broker-maintained markets enable you to squeeze needed but eccentric maturities of CDs into your portfolio, as you can buy existing CDs in a range of current maturities.

126

MORTGAGE-BACKED SECURITIES

Pass-through securities from Ginnie Mae and her home finance siblings can present exceptional opportunities for the income component. Ginnies selling at a discount feature attractive prices, par Ginnies are relatively straightforward, and Ginnies selling at premiums can offer fetching cash flow.

The obvious dilemma with mortgage-backed securities is their complexity. In nearly all cases, they require more study than other Treasury and agency securities. Further, their uncertain terms of maturity and inconstant periodic payments of principal along with interest make them less dependable income generators than other securities. They do, however, have the advantage of cash flow for investors who seek some return of principal along with interest comprising an **income stream.**

ZEROS FOR FUTURE ACCUMULATIONS— THE CLIFF STRATEGY

Thus far, our discussion has centered upon conventional coupon-paying securities for the income component. If you are investing for compound interest and future accumulations through the income component, zero coupon Treasury and agency securities can be one of your best investment choices. Zeros compound continually at the interest rate determined at purchase and therefore produce highly dependable accumulations. You can take advantage of continual compounding and predictability by structuring zeros to mature at a specific time, a strategy called **cliffing.**

Take the case of an investor who wants to accumulate money in a ten-year period. This is a very practical situation that might pertain to someone choosing taxable zeros for an IRA, for additional retirement income, for a child's tuition, or for starting a business at a known time. This investor wants a consolidated mass of capital at the end of ten years—a cliff anticipated at a known time—so each year he or she invests, say, $10,000 in zeros maturing in 2000. The prices shown in Table 11-1 are suggestive, not actual.

This investor has staged all of the zeros to mature in the same year, 2000, and has earned $200,000 on an investment of $100,000. If you are investing for future accumulations at a known time, you can do so successfully by structuring maturities of zeros. Zeros' continual compounding, range of maturities, and predictable accumulations make the cliff strategy one of the most elegant, simple, and profitable strategies for achieving future accumulations.

127

Table 11-1: CLIFFING ZEROS FOR FUTURE ACCUMULATIONS

Year	Cost Per Zero	Investment	Total Accumulations	Maturity In
1990	$333	$ 9,990	$ 30,000	2000
1991	$350	$ 9,800	$ 28,000	2000
1992	$370	$ 9,990	$ 27,000	2000
1993	$400	$10,000	$ 25,000	2000
1994	$490	$ 9,800	$ 20,000	2000
1995	$550	$ 9,900	$ 18,000	2000
1996	$600	$ 9,600	$ 16,000	2000
1997	$735	$ 9,555	$ 13,000	2000
1998	$800	$ 9,600	$ 12,000	2000
1999	$870	$ 9,570	$ 11,000	2000
INVESTMENT TOTALS		$97,805	$200,000	2000

SERIALIZING ZEROS FOR CURRENT INCOME

Serializing zeros for current income is the reverse of cliffing zeros for accumulations through compounded interest. This strategy also overcomes criticism that zeros produce no current income, for serializing can create an income stream. Serializing zeros operates effectively because zeros deliver their par as a cash payment when they mature.

When serializing zeros for cash payments, you reverse the payment schedule of the cliff strategy and extend the maturities—ten years in this example. Instead of investing $10,000 per year to produce a lump sum in ten years as we did in that example, you invest $100,000 now to produce a series of payments over ten years. One hundred thousand is a lot of money, but you can accumulate it over a lifetime of income investing through untaxed accounts and personal income portfolios.

Note in Table 11-2 that zeros provide increased income over time— $11,000 the first year and $30,000 in the tenth. You could invest more in early maturities to receive a steadier stream of equal payments, tilt zero investments to pay a longer income stream, or alter the scheme to accommodate other investment concerns. But the point remains: Serialized zeros produce cash payments. They are an excellent way to assure a source of dependable current income.

EE SAVINGS BONDS

EE savings bonds can be one of the most useful and versatile investments for the income component. You may recall many of their advantages outlined earlier, particularly their low cost, range of par values, interest rate

Table 11-2: SERIALIZING ZEROS FOR CURRENT INCOME

Year	Cost Per Zero	Investment	Cash Received	Maturity In
1	$870	$ 9,570	$ 11,000	1 year
2	$800	$ 9,600	$ 12,000	2
3	$735	$ 9,555	$ 13,000	3
4	$600	$ 9,600	$ 16,000	4
5	$550	$ 9,900	$ 18,000	5
6	$490	$ 9,800	$ 20,000	6
7	$400	$10,000	$ 25,000	7
8	$370	$ 9,990	$ 27,000	8
9	$350	$ 9,800	$ 28,000	9
10	$333	$ 9,990	$ 30,000	10
INVESTMENT TOTALS		$97,805	$200,000 in 10 years	

geared to Treasury notes, and immunity to capital fluctuation. You may also recall that you have the option to declare interest accrued from EE savings bonds each year or to defer it until the bond is cashed or matures.

The tax deferral option presents an extraordinary opportunity for tax-deferred interest accumulations. EE bonds have a normal maturity of 12 years, at which time they will reach their stated par value or greater, depending upon the fluctuating interest they have earned. But EE bonds issued after November 1965 are eligible for extended maturity. They will continue to accrue interest up to 30 years after you buy them.

Three decades of tax-deferred compounding is a compelling reason to consider EE bonds, but there's another attraction: You can exchange EE bonds, which pay accreted interest, for coupon-paying **HH bonds.** And if you have elected to defer declaring interest on EE bonds that you exchange for HH bonds, you don't have to declare that interest until the HH bonds mature or are sold. Series HH bonds issued since 1980 pay semiannual coupon interest, and their maturities have been extended to 20 years. (Series H bonds issued between 1959 and 1979 have a 30-year maturity.)

Accordingly, under the present rules the EE bond you purchase today can grow tax-deferred for 30 years. You can convert it to a current income investment that pays semiannual interest for 20 years. Only when the HH bond matures (or is sold) do you have to declare the accreted interest from your original investment. That amounts to 50 years of tax deferral—although, of course, the coupon income from HH bonds is federally taxable during the years you receive it. All interest from EE and HH bonds is exempt from state and local taxes.

HH bonds have two special features that make them versatile for investors who need current income from the income component. First, they are immune to capital fluctuation; they will never be worth less than their par value (HH bonds feature par ranging between $500 and $10,000). Second, the date you convert HH bonds establishes your payment schedule for semiannual coupon income. EE bonds converted in January will pay interest as HH bonds in July and January; in February, August and February; in March, September and March—and so on. This enables you to decide when you would like to receive semiannual coupon payments and to structure your conversions accordingly.

To convert EE to HH bonds, you can take them to a Federal Reserve Bank or branch or mail them to Bureau of the Public Debt in Washington, D.C. 20239-0001. When you convert EE bonds for HH bonds, the EEs must be at least six months old and must have grown to at least $500, the par value of the smallest HH bond.

GOVERNMENT MONEY MARKET FUNDS AND MUTUAL FUNDS

As with T-bills, interest from government money funds tracks with the general course of interest rates, presenting the positives and negatives of inflation-sensitive but unpredictable payments. Government money funds often have no loads, making them low-cost investments, but their interest payments are legally defined as dividends subject to state and local taxation, and yearly management fees apply. As constant-dollar investments carrying the assurances of government securities, they rank high in prevention of market and default risk.

Government bond funds are the best way to diversify your income component, although average portfolio maturity rather than fixed portfolio maturity renders them susceptible to market risk. Target funds help to reduce, but not eliminate, market risk. Loads in addition to management fees are customary with government bond funds. Fund fees may make you better off buying Treasury and agency bonds as a direct investor. Also, remember that some government bond funds pay fully taxable dividends, whereas interest from Treasury and some agency securities is exempt from state and local taxes.

One advantage of mutual funds is that they permit you to take interest and/or principal as current income, leaving the rest to compound. Some funds also will arrange annuity-like payments of interest and principal in regular monthly checks, a benefit for investors who intend to consume their capital. Neither advantage is available with conventional Treasury and agency securities, excepting mortgage-backed securities, which customarily pay interest and some portion of principal, although irregularly. Otherwise, funds pay and compound monthly if you are letting your income component grow, unlike the semiannual interest payments of most notes and bonds.

FREQUENCY OF PAYMENT

We have examined how different types of Treasury and agency securities can meet the income component's requirement for quality. Now it's time to address the considerations of selecting and managing them to achieve the functions of the income component. We start by arranging them to provide frequency of payment.

Treasury notes and bonds are among the easiest securities to manage for regular income. Any single note or bond makes semiannual coupon payments at established dates. For example, any Treasury maturing in May of any year will pay half of its coupon in May and the remainder the following November, six months distant from May. Similarly, a June bond will pay interest in June and December. Accordingly, six issues of bonds staged with attention to payment dates will produce income each month of the year.

For convenience, let's suppose you have $60,000 to invest and that you seek monthly income. You can invest $10,000 in each of six notes or bonds to produce monthly payments, as, of course, you would apportion greater or lesser amounts than $60,000 among six issues. Table 11-3 is an excerpt of Treasury bond quotations for maturities only in 1991. When staggering your payment dates you will want to look at maturities of many different years, but 1991 is presented here merely to illustrate the point. Note the following issues:

Table 11-3: STAGING PAYMENT DATES FOR MONTHLY INCOME

Coupon	Payment Date	Payment Date	Semiannual Payment
$90	January 91	July 91	$450.00
$91.25	February 91	August 91	$456.30
$97.50	March 91	September 91	$487.50
$92.50	April 91	October 91	$462.50
$87.50	May 91	November 91	$437.50
$82.50	June 91	December 91	$412.50

Without complicated arrangements, you have assured yourself monthly income for consumption or reinvestment. When you consider that the example includes only Treasury obligations and only one year

131

among the scores of maturities available, you can imagine the possibilities of broadening your scope to include the other types of securities. With agency securities, T-bills, CDs, and hundreds of other issues of Treasuries, your opportunity to arrange frequency of income is bounded only by the capital you have available to invest. However you enlarge this principle in practice, the principle remains robust: Align your Treasury and agency securities so that their interest payment dates produce consecutive income.

In fact, you can stage a series of regular payments using only Treasury and agency securities, substituting an appealing agency security for a Treasury note or bond, peppering in a T-bill or two for supplementary income between or in place of semiannual coupons, adding a CD or a mortgage-backed pass-through where appropriate. You also can use Treasury and agency securities as the backbone of a regular payment schedule, relying upon quarterly stock dividends, corporate and municipal bonds, real estate rentals, and royalties from limited partnerships to flesh out your income schedule.

Many investors also take advantage of government money market funds and mutual funds for monthly receipts. Funds typically credit interest from their securities monthly. If you are reinvesting for the future, monthly compounding takes place without further effort on your part. If you are consuming current income, funds will send you checks for interest or capital gains monthly, quarterly, or semiannually as you instruct. In addition, funds also will arrange for annuity-like payments of a fixed amount to be mailed to you at monthly, quarterly, or semiannual intervals. This arrangement will draw down the balance of your account with the fund, but it is highly convenient for investors who live on income from their funds.

If you are a direct investor who buys Treasury and agency securities for compounding, it is essential that you reinvest interest payments as soon as you receive them. Automatic reinvestment of interest is a good reason to work with a broker in assembling your portfolio, for payments you receive will be placed immediately in your brokerage money market fund to compound. When you receive an interest payment that you won't spend right away, reinvest it immediately.

BALANCING CAPITAL STABILITY
AND MAXIMUM INCOME

The income component generally needs some degree of capital stability, although not the immunity to price fluctuation that characterizes the savings component. Moderate capital stability is important because income investments sometimes need to be sold and realigned to take advantage of opportunity. Disposing of an income investment at a capital loss can negate the interest or dividends you receive from that security, and your subsequent investment has to be that much more productive to compensate for the capital loss. Yet the income component must not emphasize stability to the forfeiture of income, for maximum income is the goal of the income component. It is entirely logical to buy a long-term bond for an attractive coupon even though its price may fluctuate, just as you can be wise to buy a premium bond with a hefty coupon even though you lose the premium as the bond approaches maturity.

In some circumstances the income component can have both capital stability and high income in a single security. When economywide interest rates are rising, for instance, T-bills and government money market funds pay increasing yields and maintain their prices. Risk of capital loss is also eliminated with federally insured CDs from depository institutions. Despite their drawbacks, they do not decline in price prior to maturity. Savings bonds, both EE and HH bonds, also are exempt from market risk, and yields on EE bonds increase with yields on Treasury securities.

For the most part, however, reaching for extra income from Treasury and agency securities usually involves subjecting the portfolio to some capital fluctuation. This is true because higher income generally—but not always—comes from securities with longer maturities, and longer maturities are more vulnerable to price fluctuations. Thus, the first trick to balancing capital stability and income is to manage maturities—but with an eye always on income generated.

You can follow several general guidelines to achieve this balancing act. These guidelines are not mutually exclusive, even if they seem to be. You can use all of them to advantage.

1. If two securities provide the same income, select the one with shorter maturity for the income component. The longer maturity doesn't compensate for the greater risk of capital fluctuation.

2. Apportion income investments with progressive maturities. That is, arrange your notes and bonds to have a series of escalating maturities—three years, seven years, ten years, or whatever interval you deem appropriate. This arrangement will balance the capital fluctuation of your income component as a whole, for the relative stability of shorter maturities will offset the greater fluctuations of the longer.

3. Apportion maturities at opposite ends of the maturity spectrum. A less refined variant of the progressive maturities strategy, "barbelled

maturities," likewise balances the fluctuations of long maturities with the stability of shorter. It is less effective than the progressive maturities strategy overall, but it does locate your more volatile investments at higher paying areas of maturity. Remember principle 1 above when barbelling maturities, however.

4. Hold a portion of the income component in constant-dollar T-bills, money funds, and CDs. These investments will assure that some portion of the income component is exempted from capital fluctuation while providing variable (bills and money funds) and predictable (CDs) income.

5. Be prepared to buy and hold long-term securities. The buy-and-hold strategy is most effective if you plan to make repeated investments in the income component over several years. You can ride out capital fluctuation in longer maturities because your subsequent investments can be apportioned elsewhere in the maturity spectrum. Essentially, your ability to make repeated investment reduces the overall effect of price fluctuations on the income component.

DEFINING MAXIMUM INCOME

You seek maximum income consistent with quality and some capital stability for the income component, but maximum income is a concept with several interpretations. Securities with markedly different prices, coupons, dividends, and yields can rightfully claim to offer maximum income. Yet each has shortcomings that you must consider.

Nominal Yield: Certainly one definition of maximum income is maximum coupon or interest income. Otherwise known as nominal yield, the concept is simple: A bond paying $150 provides twice the income of a bond, CD, or other security paying $75. Many investors regard this definition as naive, for it omits other factors that determine the attractiveness of an investment, such as price, maturity, and other pertinent yields. These valid considerations aside, however, there are several circumstances in which you are correct in pursuing securities with the highest cash payments.

Retirees and other investors who need the most current income their portfolios can generate should investigate the big-dollar coupon securities. In fact, all investors should opt for high coupon income when economywide interest rates are rising, as they do during inflationary economies. Although there are many ways to manage the income component during inflation, high-coupon securities offer one standard advan-

134

tage: They cast off more cash to reinvest at higher rates of interest. You also want high-coupon securities when an economy crashes into a severe recession. They provide greater payments at a time when economywide income and your personal income are declining, and they boost your purchasing power when the general level of prices declines, as it sometimes does in an eroding economy.

Current Yield: Maximum dollar payments are not the only interpretation of maximum income. Another pertinent definition is maximum payments per dollar invested, otherwise known as high current yield. As you'll recall from Section I, current yield is coupon income divided by market price.

Low-coupon securities provide relatively higher income when their prices have fallen below par. On the basis of current yield, they can compete equally with high-coupon securities because it costs less to buy them—or, more accurately, you can buy their coupon payments more cheaply. For example, suppose you have a bond with a $90 coupon selling at $900 and a bond with a $150 coupon selling at $1,500. Both have current yields of 10 percent. On the basis of income received per dollar invested, current yield, they are equal investments.

To some extent, all investors can maximize income by attention to current yield, but current yield is a more significant consideration when you can purchase securities at attractive prices. As you can see in the example above and from your own reading of the Treasury pages, current yields usually are similar among Treasury and agency securities, regardless of coupon, maturity, and market price. In respect to current yield itself, all will be generally equal. However, a lower-priced security brings a competitive current yield for less capital invested and in that sense maximizes your investment capital, although perhaps not total income.

Whenever you are looking at current yield and trying to locate a fetchingly priced investment, remember one drawback of current yield: Maturity does not pertain in its calculation, which is merely coupon divided by price. Term of maturity is an important element in selecting securities for the income component, and current yield doesn't consider it.

Yield to Maturity: Many investors rightly consider yield to maturity the most important measure of maximum income, and for three reasons. First, it does consider term of maturity in its calculation. Second, it measures the total return produced by a security, including capital gains from principal paid by a discount bond. Third, yield to maturity is the commonly accepted financial standard to compare bonds, and as a common standard it enjoys credibility as a measure of return. Other things being equal, then, yield to maturity is one way to determine which bond produces maximum total return.

The dilemma is that other things aren't always equal when you are considering investments. One limitation of interpreting maximum income according to yield to maturity is apparent: It doesn't measure current income, only total return over term to maturity. Thus, a bond with a low coupon generates less current income than a bond with a high coupon, but both can theoretically have equal yields to maturity, and in practice they often do. In this case, considerations other than yield to maturity might dictate your choice of investment.

Other problems with yield to maturity as a measure of maximum income arise from the yield calculation itself. As you will remember from Section I, the first mathematical component of yield to maturity is a bond's average annual income—coupon plus capital gain from discount bonds or minus the capital loss from premium bonds, with the discount or premium amortized yearly over maturity. However, discounts and premiums don't accrue or dissipate evenly over maturity, as the calculation assumes. Mathematically, this shortcoming can be offset by weighting for time, but the problem remains: The calculation tends to overstate yields on discount bonds and understate yields on premium bonds.

Yield to maturity can be your foremost guide to detecting which securities offer maximum income if you are investing for future accumulations rather than current consumption. Yield to maturity is, after all, a measure of total returns, and as an investor compounding your gains, that's what you want to measure. Again, however, you need to be aware of a second eccentricity in the yield calculation. In order to earn a bond's true yield to maturity, you have to be able to reinvest coupon payments at the stated yield. That is, a ten-year bond with, say, an 8 percent yield to maturity doesn't actually produce a true 8 percent yield unless you can reinvest each semiannual coupon at 8 percent each year for ten years.

With the merits and flaws of each measure of maximum income before you, you're bound to wonder which one is most relevant. Actually, you have to consider each one in order to decide which is the most pertinent to your particular investment situation. You must maintain flexibility in determining how to secure maximum income. Some of the following pointers will help you do so.

- Mix securities with different income characteristics into your portfolio. A discount bond with a low coupon might not provide maximum current income, but its price and eventual capital gain might make it a commendable choice. A high-coupon bond selling above par will generate maximum coupon income, which might offset its lackluster current yield or yield to maturity. Each individual security, chosen for its merits and your investment circumstances, will contribute to the overall performance of the income component.

• View the income component as if it were a single security. At regular intervals, calculate the varying yields—nominal, current, to maturity—from all of your income securities. Then average them for the portfolio as a whole. This procedure will enable you to track your overall income performance.

• Follow the strategies discussed earlier to secure maximum frequency of income. Frequency of payment is always the ally of the income component. Whatever your choice among securities of varying yield characteristics, having a dollar in hand from immediate payments enables you to boost your return from reinvesting payments.

REINVESTMENT OPPORTUNITY AND REINVESTMENT RISK

Balancing reinvestment opportunity and reinvestment risk is inseparable from your objective of frequent income and maximum income from the income component of the portfolio. It also is an objective that ties to your need for relative capital stability. Fortunately, techniques you use in meeting these other functions of the income component also pertain to this one.

Reinvestment opportunity is a simple concept to define: You want to structure income investments so that you can secure the best returns the economy offers. Essentially, reinvestment opportunity means having the ability to reinvest as often as possible. If you are consuming interest and dividends for current living expenses, you want your income component to provide the best available income. If your strategy is to compound interest and principal for future accumulations, the same is true. The two basic elements of the income component are the capital you invest and the returns you earn on it. You want optimum reinvestment opportunity for both principal and interest.

At first blush, that seems easy. To assure optimum opportunity to reinvest principal, all you do is restrain maturities of your securities. If you restrict maturities to one or two years, every year or two you can reinvest the par value of your matured bonds, renewing your principal at the available interest rate. Similarly, it should be easy to obtain reinvestment opportunity on interest or dividends by sweeping them into a money fund as soon as you receive them. The problem with such a seemingly simple strategy is that reinvestment opportunity collides with reinvestment risk.

Having read Section I, you understand reinvestment risk. If economywide rates of interest increase, you can reinvest interest and dividends for higher returns, but your existing securities might be locked into the former, lower rate. If economywide rates decline, you no longer have the chance to reinvest principal or payments to obtain previously higher rates. Restraining maturities addresses only the first aspect of reinvestment risk, for if rates rise, you can reinvest your matured bonds in securities paying the higher rates. But if rates fall, so does your return because your new bonds will pay the new, lower rate.

This dilemma cannot be resolved entirely by extending maturities, for that exposes you to the reverse aspect of interest rate risk. When economywide rates fall, longer maturities might lock in higher payments than the new rates. But if economywide rates rise, you can be stuck with bonds that pay uncompetitive returns, in addition to which their prices likely will fall, violating the capital stability of your portfolio.

Some of the following techniques will help you to balance reinvestment opportunity and reinvestment risk.

- Stagger maturities. By apportioning maturities at even intervals— one to three years, five to seven years, and longer—you can reinvest matured principal with relative frequency to take advantage of increasing rates. Conversely, you achieve some defense against falling rates, for the longer maturities will cast off their payments at previous levels. In either case, you will be able to reinvest current payments.

   This strategy also assures a greater degree of capital stability. The shorter maturities are subject to less capital fluctuation and provide more frequent opportunity to reinvest matured principal. This strategy serves the twofold purpose of reducing market risk while balancing reinvestment opportunity and risk.

- Mix T-bills and government money funds in with other income securities. Because of their short maturities, these instruments offer more frequent reinvestment opportunity than afforded by longer maturities and semiannual or quarterly payments from notes, bonds, and CDs. Also, their payments will rise with the general level of interest rates. By mixing them with fixed-payment notes, bonds, and CDs, you defend against both aspects of reinvestment risk. Payments from bills and money funds rise with the economy, while coupon income from other securities remains constant. Conversely, payments from notes, bonds, and CDs will remain constant when returns on bills and funds decline with reductions in economywide interest rates.

Moreover, mixing bills and money funds serves other functions of the income component. First, this strategy boosts frequency of income, for T-bills provide frequent payments and money funds pay monthly. Second, it provides greater capital stability, for bills and funds hold their prices while other securities fluctuate. Third, it maximizes income because it mixes variable payments from bills and money funds with fixed payments from other securities. Once again, you see how a strategy for balancing reinvestment opportunity and reinvestment risk fits well with your other goals in managing the income component.

- Hold a reserve cash position to take advantage of unfolding market situations. This is a wise decision any time you invest, but it can be especially helpful in managing reinvestment opportunity and risk. There is no greater reinvestment opportunity than having cash you can invest when opportunity presents itself. A cash position also enables you to invest in selected maturities or identified investments that maximize returns at the moment they are offered. Obviously, you must hold your reserve position in highly liquid securities of short maturity. A money market fund is the best choice, followed by T-bills. You can move out of these investments into others without capital loss or delays.

SUMMARY

The income component of the portfolio is intended to produce current income for living expenses or for compounding to achieve future accumulations. The many types of Treasury and agency securities we've covered are excellent for these uses. In selecting securities for the income component and managing them for best results, you need to address the functions of the income component. These include producing frequent income, balancing capital stability and maximum income, and balancing reinvestment opportunity and reinvestment risk. Each of these functions can be achieved by combining Treasury and agency securities of differing price behaviors, income behaviors, and maturities within the income component. By matching different securities with appropriate characteristics, you can position the income component for the returns and other characteristics that meet your personal investment situation and take advantage of changing economic conditions.

12

Treasury and Agency Securities for Capital Growth

Growth investments are those that provide long-term capital appreciation—that is, increases in market price—as opposed to income investments, which emphasize current or compounded receipts. Treasury and agency securities typically take second place behind more customary growth investments such as corporate stocks. However, as growth investments noted for price gains, they have outperformed stocks and other investments during selected economic periods.

Many investors regularly use Treasury and agency securities as recurring parts of the capital growth component of their portfolio. They interchange them with stocks, corporate bonds, and other securities they select for capital gains. In particular, they buy Treasuries and agencies when they estimate imminent declines in interest rates, for as you recall from Section I, these securities increase in price when rates decline. When the hoped-for capital gain materializes, these investors sell their securities.

Aggressive investors use Treasury securities to seize quick capital gains. Others use Treasury and agency securities primarily as income securities, but they are aware of their capital growth opportunities. Whichever you happen to be, you need to understand how these instruments can be used as growth investments.

TREASURY AND AGENCY SECURITIES FOR GROWTH

With the exception of EE and HH savings bonds, money market funds, and conventional CDs, all the Treasury and agency securities we have covered can produce capital growth. The reason they can be growth investments is that they are traded in secondary markets. Therefore, their prices fluctuate with market conditions, and price fluctuations can produce capital gains. In fact, capital gains aren't possible without price fluctuations, and that's why constant-dollar, capital-stable securities can't provide capital gains.

A government bond fund is an excellent choice for diversified capital gains whenever interest rates fall. A Treasury fund with an intermediate or long weighted average maturity will be appropriate. Bond funds are good alternatives during periods of gently declining interest rates. You will enjoy more broad scale price appreciation from a portfolio of bonds than you would from a smaller selection purchased from your personal resources.

Remember that Ginnie Maes and Ginnie Mae funds demonstrate a perverse behavior during declines in economywide interest rates. When rates decline significantly enough for homeowners to refinance, mortgage-backed securities lose their mortgages. As a result, they're advisable capital gains investments only when rates are declining modestly. But remember, also, that periods of sharply rising rates will drive Ginnies and their funds to discounts from par. They can be excellent gains investments following a period of sharply rising interest rates.

Treasury and agency securities provide capital growth from two sources: price appreciation from securities selling at a discount and price gains from declines in economywide rates of interest. Let's examine both sources of growth.

DISCOUNTS FROM PAR

Buy-and-Hold Strategy

The first source of capital growth from Treasury and agency securities is price appreciation from discount bonds. Even if interest rates do not fall, bonds selling below par will appreciate toward par as they approach maturity, and when they mature they pay full par value. Accordingly, any time you buy a discount note or bond, the difference between your purchase price and par will be a capital gain if you hold the bond until it matures.

As you understand from Section I, notes and bonds are originally issued at or near par. Once they enter public trading, however, their prices respond to changes in the general level of interest rates. When interest rates rise, coupon payments of existing notes and bonds might become less attractive. Their prices fall until their coupon payments represent a competitive payment in the higher rate environment.

The best times to locate discount notes and bonds are during and after a period of rising economywide interest rates. Interest rates, nicknamed "inflation's twin," are usually on the increase during bouts of economic inflation. For example, during the double-digit inflation of the Carter presidency many Treasury securities sold at deep discounts from par, often at prices of $700 to $800. To a lesser degree, you can locate Treasury and agency securities at mild discounts from par—market prices around $900 or slightly less—any time the general level of interest rates is increasing.

Recognizing when to go shopping for discount bonds is a fairly straightforward matter. Your best buying opportunity occurs at the end of a cycle of inflation or during any period of increasing interest rates. Recognizing which securities to buy is the second part of the discount bond strategy for capital growth. Treasury and agency securities of any coupon or maturity can theoretically sell at discounts. As a general rule, two types of Treasury and agency securities are likely to sell at discounts: those with lower coupons and those with longer maturities.

Lower coupon bonds are more likely to sell at discounts than bonds with higher coupons because their comparatively smaller interest payments make their prices more volatile. When economywide rates rise, the smaller coupon produces a smaller outright payment, and it also provides less interest to reinvest. Logically, then, its price decreases faster and farther than bonds with prices supported by higher coupons. It is common to find deep discounts among the longer maturities, usually ten years or more, because longer bonds typically fluctuate more in price than shorter bonds. Therefore, you are also likely to find battered prices among longer bonds.

The discount growth strategy implies (but does not insist, as you'll see momentarily) that you will hold your discount bond to maturity. If you follow the buy-and-hold strategy, you will seek discount bonds with shorter maturities because the shorter bond matures and pays its full capital gain sooner than a bond with longer maturity.

Trading Strategy

Unfortunately, changing economies don't always produce discounts at short terms of maturity. Sometimes the term structure of interest rates, discussed later in Chapter 15, produces the deepest discounts on bonds of distant maturities. Buying a long-term bond at a discount requires great patience if you are following a buy-and-hold strategy, for you may have to wait many years, perhaps decades, until the bond matures at par and produces its capital gain. However, the happy circumstance is that you don't necessarily have to wait for a discounted long bond to mature before enjoying a capital gain.

Changes in economywide interest rates customarily follow cycles of increase and decrease. Interest rate cycles are accompanied by price changes in bonds, especially long-term bonds. Accordingly, you don't have to wait for the long bond to mature. You can sell it at a capital gain when its price increases during a cycle of falling interest rates.

For example: Suppose a 20-year Treasury bond is issued with a coupon of 8 percent ($80) at a time when the general level of interest rates and investors' requirements dictate 8 percent as a competitive return. Two years later, the general level of rates had increased to 10 percent. As a rule, the price of the bond would decline until its coupon represented a return competitive in the new rate environment. The revised market price would be $800, for at that price the bond's $80 coupon presents a 10 percent current yield competitive in the changed economy.

At this point, the bond is selling for $800 and matures in 18 years. If things stayed the same, you would wait upwards of 18 years for this bond to produce its $200 capital gain. Fortunately, things change, and one of the changes could be a decrease in economywide interest rates.

Just as rates can increase from 8 to 10 percent or higher, so can they return to 8 percent or lower. For the sake of example, let's suppose that interest rates decline back to 8 percent the following year. When this happens, the price of the bond will recover to full par because its $80 coupon once again becomes competitive. The bond you purchased for $800 is now worth $1,000 again. You secured your capital gain of $200 without having to wait 17 more years until the bond matures.

As you can see, you don't have to follow a buy-and-hold strategy with discount bonds. You can sell them any time they produce a capital gain. As a trader rather than a buy-and-hold investor, however, you'll look at a specific type of discount bond. Specifically, you will center your attention on low-coupon bonds with distant maturities selling at discounts. These bonds combine both elements of price volatility—the low coupon and the distant maturity. Having been beaten the most in price when interest rates increase, low-coupon, long maturity bonds will recover their prices more quickly when rates decrease. They are your best possibilities for capital gains without having to hold bonds until maturity.

DECLINE IN INTEREST RATES

Whenever interest rates in the economy decrease, nearly all publicly traded Treasury and agency securities will produce capital gains. You don't have to concentrate upon discount bonds. You can take advantage of rising prices for capital growth among the full spectrum of Treasury and agency securities. In addition, you don't have to concentrate your investment only after periods of sharp interest rate increases. Whenever interest rates are trending downward, you can invest for capital gains.

Even bonds selling at par will produce capital when general interest rates decline. The most dramatic evidence of that fact is the substantial premiums that high-coupon, long-term bonds have commanded when rates declined. For example, during the late summer of 1989 general interest rates hovered around 8 percent. That rate was far below the $100 to $150 coupons offered by selected Treasury issues with maturities beyond the year 2000. As a result, those bonds escalated in price, reaching levels of $1,200 to $1,600 and higher.

High-coupon bonds with shorter maturities also participated in the price rally. For instance, a few Treasuries with coupons of $100 to $120 maturing in the early 1990s rose to prices of $1,070 to $1,200. Lower-coupon bonds with longer maturities also increased in price. Long-term bonds with coupons approaching $90 and $100 posted prices exceeding $1,100.

CAPITAL GAINS RELATIONSHIPS

Capital gains occur widely across the spectrum of maturities and coupons when overall interest rates decline. Nonetheless, there are important general relationships between rate declines, price movements, coupon rates, and maturities. You need to understand these relationships so that you can select securities most likely to produce gains.

Relation Between Nominal Yield and Rate Change: When two bonds of identical maturity sell at par, the most important price gains relationship is between the bond's coupon and the changing level of interest rates. When interest rates decline, bonds with coupons closest to the new level of rates will increase less in price. Logically, then, bonds with coupons substantially above the new, lower rate increase more in price.

However—and this is an important point—this general relationship prevails only for bonds selling at par. It is most pertinent when you are evaluating two newly issued bonds, both of which are issued at par, and you are trying to gauge which has greater gains potential. But this is not always the case. Often, you will be looking at existing bonds trading in secondary markets. In secondary markets, two bonds of identical maturity rarely trade equally at par if their coupons differ, for they will have different prices. When bonds have different prices, yield to maturity changes this general relationship between coupon and rate changes.

Relationship Between Yield to Maturity and Rate Change: Let's take the case of two bonds with identical maturities and yields to maturity but different coupons. In this case, the lower-coupon bond will have a lower price. When the general level of rates declines, the discount bond with the lower coupon will appreciate more in price.

To demonstrate, suppose you are comparing two 20-year bonds with yields to maturity of 10 percent. The first bond has a coupon of $100, and its price is par. The second bond has a coupon of $90, and its price is $914.20. If general rates fall to 8 percent, the first bond will appreciate to $1,197.92, producing a gain of 19.79 percent. The second bond will increase to $1,098.96, producing a gain of 20.21 percent.

Let's make the circumstances more dramatic to illustrate the point. Suppose you have two 20-year bonds with yields to maturity of 10 percent. The first bond has a coupon of $70, and its price is $742.61. The second bond has a coupon of $30, and its price is $399.43. If general interest rates fall to 7 percent, the first bond will increase to par, producing a gain of 34.66 percent. However, the second bond will appreciate to $572.90, producing a gain of 43.43 percent.

Years to Maturity: When other factors of two bonds are equal, the bond with the longer maturity will increase more in price when general interest rates fall. That is, a 20-year bond with any nominal yield or yield to maturity will increase more in price than a ten-year bond with identical yields.

CAPITAL GAINS WITH ZERO COUPON BONDS

Lower coupon bonds are generally more volatile in price, so it's logical that zero coupon bonds and zero coupon bond funds, which pay no coupon income, are the most volatile in price. This logic is confirmed by market experience. Over the decade that CATS, TIGRs, and other derivative zeros have been widely available, these securities have shown dramatic price movements resulting from changes in economywide interest rates. Zero coupon bond funds have been the most rewarding of all bond funds and have outperformed nearly all other types of mutual funds several times since the general decline in interest rates starting in 1982.

Table 12-1: VOLATILITY OF ZERO COUPON SECURITIES (8% initial yield. Rates fall to 7%)

	Price			
Years to Maturity	5	10	20	30
At 8% Yield	$675	$456	$208	$95
At 7% Yield	$709	$503	$252	$127
Percentage Change	+5%	+10%	+21%	+33%

Table 12-1 shows what happens to the market price of zeros when interest rates decline by 1 percent.

As Table 12-1 demonstrates, price moves are greatest for zeros and zero funds with longer maturity. However, even shorter maturities are highly responsive to changes in economywide interest rates. All zeros are more volatile in price than coupon bonds of similar maturity. That's why many capital growth investors buy them when rates are on the downswing. Compare the results of Table 12-1 with those of Table 12-2, which shows the price behavior of a conventional coupon bond when interest rates decline one percent.

SPLIT FUNDS

One of the miscellaneous Treasury and agency securities, and one of the vehicles mentioned in Chapter 9 was the unit trust that mated zero coupon securities with other types of investments, including common stocks, precious metals, and commodities futures. For conservative investors, the chief attraction of these split funds is their immunity against absolute capital loss. Held to maturity, split funds return all of your original capital, for zeros in the portfolio will compound to the amount of your initial investment. Conservative appeal notwithstanding, split funds do more than conserve principal; they also can provide capital gains.

Admittedly, split funds do not procure capital gains from Treasury securities. The zeros hedge the portfolio against losses and are held to maturity for their predictable accumulations rather than sold for gain if interest rates decline. However, split funds consolidate Treasury and other securities in a single investment. The collateral investments alongside the zeros can appreciate in price, and in this sense you can achieve

Table 12-2: **VOLATILITY OF 8% COUPON BOND VS. ZERO WITH 8% YIELD (8% initial yield. Rates fall to 7%)**

	Price			
Years to Maturity	5	10	20	30
At 8% Yield	$1,000	$1,000	$1,000	$1,000
At 7% Yield	$1,041	$1,071	$1,107	$1,125
Percentage Change	+4.1%	+7.1%	+10.7%	+12.5%
Zeros	+5.0%	+10%	+21%	+33%

capital growth from a Treasury portfolio diversified among other types of securities. As a capital gains investor using split funds, you can own Treasury securities and secure price appreciation from related investments.

AGGRESSIVE GROWTH WITH TREASURY SECURITIES

Treasury and agency securities are the most default-free investments available in our economy. In most circumstances, they could hardly qualify as aggressive growth investments—investments that offer the chance for very rapid price gains and equally dramatic financial losses, as opposed to moderate, longer-term price appreciation associated with ordinary capital gains. Yet under selected economic circumstances, aggressive growth is exactly what Treasury and agency securities can provide.

Abrupt plummets of economywide interest rates can turn Treasury bonds into aggressive growth investments because their prices will soar phenomenally in response. In 1982, for example, long-term Treasury bonds produced a startling 40.4 percent return in a single year because economywide interest rates caved in. If you owned long-term Treasuries during that period, you would have enjoyed extraordinary price appreciation in a very brief time. As always with aggressive price moves, volatility has a downside when interest rates rise sharply. As a matter of fact, in the period surrounding 1982, interest rates rose from 11 percent to 15 percent, fell back to 11 percent, and rose again. Two sides of that triangle represented substantial losses within a year from rebounding interest rates.

Fortunately, such rapid movements in interest rates are rare. Most growth investors are content with moderate gains from smoothly declining rates. But some investors aren't content with the moderate price growth that Treasuries and agencies provide during less abrupt rate declines. They seek aggressive capital growth through techniques that magnify small price gains.

BUYING ON MARGIN

One such technique is to buy Treasury and agency securities on **margin.** That is, investors borrow money from their bank or broker to buy bonds, hoping their prices will increase suddenly and soon. If the bonds perform accordingly, investors sell, repay the loan, and walk away with the remaining profit. The maximum amount of money you can borrow to purchase securities is called initial margin, which is established and changed by the Federal Reserve. At present, Fed regulations permit investors to borrow up to 50 percent of the purchase price of securities so long as they meet other financial requirements, such as a minimum account size. Buying on margin magnifies price gains through leverage because you buy more securities than your capital in hand permits.

For example: Suppose you think interest rates are about to fall from 9 percent to 8. You want to invest $10,000 in 20-year bonds selling at par with a $90 coupon, believing long bonds more likely to increase than other maturities. You instruct your broker to take $10,000 from your government money market fund, and you buy the bonds. If interest rates do fall to 8 percent, your bonds will appreciate to $10,989.64, a gain of 9.9 percent.

However, if you margined your purchase, you could buy $20,000 worth of bonds, borrowing $10,000 from your bank or broker. If interest rates fall, your bonds increase to $21,979.28. In this case, you double your return because you only invested $10,000 of your own funds. The gain of $1,979.28 represents a 19.8 percent return on your personal capital.

Margin transactions are not all gravy, however. For them to be profitable, prices need to move sharply, swiftly, and in the right direction. If the bonds do not increase in price, you are stuck with the bonds and with hefty interest payments to the bank or broker, offset only partially by coupon interest on the bonds. Worse, if bond prices fall rather than rise, you are stuck with double capital losses and hefty interest payments on the borrowed money. If prices fall far enough, your broker will require you to add money to your account, and if you don't your position will be closed out at a capital loss.

ASSESSING INTEREST RATE CHANGES

If you intend to invest for capital growth from Treasury and agency securities, you have to follow economywide interest rates. Predicting interest rates is a frustrating task even for full-time professionals who are skilled and experienced at it. But amateur investors don't always have to anticipate interest rate changes *before* they occur; you can learn to follow selected economic and market signals to take advantage of changes *as* they occur.

Follow Money Funds and T-bills: Yields on money market funds and Treasury bills are highly responsive to economic conditions reflected in interest rates. They also are reported daily in the financial media. Apart from monitoring their changes in the daily financial pages, be alert to rates posted at the weekly T-bill auctions.

Relatedly, track the average maturities reported for money market funds. When portfolio managers lengthen the maturity of securities in money funds, they are telling you they expect rates to fall. When the average maturities are shortening, professionals are undecided about rates, or they expect them to rise. Use money fund maturities as an estimate of what professionals believe to be the course of rates.

Track the Trend in Inflation: Expectations of inflation are the driving determinant of interest rates, and they are constantly reported in financial media. Heightened expectations for inflation will be reflected in higher interest rates. Lower inflationary expectations portend lower rates and capital gains in Treasury and agency securities.

Become Conversant with Key Economic Signals: Economic slowdown is generally positive for prices of Treasury and agency securities. Such key economic signals as leading indicators, industrial production, nonfarm employment, and consumer and wholesale prices intimate the level of economic activity and suggest opportunity for capital gains among Treasury and agency securities. To learn more about investing with economic cycles of inflation and recession, pick up a copy of *Investing in Uncertain Times* by your author and Longman Financial Services.

Monitor Price Changes at All Maturities of Treasury Securities: Daily note and bond quotations reflect daily estimates of investors' feelings about rates. Over a period of time, the daily fluctuations in prices reflect a more consistent estimate of the trend in rates. You can follow other investors' estimates as a guide to your own investment decisions.

CAPITAL LOSSES VERSUS CAPITAL GAINS

Whenever you strive for capital growth from any investment, including Treasury and agency securities, you have to face the prospect of capital losses. The same price volatility that can produce gains also subjects you to the possibility of capital loss.

Besides confirming what you have already learned about interest rates, coupons, yields, prices, and price behaviors, the previous examples also demonstrate the kinds of bonds you want to avoid when you are defending against capital loss. You not only want to defend against capital loss in the savings and income components of the portfolio, but you also want to defend the capital gains component when interest rates are increasing and bond prices threaten to fall.

Therefore, remember the reverse of these examples when economy-wide interest rates are increasing. Select bonds of shorter maturity and higher coupons, for they are less vulnerable to price volatility and will decline less in price when rates increase. Wait until rate increases have peaked and prices of bonds have been battered. Then step in with the discount gains or interest rate strategies outlined in this chapter. Capital gains will be yours for the taking.

GENERAL GUIDELINES IN MANAGING FOR CAPITAL GROWTH

Investing for capital gains from Treasury and agency securities looks like an easy proposition: Buy after prices have been battered or when general interest rates are softening. But no one is ever 100 percent on the money 100 percent of the time, especially when investing for capital gains from a security. There are several rules of thumb you can follow that will help to reduce the effects of the inevitable mistakes you will make when reaching for capital gains.

Hold Capital in Reserve: Again, this constant piece of proven counsel reappears. Many investors have made a bundle by betting the ranch when interest rates moved the right way. Equal numbers wound up mortgaged to the hilt. When you are following the trend in rates, be disciplined enough to restrain your eagerness, even when things are going your way. A sound portfolio is created over time with measured investments, and that means having capital in reserve to invest during recurring opportunities.

Buy into Weakness: During any market trend, even an upward trend in prices, intermittent pull-backs occur. These reversals in the midst of a general trend present buying opportunities. They are an excellent reason to hold cash in reserve that you can commit during periods of market weakness.

Dollar Cost Average: Dollar cost averaging is the easiest way to take advantage of any long-term market trend, including the trend in rates, without having to hop on every opportune movement. Chapter 8 demonstrated how dollar cost averaging works with government bond mutual funds. If your capital permits, you also can use the technique for direct purchases of Treasury and agency obligations, buying a few notes and bonds in regular, disciplined purchases of a few thousand dollars at recurring intervals.

Spread Your Risk: Although long-term maturities typically produce the greatest capital gains, it's wise to apportion investments across a range of maturities. You might not optimize your gains by diversifying across maturities, but you will be better positioned to take advantage of price gains wherever they occur in the spectrum of maturities.

Be Prepared to Wait: Patience is particularly rewarded with Treasury and agency securities because they pay default-free interest while you are waiting for their prices to increase. No other group of securities can make that claim. If your strategy doesn't produce anticipated gains in the expected time, you can take your income, wait out the market, and sell when opportunity finally arises.

SUMMARY

Although Treasury and agency obligations are widely used for their income, they can also produce capital gains when the general level of interest rates declines. Unlike buy-and-hold investors who generally keep their securities until maturity, capital gains investors take advantage of broad, public markets to sell appreciated securities before maturity. They also can buy Treasuries and agencies at discounts from par and hold them until maturity.

As a general rule, long-term maturities and low-coupon securities produce the greatest gains from declines in economywide interest rates. However, capital gains can and do occur across a broad front of issues. In addition, zero coupon bonds of all maturities are favored growth investments because their prices move most dramatically when rates change. Similarly, split funding concepts that mate Treasuries with other types of investments permit you to hold default-free investments diversified by capital growth from other securities. Highly aggressive investors who hope for rapid capital gains from rate declines can buy Treasury and agency securities on margin.

Investors who strive for capital gains must follow market, economic, and interest rate trends for signals of unfolding investment opportunity. Finally, capital gains investors are always aware of the prospect of capital losses. To mitigate those inevitable periods of error, they also learn to manage the growth portfolio with caution.

13

Treasury and Agency Securities for Retirement

Treasury and agency securities can be—and arguably should be—the backbone of your individual retirement account, employer investment plan, or self-employed retirement plan because these securities produce extraordinary sums when permitted to compound tax deferred. Further, their low risk of default makes them ideal for long-term investment holdings, and their wide markets enable you to buy and sell them with ease in managing these accounts. Equally important, when you do retire you need to convert retirement accumulations into current income for living expenses. Again, Treasury and agency securities provide the dependable income you need.

Investing for retirement accumulations and investing accumulated sums to produce current income during retirement call upon techniques covered in Chapter 11, which discussed the income component of the portfolio. As you will recall, the income component can be used to produce future accumulations from compounded interest and dividends. Essentially, tax-deferred retirement plans are long-term instances of managing the income component for compounding. The income component also can be managed to produce current receipts. In large measure, the income component becomes the dominant portfolio element of retired investors. So structuring retirement plans for current income during retirement also calls upon strategies Chapter 11 discussed to produce maximum and frequent current receipts.

Accordingly, this chapter builds upon both aspects of Chapter 11 and the income component with specific reference to retirement plans. It starts by discussing ways to use Treasury and agency securities for tax-deferred compounding. Then it refreshes your recall of Chapter 11 in discussing ways to convert your retirement accounts to produce current income.

EMPLOYER INVESTMENT PLANS

One source of tax-free compounding available to you if you are employed by a corporation is the employer investment plan, or EIP. Typically, your EIP offers several investment selections, including purchases of your company's stock, investment in one or several growth or income mutual funds, a guaranteed-return plan for older employees, and a government securities mutual fund. Each of these investment alternatives has a justifiable place in your EIP. But there are many reasons why you should use the government securities fund when apportioning investments within your EIP.

The first reason to invest some company-sponsored retirement dollars in a government securities fund is tax-free compounding of interest. Figure 3-6 in Chapter 3 demonstrated the formidable sums that you can accumulate by reinvesting interest payments, even at modest rates of return. Considering that a government securities fund also provides default-free returns, the compounded returns possible over an employment career commend these funds strongly.

Apart from tax-free compounding of interest, there are several additional reasons why you might include the government securities fund in your employer plan. First, any deterioration in earnings or dividends will make your company stock less appealing for your employer-sponsored retirement account. The key to retirement accumulations is steady growth over an extended period; if your company stock isn't providing it through increases in dividends and share price, the steady accumulations of government securities funds become much more attractive.

It is worth remembering that when you hold heavy concentrations of your company's stock in your investment plan, you leverage your retirement and financial future unacceptably. If financial dislocations befall your employer, not only your salary and job, but also your pension and investment plan are jeopardized. This in itself is reason to diversify your employer plan into another investment, especially the obligated payments of bonds and the top quality of Treasuries.

Second, deterioration in comparative yields on other investments within your employer plan will make the government securities more attractive. Market risk or a reduction in short-term interest rates might make a stock mutual fund or a money fund less attractive than the government securities fund in your employer plan.

Third, emergence of wholesale economic risk or widespread market fluctuations might lead you to seek the quality and stability of Treasury securities. When economic and market instability befall other securities in an employer investment plan, the government bond fund might save your retirement and financial future.

For all of these reasons, the government securities fund offered by your employer investment plan deserves your consideration. You need not devote your total contributions to the bond component of an EIP, except perhaps during wholesale economic risk or market collapse, but remember that government securities offer compounding, a degree of certainty, and diversification away from leveraging your financial future entirely upon your employer's business performance.

TREASURY SECURITIES FOR IRAS OR SELF-EMPLOYED RETIREMENT PLANS

Not enough can be said about the attractiveness of Treasury and agency securities for IRAs and self-employed retirement plans (SERPs, formerly Keogh Plans). They are easier to analyze than stocks, for they carry no default risk or business risk. Predictable maturities and predictable semiannual income give you one of the greatest benefits of a retirement portfolio—predictable accumulations.

In addition to their customary advantages, government securities offer two particular advantages when you hold them in your IRA or retirement plans for the self-employed. The first is your ability to buy quality securities and hold them for whatever term you select. Knowing that default-free issues will mature at par and pay continuing interest, you feel more confident that your investment won't suffer an absolute loss of principal. Second, knowing that quality bonds will mature at par enables you to ride out price fluctuations with greater confidence. You don't have to fear for your ultimate capital and sell to avoid losses, as your principal will be reclaimed at par. This is a special advantage in tax-deferred accounts, for capital losses aren't deductible from income tax.

THE GRADUALIST APPROACH

Beyond these general advantages, Treasury and agency securities also give you many alternatives in managing your retirement accumulations. Many investors prefer to invest for gradual accumulations. They buy

155

bonds that mature before they retire, intending to reinvest matured principal many times over the course of their working careers. They restrain maturities, accepting the interest payments offered by shorter maturities, and look for greater investment opportunities if interest rates rise at a future date. When the opportune moment of higher rates arrives, their capital is available.

The gradualist approach to retirement accumulations has much to commend it. Certainly one advantage is that it maximizes reinvestment opportunity. As you now know, the general course of interest rates will rise and fall during the time that you are investing for retirement. Restraining maturities gives you the chance to reapportion bonds in your IRA or SERP when interest rates rise. The gradualist approach gives you greater responsiveness in taking advantage of future opportunities while you are compounding returns.

In addition, the gradualist approach of restraining maturities gives you greater flexibility in converting your IRA or SERP for current income when the time arrives to do so. When you buy bonds with maturities prior to your retirement, you acquire a consolidated mass of capital for reapportioning when you do retire. You then can decide how to allocate your consolidated capital mass for income rather than tax-deferred compounding.

Finally, the gradualist approach is especially warranted when short-term interest rates are essentially the same as rates on bonds with longer maturities. As sometimes happens during economic cycles, yields to maturity on Treasury and agency securities may be undifferentiated across maturities—that is, short-term rates are not markedly different from long rates. When this situation occurs, you are not rewarded for extending maturities. The gradualist approach provides essentially the same yields as buying longer bonds, and it gives you greater capital stability and reinvestment opportunity.

THE LONG-TERM BUY-AND-HOLD APPROACH

Other investors prefer to take the long view when they start making IRA or SERP contributions. They buy Treasury and agency securities that mature when they expect to retire, even if that date is decades away. They hold the bonds to maturity, rigorously reinvesting semiannual coupons at prevailing rates of interest. These investors accept the uncertainty of changing interest rates affecting their compounding in exchange for the certainty of predictable coupon income for many years.

For example, say that you will be retiring in 2012. You can select securities maturing thereabouts, hold them to maturity knowing that their par value will be paid in that year, and rely upon reinvesting continual coupons for tax-deferred compounding until the bonds mature. You have predictability in that your par value will be preserved, and you will have predictable income to compound because the bond coupon casts off a known payment—even though the rates at which reinvested coupons compound will change. When the securities mature at the time of retirement, you can reapportion the proceeds as retirement needs and market conditions dictate.

One compelling advantage of this strategy is its simplicity. The long-term buy-and-hold approach requires no complicated portfolio maneuvering, for each year you purchase securities with the same or nearly the same maturity. In addition, this strategy produces ultimate accumulations at the point of retirement, when you need them. A further advantage if you are many years from retiring is that you often can buy long-term bonds at discounts from par, putting more of your yearly IRA or SERP contribution to work.

THE INCREMENTAL STRATEGY

Not every investor can set aside the full $2,000 per wage earner that IRA rules permit or the maximum amount that might be permitted under rules governing self-employed retirement plans. In the case of IRAs, perhaps the financial obligations of a family keep you from making maximum contributions. In the case of self-employed persons, perhaps the demands of building a business unavoidably take precedence over retirement anticipation investments. Even if money isn't a problem, perhaps time or impatience with managing a retirement plan keep you from one of the strategies discussed above. In all cases, however, you can still invest something toward retirement by calling upon government securities mutual funds and the strategy of incremental investing.

The incremental strategy is as its name implies. You invest small sums in the government securities fund as your time, temperament, or budget permit. Over many years, your incremental contributions to the fund compound as interest and continuing contributions are credited to your account. Modest amounts added on a regular basis can accrue to surprising magnitudes over time. In fact, the incremental strategy using mutual funds can be as rewarding as any long-term tax-deferred investment, including contributions you make to your EIP.

Government bond mutual funds are perfect for the incremental strategy. You can subscribe to a government bond fund for small amounts, often $1,000, and you can add convenient sums, sometimes as little as $50, through subsequent investments. Because they permit small investments, you build retirement accumulations gradually and without large dents from your household or business budget. As a further advantage, the incremental strategy lets you use dollar cost averaging, one of the long-term investor's most powerful tools. Over a number of years, perhaps even decades, steady contributions of an affordable amount monthly or quarterly provide built-in capital gains as well as compounded interest. Both equate to substantial sums upon retirement.

In addition, don't forget the other advantages that government bond funds offer—convenience, accessibility, a professionally diversified portfolio, record keeping, and switch privileges. Virtually all government bond funds are approved for retirement accounts and are equipped to process the necessary paperwork. As you remember from Chapter 8, however, look for funds with no loads and low management fees.

THE CLIFF STRATEGY WITH ZEROS

Zero coupon bonds have become the securities of choice for IRAs because of their range of maturities, highly predictable accumulations, continual compounding, and exemption from taxation on phantom interest in tax-deferred accounts. Their highly predictable returns enable you to know exactly how much your plan will be worth when they mature. Their range of maturities fits your retirement plan whether you are retiring this year or 25 years from now. Their low prices for distant maturities permit younger, lesser-salaried investors to have long-term growth with modest investments. Zeros are ideal for tax-deferred plans because their phantom interest isn't taxed until you withdraw funds at retirement.

The cliff strategy for managing zeros outlined in Chapter 11 is one way to accumulate sums for retirement. In following this strategy, you purchase zeros that mature during the year you expect to retire. When retirement arrives, the matured value of your zeros presents a sizable sum that you can convert into current income investments.

If the year of your retirement is distant and you are buying long-term zeros, you must be aware that long zeros will fluctuate more dramatically in price while you own them. As a buy-and-hold investor, you will have to tolerate that capital fluctuation, but you have the confidence of knowing the par value of your default-free Treasury zeros will be there when you retire.

OTHER STRATEGIES WITH ZEROS—ANALYZING MATURITY AND YIELD

You might buy zeros because you want them to mature in a specific year, as you do with the cliff strategy. On the other hand, there are other ways to maximize the attractiveness of zeros for retirement accumulations. More specifically, you can select zeros by following one of three strategies: You can select zeros that offer the highest yield for the shortest term of maturity; zeros that offer the highest yield; or zeros that offer maximum accumulations.

You saw in Chapter 6 that a zero's yield is a function of price and term of maturity. Although prices for long-term zeros are lower, zeros of varying maturity may produce the same yield to maturity. Look at the three zeros displayed below. Yields are hypothetical, and let's assume an investment of $10,000.

Maturity	Yield to Maturity	Accumulations
10 years	9.2%	$25,000
15 years	9.6%	$60,000
20 years	9.7%	$80,000

If you want the highest yield for the shortest time, you will want ten-year zeros yielding 9.2 percent. Shorter maturity presents an acceptable yield and sooner reinvestment opportunity. If economywide rates have increased in ten years, you can reinvest at those higher rates. By selecting ten-year zeros in this example, you receive the highest yield for the shortest time.

However, you don't know that interest rates will be higher in ten years, when the zeros yielding 9.2 percent mature, so you may decide to invest in zeros offering the highest yield now and take your chances with later rates. If that's your decision, you'll want the 15-year zeros offering 9.6 percent yields to maturity. In this example, the 9.6 percent zeros effectively offer the highest yields because the 20-year zeros yield only one-tenth percent more despite their five additional years until maturity.

Other things being equal, you might consider the 20-year zeros to be the poorest choice. They scarcely out-yield the ten-year zeros offering 9.2 percent, and their negligible yield difference over the 15-year zeros seems hardly worth noticing. However, the 20-year zeros offer maximum accumulations for a buy-and-hold strategy. Even though their yield is not compelling, they will have a lower price than the other two series of zeros. Accordingly, the 20-year zeros produce greater accumulations— $80,000 as opposed to $25,000 and $60,000—than the others because of their lower price. If you are looking for maximum accumulations, the 20-year zeros provide it, and that makes them a legitimate choice for tax-deferred compounding.

None of your preferences in yield or accumulations is necessarily wrong when compared to another choice. The point is to invest with knowledge of maturity, yield, and your particular investment orientation when using zeros for retirement planning.

RETIREMENT ACCUMULATIONS OUTSIDE TAX-DEFERRED ACCOUNTS

Although most Americans hold their retirement accumulations in EIPs, IRAs, and related vehicles, they supplement formal retirement plans with other Treasury and agency securities. One security of growing importance for retirement-minded investors is the EE savings bond. EE bonds have the special advantages of being exempt from state and local income taxation and of being eligible for deferral of federal income taxes if you choose. The former advantage isn't available from conventional retirement plans, as income from IRAs, SERPs, EIPs, and employer pensions is fully taxable when you begin to receive it.

Now that EE bonds are eligible for extended maturity of up to 30 years, they fit well with almost any investor's retirement horizon. They continue to accrue interest beyond their nominal maturity of 12 years, so you can buy EE bonds each year and cash them as retirement needs dictate. Also, they are indexed to rates paid by Treasury notes, and their potentially escalating interest accruals offer some protection against inflationary increases in interest rates.

Finally, don't forget that you can exchange EE bonds for coupon-paying HH bonds. Not only do you retain tax deferral of the EE bond interest when converting, but you also obtain regular income for current expenses during retirement. This combination of features makes EE savings bonds excellent investments to hold in addition to retirement accounts.

CURRENT INCOME FROM RETIREMENT INVESTMENTS

Investors can spend their entire working career accumulating tax-deferred sums for retirement, but at some point nearly all Americans retire, and upon retiring they need to arrange for income to meet living expenses. The retirement anticipation portfolio, long cultivated for future accumulations, becomes the retirement portfolio that supports an investor. Prior to retirement Treasury and agency securities are managed

Table 13-1: SERIALIZED ZEROS FOR CURRENT INCOME

Year of Investment	Year of Maturity	Investor's Age During Retirement	Par Value of Zeros
1982	2008	60	$50,000
1983	2009	61	$50,000
1984	2010	62	$50,000
1985	2011	63	$50,000
1986	2012	64	$50,000
1987	2013	65	$50,000
1988	2014	66	$50,000
1989	2015	67	$50,000
1990	2016	68	$50,000

for capital accumulations. Upon retirement, they need to be managed for current income. Some investors don't wait until the day of retirement to structure their IRA or SERP for current income. Rather, they anticipate their eventual need for current income while they are managing for future accumulations. Instead of accumulating capital that they eventually convert to income, they stage retirement investments to produce income over a sequence of years while they are accumulating capital.

SERIALIZING ZEROS FOR FUTURE INCOME

The income stream strategy, also discussed in Chapter 11, showed how to serialize zero coupon securities to provide a stream of income. In that example, however, we took the case of an investor who reapportioned a $100,000 lump sum to provide income over ten years. Now we see how to serialize income with a series of IRA and SERP contributions during working years.

Table 13-1 is an actual page from the retirement journal of a self-employed, 41 year-old investor. For the past several years, he has been serializing future income with each year's contribution to his SERP. Each year, he is able to contribute between $4,000 and $5,000 to his plan. With those yearly contributions, he has been structuring one series of zeros to mature at age 60, another at age 61, and so on. Because he is many years from retirement, he is able to buy zeros at low prices to produce attractive accumulations. He intends to hold the zeros to maturity and cash them for current income when they mature during successive years of his retirement.

As you see from Table 13-1, this investor will not need to realign investments in his SERP to produce current income. He has already assured himself of $50,000 yearly starting at age 60 by serializing each year's SERP contributions in zeros. In 1991 and beyond, he will continue to buy zeros with maturities in 2017 and beyond. Over his working years he will have secured a long-term supply of predictable income well into his eighties.

SERIALIZING COUPON BONDS

You can follow a strategy similar to that outlined in Table 13-1 by serializing conventional coupon bonds during the years you contribute to an IRA or SERP.

Let's say that a married couple starts their IRA contributions in 1990 and intends to contribute $4,000 per year for 20 years. For the sake of simplicity, let's say that the couple buys all of their bonds at par and all bonds will pay an $80 yearly coupon. We will also assume the couple earns a 5.5 percent rate of compounding on their interest payments.

Table 13-2 presents a more complicated picture than serializing zeros during years of accumulations, so a bit of deciphering is warranted. Each year, the two investors contributed $4,000 toward bonds maturing 20 years distant. That is, in 1990 they bought bonds maturing in 2010, the year they expect to retire; in 1991 they bought bonds maturing in 2011, the second year of their retirement; in 1992 forward they did the same, so that by year 2010 they had bonds maturing from 2010 to 2030.

During the years of accumulation, their $4,000 produced $320 in yearly interest payments, for we assumed that each bond had a coupon of $80. We have also assumed the yearly $320 interest payments compounded at a modest 5.5 percent each year. Interest from bonds purchased in 1990 compounded to $11,402 by 2010; bonds purchased in 1991 compounded to $10,493 by 2010; and so on through the bonds purchased in 2010, which produced $320 in 2010. The total of all compounded interest payments reached $99,865 in 2010.

Therefore, when the year 2010 arrived, these two investors had earned $99,865 by reinvesting coupon payments. That sum was available for converting to current income. We have also assumed they earned only 5.5 percent on their $99,865, producing $5,493 current income each year.

However, that $5,493 is not all the income available from their IRAs. These investors also have bonds maturing each year until 2030. Each year during retirement, maturing bonds will pay their $4,000 par value plus interest earned during their final year of maturity. In addition, bonds that have not yet matured will continue to cast off $320 in yearly income

Table 13-2: SERIALIZED COUPON BONDS FOR CURRENT INCOME

Year of Investment	Year of Maturity	Investor's Age at Maturity	Par Value of Bonds	Yearly Interest	Compounded to 2010	Current Income From Reinvested Compounding	Current Income From Bonds (par + coupon)	Total Yearly Income
1990	2010	60	$4,000	$320	$11,402	$5,493	$10,720	$16,213
1991	2011	61	4,000	320	10,493	5,493	10,400	15,893
1992	2012	62	4,000	320	9,632	5,493	10,080	15,573
1993	2013	63	4,000	320	8,816	5,493	9,760	15,253
1994	2014	64	4,000	320	8,043	5,493	9,440	14,933
1995	2015	65	4,000	320	7,311	5,493	9,120	14,613
1996	2016	66	4,000	320	6,618	5,493	8,800	14,293
1997	2017	67	4,000	320	5,961	5,493	8,480	13,973
1998	2018	68	4,000	320	5,339	5,493	8,160	13,653
1999	2019	69	4,000	320	4,750	5,493	7,840	13,333
2000	2020	70	4,000	320	4,192	5,493	7,520	13,013
2001	2021	71	4,000	320	3,663	5,493	7,200	12,693
2002	2022	72	4,000	320	3,162	5,493	6,880	12,373
2003	2023	73	4,000	320	2,688	5,493	6,560	12,053
2004	2024	74	4,000	320	2,233	5,493	6,240	11,733
2005	2025	75	4,000	320	1,813	5,493	5,920	11,413
2006	2026	76	4,000	320	1,410	5,493	5,600	11,093
2007	2027	77	4,000	320	1,028	5,493	5,280	10,773
2008	2028	78	4,000	320	667	5,493	4,960	10,453
2009	2029	79	4,000	320	324	5,493	4,640	10,133
2010	2030	80	4,000	320	320	5,493	4,320	9,813
					TOTAL $99,865			

until they do mature. Interest earned from reinvesting the $99,865 plus the par value of bonds maturing each year plus interest earned from bonds that had not matured produces the amount recorded in the final column as yearly cash available for consumption.

Table 13-2 is only a very approximate calculation. Its purpose is simply to illustrate the concept of serializing coupon bonds for retirement income while you build retirement accumulations in an IRA or SERP. Although the mathematics is laborious, the concept is straightforward. This strategy anticipates the need for current income in the future while you are investing today for accumulations. Bonds you purchase will cast off interest payments that compound until you retire. That sum can be converted into income securities that pay cash-in-hand current income. Further, the par value of each serialized bond becomes cash income when it matures, and bonds not yet matured will continue to pay coupon income that can be used for current comsumption during retirement.

CONVERTING ACCUMULATION PORTFOLIOS TO CURRENT INCOME

Not all investors anticipate their need for retirement income while they are contributing to their retirement portfolios. Some investors pursue a cliff strategy so that all their accumulations come due when they retire. Some sources of retirement accumulations, such as an EIP, pay a lump sum distribution at retirement. In addition, investors might receive other large, one-time disbursements when they retire, perhaps proceeds from selling a home or cashing in other long-accumulated assets from personal portfolios. In all of these cases, these investors need to reapportion their accumulations to produce current income.

Bundling up a working lifetime of investments into a current income portfolio requires a great deal of consolidation. When reapportioning your accumulated investments to produce current income, bear in mind that the nature of your portfolio changes when you enter retirement. Prior to retirement, you may have held many different types of investments, such as stocks intended for greater or lesser levels of capital growth, mutual funds for a balance of compounded income and capital growth, or several varieties of bonds for a combination of current yields or yields to maturity. When you retire, those investments may no longer be appropriate for the presiding duty of your portfolio—providing current income with some attention to capital growth. Accordingly, the investments in your portfolio may need to be revised.

You might not make all of your allocation decisions at once, but you don't want your portfolio to be fallow while you are reviewing your possibilities. As you decide to dispose of a certain class of investments or some specific investments, hold the proceeds in T-bills and government money funds for market-level returns and capital stability while making your reallocation decisions.

EVALUATING SECURITIES FOR INCOME

As you begin to reapportion your accumulations for current income, your first task should be to familiarize yourself with the range of Treasury or agency securities, maturities, coupons, current yields, and yields to maturity. It might be a good start to look through the Treasury bond quotations in the financial pages, creating an estimated portfolio based on the highest coupons or current yields you see.

Most retired investors concentrate first on current yields from discount when measuring bonds for investment. As you recall, current yield is a bond's coupon divided by its market price, and it is a measure of current income received for current investment made. Current yield is important because it gauges immediate bang for the buck. For instance, a bond with a $70 coupon might not, at first glance, offer attractive returns. But if you only pay, for instance, $700 for the bond, you earn a 10 percent current yield on your investment.

An attractive current yield represents a good use for your retirement dollars, but you also want to examine nominal yield—the outright coupon payment. You recall from Chapter 11 that the income component needs to produce maximum income. Although there are many possible definitions of maximum, including current yield, big-dollar payments are one effective definition. You are going to live on portfolio income, after all, so it makes sense to look at bonds with high coupons because they provide the income.

In most normal economies, bonds with hefty coupons will sell above par. Most investors resist par bonds, but you should reconsider your own resistance to them. Remember that you're looking for maximum income. With Treasury and agency securities, you get what you pay for. When considering high-coupon bonds, though, it is best to concentrate on longer maturities. First, longer maturities offer a longer stream of assured, high-coupon income. Second, longer bonds defer your loss of the bond premium for many years. Third, longer premium bonds offer a greater chance for you to earn high income and break even on your purchase of a bond above par.

When evaluating high coupon bonds, calculate a breakeven point. Breakeven measures the number of years at which interest income pays for the bond premium. For instance, suppose you buy a bond with a $150 coupon at $1,500. Your breakeven point is approximately three years and four months. Over that period, the bond will pay you $500 in income, enough to offset the $500 premium. Other things being equal, you want this high-coupon premium bond to have a maturity of at least 3-1/3 years, for that is the horizon at which the bond pays for its premium. If the bond has a maturity below breakeven, you need to decide if the bond's income is sufficient despite the loss of the premium as the bond approaches maturity. If the bond has a maturity longer than breakeven, it obviously pays for itself and rewards your purchase for a greater length of time.

Capital stability is moderately important when selecting bonds for current income, and investors usually look first at bonds with shorter maturities when making their investment selections, for shorter maturities have more stable prices. Another point in favor of shorter maturities is reinvestment opportunity. Over a continuing span of time—and you are likely to be managing your retirement portfolio for decades—the capital stability of short maturities plus their sooner reinvestment opportunity offers more consistent returns.

However, capital stability is not a paramount concern, and the argument in favor of shorter maturities requires some reconsideration. Shorter maturities are more stable than longer maturities, but they may not offer the proportionately higher yields that longer, less stable maturities often provide. In retirement, your portfolio supports you, and long-term bonds might provide the higher income to support your retirement. Long bonds will be less stable, but income advantages may outweigh instability.

Remember that you are choosing bonds primarily for their payments—current yield or coupon yield. That you are 60 or 65 years old shouldn't in and of itself dissuade you from buying 20-year or 30-year maturities. You should not be afraid to include longer maturities in your reapportioned portfolio, provided that the inducement of coupon or current yield is attractive. Do not be shortsighted about longer maturities.

As you have seen many times, your evaluations are not either-or deliberations. You definitely are not constrained to considering only short or long bonds, current yields or coupon yields, or any one aspect of an investment to the exclusion of another. You should mix maturities, include varying yields, and diversify other characteristics of Treasury and agency securities in your total income portfolio.

STRUCTURING INCOME

You remember from Chapter 11 that the foremost goal of the income component is regular income. In retirement, you need to assure that your investment income parallels your working years income in frequency of payment. Therefore, your first consideration is to align your holdings to provide at least monthly payments.

It is simple enough to structure corporate and Treasury bonds for monthly income by purchasing bonds with staggered payment schedules, as Chapter 11 demonstrated. Coupon bonds pay interest semiannually during the month they are issued and six months distant—January and July, February and August, March and September, and so on. Six issues of properly chosen Treasury or agency securities can provide monthly receipts throughout their terms of maturity.

Accordingly, you should arrange your core retirement portfolio around six well-chosen issues of Treasury and agency securities. As you are picking bonds for yields and maturities, itemize your identified bonds according to payment schedules. Whichever securities you select for attractive payments and maturities, make sure that your final choices do stage income at monthly intervals.

Having chosen mutual funds for retirement accumulations, you can retain mutual funds for retirement income in your IRA. You can transfer funds from one IRA to an appropriate mutual fund IRA if you don't already have a fund. Your broker may also have an appropriate fund. Funds' many advantages, including the advantage of taking monthly payments and all returns cash-in-hand, commend them for income. Remember, however, the indefinite capital fluctuation of bond funds and their fees.

In addition, mortgage-backed pass-through securities are known for monthly payments. Although their monthly income is not as unvaryingly predictable as income from other Treasury and agency securities, Ginnie Maes and Ginnie funds do make payments monthly without your having to structure them to do so. Because of their unpredictable payments you'll not want mortgage-backed securities to be the total of your retirement investments, but you do want to include them for their regular receipts.

Finally, you want to round out your income portfolio with T-bills and government money market funds. These securities can provide additional cash between bond interest dates for further flexibility of income. In addition, their rates of interest will rise with the level of economywide interest rates, providing a hedge against inflation.

If you have been using EE savings bonds outside your normal retirement plans, don't forget that you can exchange them for HH bonds that pay current income. Interest from HH bonds can be an attractive supplement to other securities in your retirement accounts.

You can become innovative in planning current income from investments. You can combine semiannual bond payments with monthly interest checks from bond funds and other investments. You can use zero coupon bonds to produce income by serializing their maturities in an income stream. You can make full use of current income opportunities afforded by innovative strategies using Treasury and agency securities. All that is required is knowledge of Treasury and agency securities and imagination in making the most of their income possibilities.

SUMMARY

Planning for retirement and arranging portfolios to provide retirement income are the chief uses of the income component of the portfolio. In both instances, Treasury and agency securities are excellent investments, for their dependable payments, liquid markets, and diversity serve the goals of retirement planning and retirement investing.

As a working adult, you can make use of Treasury and agency securities in IRAs, SERPs, and employer-sponsored investment programs. You can follow several strategies in building retirement accumulations, achieving retirement accumulations with a gradualist approach, a long-term buy-and-hold strategy, or an incremental approach using mutual funds.

Some retirees anticipate the need for future income as they are accumulating sums for retirement. During their working years, they serialize zero coupon or coupon-paying securities for future accumulations. The task of reapportioning their portfolio at retirement is already completed. Other investors regard retirement accumulations and retirement income as separate investment decisions. They reapportion their accumulated sums at retirement to provide current income.

As a retiree, you convert retirement anticipation investments into current income producers. Again, Treasury and agency securities are wise investments, for they provide the economy's most assured payments. The range of maturities, coupons, and yields gives you flexibility in arranging current income, and the variety of types of securities available permits you to stage income as you need it.

In general, retirees seek monthly payments from their investments. They achieve them by staging coupon-paying Treasuries and agencies to provide monthly income from semiannual coupons. Retirees also rely upon government securities funds and mortgage-backed securities to provide monthly payments without portfolio maneuvering.

14

Treasury and Agency Securities
for Tuition Planning

Next to retirement, investing to meet tuition expenses is Americans' foremost financial concern. This is not surprising, as some authorities estimate rearing one child to age 18 will require one-third of your after-tax income—and that's before college expenses begin at 18.

The customary problem with tuition planning is that most parents start too late. It's tough to meet four years of college education by starting two years before sons and daughters start college. The second customary problem is that parents hold securities earmarked for children's tuition in their personal names. You may have it in mind that the investment belongs to your child, but the tax authorities won't see it that way. They will expect securities held in your name to be taxed at your personal rates, and taxes reduce investment returns.

Finally, parents don't realize that tuition planning is a fixed-sum, fixed-time investment problem—in short, a circumstance more suited to the lump sum component of the portfolio than the growth component. You're going to need a relatively predictable amount at a predictable time, and as that time approaches, you can less tolerate capital losses associated with capital growth. All of these circumstances make a general strategy of capital growth less appropriate for tuition planning. In converse, these circumstances make Treasury and agency securities ideal for tuition planning.

UNIFORM GIFTS TO MINORS ACCOUNTS (UGMA)

Assuming that you are not in a position to establish elaborate legal trusts, the favored way to accommodate children's tuition expenses is by opening Uniform Gifts to Minors Accounts. These are specialized accounts to which parents or related parties contribute cash or investments. Established with a bank, broker, or mutual fund, the account belongs to the child, as do the securities that are purchased or contributed to it. Each parent can contribute up to $10,000 yearly to each child without incurring gift taxes. One parent is usually the custodian for the account, although some states require a trustee to fulfill this obligation. The custodian directs investments in the account, and the proceeds revert to the child when he or she attains majority.

Two advantages commend the UGMA. First, its assets are separate from your assets. Should estate taxes become a consideration, the UGMA is not part of your estate and therefore is separate from estate proceedings. Second, a portion of investment returns in the UGMA will escape taxation.

Tax merits of UGMAs are not now as broad as before the Internal Revenue Code of 1986. Under present law, the first $500 of investment returns in the account escapes taxation because that sum is offset by the child's personal income tax exclusion. The $500 of investment income that otherwise would be fully taxed is untaxed.

The next tier of $500 in investment income in the UGMA is taxed at the child's personal rate—15 percent in most cases under 1988 law. However, investment returns above $1,000 are taxed at parents' personal tax rates, not the child's, as under previous law, until the child reaches age 14. At age 14, the child pays income tax at his or her personal tax rate on all investment returns in the UGMA. If you hold the child's securities in your name, investment returns are taxed to you at your personal rate. You lose the advantages the UGMA offers.

ZEROS FOR THE UGMA

Otherwise fully taxable, Treasury and zeros are especially advantaged if their phantom yearly interest accrues to less than $500 in UGMAs for preadolescent children. If managed with regard for the compound taxable interest formula in Chapter 6, their phantom interest won't be taxed. Being untaxed, their tax-equivalent yield will be even higher.

As you've seen, corporate zeros typically cost less and yield more than comparable Treasury zeros while providing the same advantages of a known maturity value. For this reason, combined with the $500 untaxed yearly accumulation now possible in UGMAs, you can buy corporate zeros for your child and enjoy the higher yield untaxed.

The problem for children under age 14, if it becomes a problem, occurs when phantom yearly interest on Treasury zeros exceeds $500. Beyond that threshold, the next $500 of interest is taxed at the child's rate, and all above that is taxed at your personal rates, and taxes offset the advantages of the UGMA. You have two alternatives in managing this situation.

First, you can concentrate fully taxable zeros in short maturities and reinvest par value of the bonds when they mature. You buy that quantity of short-term bonds which will not exceed $500 in yearly phantom interest, take advantage of the UGMA tax break, and position your child for later investment that preserves yield and tax features, as we'll discuss in a moment.

Second, you can buy fully taxable zeros of longer maturity as the floor of a continuing portfolio, a particularly advantaged strategy if you start the UGMA early. In this case, you select zeros that will produce less than $500 of phantom yearly interest for a longer period—say, until your child is 14. You will enjoy the sustained, untaxed compounding for a longer period.

If you are willing, you can buy enough zeros to produce $1,000 in taxable phantom interest in the UGMA, taking your smaller tax lumps on that second $500 taxable to the child, but postponing income taxable at your rates.

Also, the key tax phrase is *all returns* in the UGMA, including capital growth. If you buy long-term zeros that appreciate in price beyond compound accreted value to date, you can sell to preserve the capital gain and reinvest in shorter zeros or other types of bonds. Fully taxable zeros can work for adolescents 14 and older, as all phantom taxable interest will be taxed at their rates, not your presumably higher income tax rates.

An Example of Serialized Zeros in the UGMA

If you opt for zeros, the easiest strategy to follow is to buy zeros maturing during the years of your child's college education, anticipating how much you'll need for freshman year, sophomore, and so on. You stage zeros to mature over a span of four, or whatever many, college years, and you allocate your zeros accordingly. When the zeros mature, the money is there for college.

In general, financial advisors suggest that you'll want at least $10,000 as a base level of accumulations for each college year of each child. Obvi-

Table 14-1: ZEROS FOR THE UGMA

Year	Yield to Maturity	Price per $10,000	Maturity Value
2003	9.40%	$2,540	$10,000
2004	9.43%	$2,300	$10,000
2005	9.43%	$2,100	$10,000
2006	9.46%	$1,900	$10,000
Totals		$8,840	$40,000

ously, $10,000 may not be enough when your children are ready for college, but $10,000 is a base level for planning. Table 14-1 is a hypothetical UGMA portfolio based on Treasury zeros. Let's assume that a child will start college in 2003 and remain through 2006.

As you see, an investment of $8,840 serialized in these Treasury zeros will produce $40,000 in $10,000 increments between 2003 and 2006. These four issues of zeros will produce approximately $852.45 in phantom interest during the first year. Therefore, you'll have to declare $352.45 in taxable phantom interest. Taxed at the child's rate of presumably 15 percent, that's a $52.87 tax bill the first year. The tax bill will, of course, increase as the zeros compound toward maturity. If you invest in federally untaxed municipals, you avoid the federal tax problem.

Should you be financially fortunate, you can buy a sufficient quantity of zeros at one time, or you can patch the UGMA together piecemeal, buying a few thousand dollars face value this year, next year, and so on. In either case, you'll be able to assemble a base level of accumulations for college expenses during the years indicated.

COUPON BONDS FOR UGMAS

Preferred as they are for a UGMA, zeros aren't your only bond alternatives. You can purchase conventional coupon bonds and reinvest the interest coupons. The basic difference is that in the former case the par value of the bonds is your tuition fund, whereas in the latter case the accumulated interest payments amount to the tuition fund.

One advantage of coupon bonds is their visibility in that they crank out a fixed semiannual interest payment. There's no need to calculate phantom taxable income because you know exactly what interest has been received. You can purchase quality corporate, Treasury, or municipal bonds for their visible interest payments, and you can pursue several strategies in doing so.

One disadvantage of coupon bonds is that your total accumulations depend upon your ability to reinvest semiannual coupons for compounding in a money market fund, savings account, or other vehicle. Interest rates that these investments pay can change often. You'll have greater difficulty producing a consistent, predictable investment return at a known time.

One strategy is inactive management. If you're content with their interest payments, you can buy long-term bonds—say, those maturing when your young child will start college—and hold them for the sake of locking in the interest for the UGMA. If you're confirmed in this legitimate strategy, you'll be indifferent for three reasons to capital fluctuation that may result before long bonds mature. First, you know that you're buying bonds for continuing payments, not current market price. Second, you know increases in interest rates present offsetting circumstances: market price of bonds fall, but you'll reinvest coupons at higher rates of compounding. Third, par value will be safe at maturity when you need the money if you've bought quality bonds. In short, you can buy long bonds for UGMAs because, having read this far, you know what behaviors are significant about them and which aren't.

Yet you also know about reinvestment risk, reinvestment opportunity, and liquidity. As a consequence of this knowledge, you may prefer to hold shorter maturities in your UGMA coupon bonds and manage them more actively. This, too, is a legitimate investment strategy for the UGMA. By restraining maturities, you'll be able to reinvest the entire par value of matured bonds if interest rates rise, not merely the coupon payments, as in the strategy above. Conversely, if you do intend to manage UGMA bonds more actively, you'll want the resistance to capital fluctuation that short maturities offer. There's no merit in losing market price if you'll be turning the bonds over more often in the UGMA portfolio.

Remember, however, that the UGMA is a selected investment situation, and disproportionate concern with capital stability can be misplaced. Capital stability has two chief advantages: the opportunity to reinvest for higher continuing gains without capital loss and the opportunity to preserve capital for current consumption. In the UGMA, you're not investing for continuing returns but for a known investment horizon. Further, your goal is to accumulate a mass of capital that will be consumed in single payments; it's that future date and consumption that matter, not today's consumption. You'll have capital stability when it's time to consume the bond because the bond will reach its par of $1,000.

Table 14-2: COUPON TREASURIES FOR THE UGMA

Interest Paid		Accumulations*	Par Value	Total
Bond 1	$125	$2,856	$1,000	$3,856 (15 years)
Bond 2	$125	$4,141	$1,000	$5,141 (16 years)
Bond 3	$125	$3,444	$1,000	$4,444 (17 years)
Bond 4	$125	$3,763	$1,000	$4,763 (18 years)
				$18,205

* Assuming coupon payments reinvested at 5.5% compounded semiannually

---

Example of Coupon Bonds in the UGMA

It's difficult to pursue the twin purposes of UGMAs—untaxed compounding and adequate capital accumulations—with taxable coupon bonds. Consider the example in Table 14-2 of four bonds purchased at par that produce $500 interest yearly, reinvested in a savings account paying 5.5 percent compounded semiannually. Again, the bonds are staggered to mature in 15, 16, 17, and 18 years.

In this case, you secure $500 yearly in federally untaxed bond interest, although interest earned by reinvesting the coupon payments will be taxed at the child's rate because the UGMA produces more than $500 yearly. You've taken advantage of the tax code, but your accumulations are far below the $10,000 base level of tuition support you want to achieve. In addition, the tax consequences will be more severe as the coupons are left to compound. As interest in the savings account grows, so do the taxes paid on the compounded interest.

You can reduce this latter problem by restraining maturities, buying enough short-term bonds to give $500 yearly in untaxed interest, and then reinvesting the total amount in another bond for another year of $500 untaxed interest. By following this option, the UGMA essentially starts over each year insofar as the taxman is concerned.

The following illustrates an example of a parent who buys one-year Treasury bonds to produce $500 in interest. Each year, the matured bonds and their $500 interest are reinvested in another set of bonds producing $500 yearly interest. Consider this course of action:

In June 1990, a parent puts $5,000 into a UGMA containing the $82.50 Treasuries of June 1991, paying $412.50 in yearly interest. Having a short maturity, the bonds sell at par, and their interest payment is below the $500 tax threshold. The UGMA accrues until June 1991 without tax liability for 1990.

In June 1991, the UGMA contains $5,412.50. To round the numbers out, the parent contributes an additional $600 or so to the UGMA and purchases $6,000 of the $82.50 Treasuries of June 1992. The six bonds produce $495 in yearly interest, again untaxed because that amount is below the $500 threshold.

In June 1992, the UGMA has grown to $6,495 without tax. The parent adds an additional $600 or so to the account and invests $7,000 in another set of Treasuries that, again, will be priced near par because of their near maturity. This strategy will function effectively so long as the parent can manage cash and accumulations and maturities to take advantage of existing bonds and their coupons.

EE SAVINGS BONDS

EE savings bonds have become exceptional tuition planning investments thanks to a new wrinkle added to the bonds. Starting in January 1990, the Education Bond Program permits parents who meet certain income limits to exclude EE bond interest from their gross income if it is used to pay college tuition.

To qualify, parents must use all EE bond proceeds (principal and interest) to pay tuition and expenses for themselves or their dependent children attending postsecondary institutions. Colleges, universities, and vocational schools that qualify for federal financial aid programs qualify for the exemption under the Education Bond Program, but proprietary schools, such as beauty or secretarial colleges, usually don't qualify.

The full interest exclusion is available to married couples filing joint returns with adjusted gross incomes of $60,000 or less and to single filers with adjusted gross income of $40,000 or less. Interest exclusion phases down for joint filers with incomes between $60,000 and $90,000 and for single filers with incomes between $40,000 and $55,000.

The program applies to standard EE bonds—that is, no special series of EEs will be issued. The bond must be registered in the name of the taxpayer or taxpayer and spouse, not the name of the dependent children. Even EE bonds you have already purchased can qualify for the interest exemption, provided you were at least 24 years old before the bond was issued.

Even if you don't qualify for interest exemption under the Education Bond Program, EE savings bonds still can be excellent college planning investments. In place of or in addition to the UGMA, you can buy EE savings bonds for your children. Name the child as sole owner at the time the bond is purchased, and no further paperwork is required for accreted interest to be taxable at the child's rate.

176

Tax on accreted interest can be deferred until the bond is paid at maturity or upon being cashed, so you can attend to compounding in the UGMA and deal with EE bond interest later. Interest is exempt from state and local taxation, as always with EE bonds. However, one problem you face in deferring tax on EE bond interest is that Congress may have raised personal tax rates by the time the bond matures and tax on accreted interest becomes payable. Higher tax brackets cut into the child's accumulations. Accordingly, you may want to consider declaring federally taxable interest each year. Odds are that you will owe no tax liability for many years.

GOVERNMENT BOND FUNDS

Government bond funds permit low initial investments and lower subsequent investments as you begin paying tuition. They contain the bonds you would normally select for the UGMA, and they permit you to accumulate shares as you can afford them. The fund also will maintain all your records, a welcome function at year-end tax time. Zero coupon bond funds can be particularly useful for the piecemeal investor. Maturing in set years—perhaps year that coincide with your child's college years—zero funds let you buy zeros a little bit at a time and still preserve the advantages of directly purchased zeros.

You will want all returns reinvested in additional shares of the fund for maximum accumulations. A further consideration is that you can use switch privileges to move among bond funds—particularly from a corporate or Treasury fund into a municipal fund as taxes become a consideration.

THE PROBLEM OF TOO LITTLE TOO LATE

If you wake up one morning and discover that your baby is suddenly three years from freshmanhood, there's not a lot you can do to prepare unless you have substantial capital at your disposal. Lacking it, you still have some options.

First, remember that you have four years of college to prepare for, and that fourth year is seven years away. Zero coupon bonds maturing in seven years will carry some fair prices and yields. You can take care of the more distant college years first, and that's better than throwing up your hands in resignation. Second, consider bonds maturing beyond the years your child will be in college—say ten years rather than seven as in this example. A longer zero will carry a more advantaged price, and that price will stabilize near par as the zeros mature. You can sell the zero before maturity to pay some part of college tuition, taking advantage of its lower initial cost. Further, if interest rates fall, your zero will appreciate. Capital appreciation might add an extra increment to your tuition funds.

In addition, longer bonds typically offer a higher coupon or current yield than shorter bonds. You can increase tuition funds, at least slightly, with yields from longer bonds. Prices might also increase, providing another source of income. Don't forget discount bonds. Treasury and agency securities don't always sell at discounts, but you can watch for occasions when they are as you prepare a tuition portfolio. Bonds selling at discounts will provide capital gains as they mature or if interest rates fall. That's another source of tuition funds in addition to interest payments.

SUMMARY

By starting early, holding assets in UGMAs, and relying upon the features of zero coupon and coupon-paying bonds, parents can achieve a base level of tuition support for children with minimal distortion to their own portfolios. The most straightforward strategy is to purchase zero coupon bonds maturing during the years of your child's education. Coupon bonds can likewise assist tuition planning, although perhaps not as effectively in managing the tax advantages of UGMAs and receiving maximum accumulations. Relatedly, EE savings bonds are now particularly advantaged for tuition planning, as their interest is totally untaxed if turned to that purpose. Bond funds are your best choice for long-term accumulations through small, regular investments. The choice of funds, switch privileges, and record-keeping services commend funds for many tuition-minded investors.

15

Managing Treasury and Agency Securities During Changing Economies

Fitting Treasury and agency securities into your portfolio is only the first part of managing them astutely. More difficult is steering them through a landscape of changing economies and interest rates. We have noted many times that prices and yields of Treasury and agency securities rise and fall with the economy, producing capital gains and losses, alternately presenting and withdrawing attractive income opportunities. Fortunately, the economy doesn't work these changes in secret. It produces a record you can consult in choosing the type and maturity of securities available. The economic record is called the term structure of interest rates, or more commonly the **yield curve,** and it is your chief tool for directing your portfolio.

THE BROAD PICTURE—YIELD AND TIME

The term-yield graph reflects simple reality. At any moment, bonds of both short and long maturities will be offering a certain yield to maturity. That span of yields is the term structure of interest rates. The yield curve is a line that relates those yields (vertical axis) and time (years to maturity on the horizontal axis) in a meaningful picture.

It's easy to construct a yield curve, and you should do so weekly or at least monthly. Easier yet, your broker no doubt publishes regular reports

---

Figure 15–1: TERM STRUCTURE OF INTEREST RATES

Yield to
Maturity %

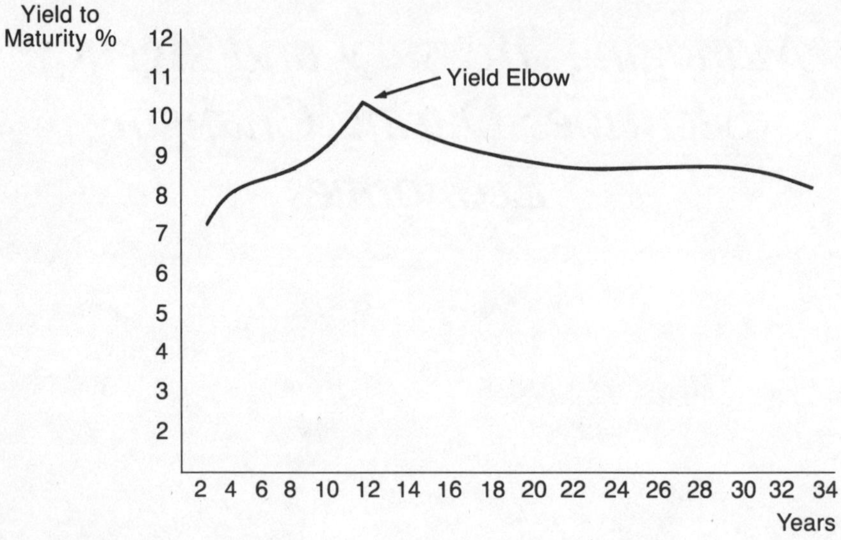

on the yield curve, and financial media print them almost daily. To build your own, refer to the final entry behind bonds listed in the Treasury section of the financial pages. That's yield to maturity. At two-year or five-year intervals, trace the yield across one year to 30 years as shown in Figure 15-1. (You can do the same with corporate and municipal bonds to compare different kinds of bonds on one graph.) The line connecting the spectrum of yields is the yield curve, and the years where yields are highest produce the **yield elbow.**

Figure 15-1 shows one possible term structure of interest rates and its yield curve. The yield curve displays several important pieces of information.

- First, it shows the range of yields available from Treasury securities. Yields in this hypothetical example range between 7 and 11 percent.

- Second, the yield curve shows at which year of maturity Treasury bonds offer their highest yields (the yield elbow). Left of the elbow, earlier in the term structure of rates, bond yields are increasing; to the right, yields to maturity decrease. Note that in Figure 15-1 yields increase out to about 12 years, after which they plateau and then decline. The yield elbow occurs at about 12 years of maturity, indicating that the economy is offering its highest yields for 12-year maturities. Beyond maturities of 12 years, the economy does not produce higher yields.

- Third, changes in the yield curve reflect changes in the economy. Recession and inflation produce changes in economywide interest rates that cause bond prices to fall and yields to rise, or, conversely, prices to rise and yields to fall. As the economy changes, the yield elbow shifts left or right, and the yield curve rises, falls, or flattens. More specifically, economic patterns create telltale shifts in the yield curve and elbow *at specific terms of maturity,* short or long. Recognizing those shifts is the key to managing Treasury securities during changing economies.

THE NORMAL ECONOMY—A POSITIVE YIELD CURVE

The first step in reading yield curves is to see what term-yield would be in a normal economy without undue inflationary or recessionary pressures. The picture of normalcy is the positive yield curve of Figure 15-2. Its central feature is bond yields that ascend gradually to their elbow at distant maturities.

Behind this gently sweeping yield curve little is happening with new bonds, old bonds, and the economy. Optimistic about economic conditions, bond issuers would be paying higher coupons for "borrowing long" when they issue new bonds. Yields on newly issued Treasury securities would follow the economic pattern, increasing perceptibly at each term of maturity, five years, ten, and so on.

Existing bonds would be responding in sync, with prices at all maturities edging up and down to sustain higher yields at distant years. Price movements—capital gains and losses—would be uneventful on Treasury and agency securities and government securities mutual funds. Mortgage-backed securities would be progressing at FHA speed without undue prepayments. Seeing little call to alarm, the Federal Reserve moderates operations to adjust the economy through interest rates.

A positive yield curve would be an inducement to extend maturities to capture higher yields on longer bonds. Otherwise, you could pick bonds of maturity and yield serving your personal situation, for the economy would not be penalizing your choice. But changing economies alter the yield curve, and the new picture calls for action. One departure from normalcy is that the economy can enter a conventional recession. If

---

Figure 15–2: POSITIVE YIELD CURVE

Yield to
Maturity %

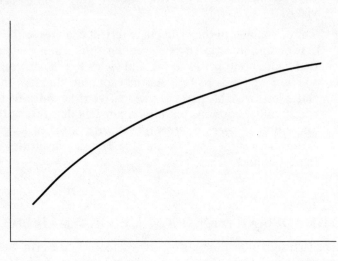

Years

---

you understand what happens to produce its characteristic yield curve, you know your choices as a bond investor.

THE YIELD CURVE OF RECESSION

Figure 15–3 is the yield curve of a conventional business cycle recession. Bond yields generally decline during recession, and the recessionary yield elbow customarily occurs earlier in the term structure of rates.

Several simultaneous events produce this configuration. Competing investments become less profitable in a softening business cycle, drawing investors to Treasury and some agency securities. Investor demand increases bond prices, lowering yields. Also, the Fed pumps money into the economy to fight recession, thereby reducing economywide interest rates and adding to price gains in bonds. The price/interest effect usually is greatest on long-term bonds. Accordingly, the yield elbow shifts to an earlier year, as Figure 15–3 illustrates, because of price increase and yield decline on the long end of the spectrum.

As an investor during conventional recession, you capture price gains by buying longer-term securities, especially bonds maturing behind the

Figure 15–3: RECESSIONARY YIELD CURVE

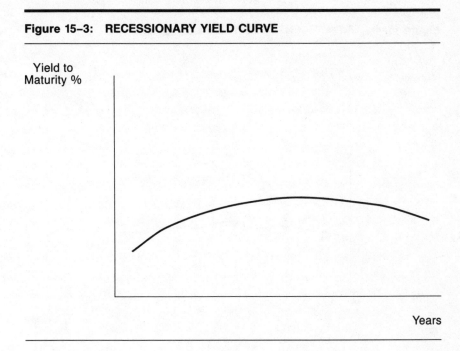

Yield to
Maturity %

Years

yield elbow. Further, those bonds lock in yields at a time when economy-wide interest rates are falling. Thus, buying longer bonds gives you capital gains while improving income. Those longer maturities are especially productive if recession deepens, because the Fed will continue to ease interest rates, and longer bonds will continue to appreciate in price.

However, if you are strictly an income investor—that is, if price gains aren't part of your strategy—you buy bonds maturing at the yield elbow during a conventional recession. As an income investor you are interested in the highest yields, and the elbow shows which term of maturity offers them. Therefore, you go with the elbow, and the yield curve identifies your selection of maturity.

Why choose shorter maturities when you might have income plus capital gains with longer maturities? Because gains turn to capital losses if the economy beats recession. When recession abates, the positive yield curve will reestablish itself. Longer bonds will lose recession's price gains as long-term rates increase, whereas shorter bonds will not. So if you are holding long-term bonds when the positive yield curve starts to reappear, sell to seize your gains. You can hold your shorter bonds.

Figure 15–4: UNDIFFERENTIATED YIELD CURVE

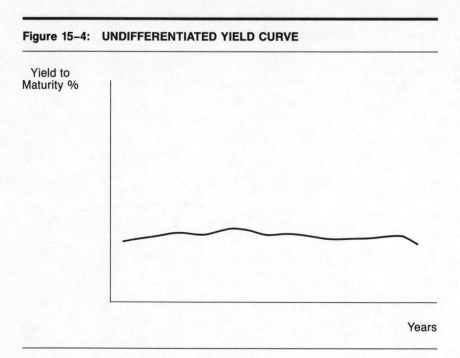

Yield to
Maturity %

Years

THE FLAT YIELD CURVE—A DANGER SIGNAL

As economic trends emerge, remain alert for the reddest danger signal, the flat yield curve of Figure 15-4. During flat term-yield—"undifferentiated" is its scholarly name—yields are essentially the same across all maturities. Such was the case throughout much of 1987, 1988, and into 1989, when one-year and 30-year bonds offered yields identical within two-hundredths of a point. A flat yield curve characterizes any economy in transition. However, flat term-yield may also signal inflationary recession, the "stagflation" that strangled the Carter era economy.

When you see a flat yield curve, don't buy bonds with maturities beyond a few years. You might even sell long-term bonds you already own. One reason why is that yields are the same short-term or long-term, which favors shorter maturities. More significant, an economy cannot operate indefinitely with undifferentiated yields. While the economy and bond markets sort out, a flat yield curve can produce gains or losses at any maturity—and without improving income from your bonds.

184

Figure 15–5: NEGATIVE YIELD CURVE

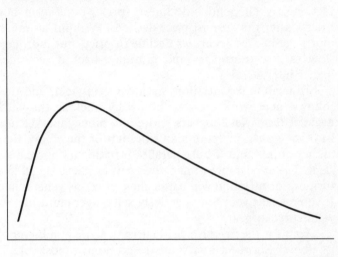

Yield to
Maturity %

Years

For all but aggressive, sophisticated, and lucky investors, flat term-yield sends one message: Preserve capital until the yield curve indicates what else to do. Invest in money market funds, Treasury bills, six-month or one-year certificates, and short-term bonds or bond funds. These choices will yield adequate returns, keep principal intact, and situate capital to reinvest when economic and term-yield pictures clear.

THE NEGATIVE YIELD CURVE OF INFLATION

One clearer picture is that of inflation and its hallmark, the negative yield curve in Figure 15–5. Negative term-yield means bonds offer higher short-term yields than long-term. During March of 1989, for example, one-year and two-year Treasury notes offered 9.8 percent yields to maturity while three-year to six-year bond yields shaved to 9.6 percent and yields on 30-year bonds declined to 9.3 percent.

Negative term-yield occurs chiefly from Federal Reserve actions to extinguish inflation. When the economy inflates, the Fed siphons money from it, which raises interest rates. All interest rates rise during inflation, but the Fed's attempts to counter inflation are most pronounced in rais-

185

ing short-term interest rates, and its attempts are amplified by related market forces.

With the advent of inflation, Treasury and agency securities—in fact, nearly all bonds—decline in price. Long-term bonds and bond funds suffer the greatest price declines. With inflationary interest rates, mortgage-backed securities decline in price, but mortgage prepayments slow as new mortgages and mortgage-backed securities appear with higher interest rates.

You can make inflation, negative term-yield, and the economy that follows them work for your bonds by tracking the yield curve. When negative term-yield appears, move into money market funds and T-bills. In other words, invest in maturities left of the elbow. Being short-term, money funds and T-bills parallel inflationary increases in short-term rates. The appearance of negative term-yield is a signal to avoid long maturities, for inflation will batter their prices as general interest rates rise. If you manage your bonds actively, sell longer maturities when a negative yield curve appears.

Wait for the negative yield curve to settle at a high point—"confirm its elbow." Short-term rates are the economy's most volatile. It takes time for the yield elbow to stabilize as the economy and the Federal Reserve play out their agendas. At the height of an inflationary cycle, you are waiting for short-term yields to stabilize at a point or slightly higher than longer yields. When the negative yield curve is fully confirmed and the highest interest rates have stabilized around short maturities, the economy is wringing out its inflation. You have conservative and aggressive choices for managing your portfolio at this point.

If you are conservative, exit money funds and T-bills and buy bonds maturing at the inflationary yield elbow. Bonds maturing at the elbow lock in yields as inflation abates, general interest rates fall, and positive term-yield reasserts itself.

If you are aggressive, also buy longer bonds. Extending maturities takes advantage of declining, postinflation interest rates. This strategy locks in long-term yields as economywide interest rates fall, and it produces capital gains as long bonds battered by inflation reclaim their preinflation prices.

This aggressive strategy assumes danger of capital losses. If you misjudge inflation, longer bonds will continue to relinquish prices as economywide interest rates and bond yields continue increasing. You can reduce some capital risk by substituting long-term, federally insured certificates of deposit for long Treasury and agency securities. Although CDs have many disadvantages, they don't fluctuate in price, and you won't lose capital if you extend maturities too soon.

TREASURY SECURITIES FOR DEPRESSION

A depression is total and continuing macroeconomic decline in a national economy's business output, business income, employment, personal income, values of corporate and personal assets, consumer confidence, prices, and virtually any economic measure—business cycle recession at its most severe. When an economy and business earnings are deteriorating massively, you do not want to own corporate investments because market risk, default risk, and economic risk are too severe. You do, however, want Treasuries.

Minimal risk of default and absence of business risk commend Treasuries, bond funds investing in Treasuries, and governmental agency debt with a pledge of Treasury assistance. Above all other investments during depression, these are your securities. In fact, you might want to stay away from securities that are presumed to have Treasury backing, but in fact do not. The real thing is so plentiful that you don't need to look beyond Treasuries.

The primary advantage to Treasury securities during this kind of economy is their assured income. After all, the economic problem of depression is an absence of income, and Treasuries, especially those with the high coupons, offer assured income. Above all other investments you can choose for depression, wed your portfolio to high-coupon Treasuries. You will pay prices above par for them, but you want their higher income.

The second advantage to Treasuries during a depression is that they produce capital gains. Responding to loose monetary and fiscal policies, the doctrinaire response to depression, premiums on Treasuries will accelerate further above par as those policies expand the money supply and lower interest rates. Having locked in the income you need for depression, Treasuries also will produce capital gains from market and policy forces.

SUMMARY

The term structure of interest rates and the yield curve offer straightforward signals for managing your Treasury and agency securities. For the economy of a given moment, the yield curve and yield elbow identify the range of interest rates across a spectrum of maturities and the maturity at which the economy presents its highest yields. As economies change, they present characteristic shifts in the yield curve. By learning to identify those shifts, you can anticipate the effects of economic change on your present portfolio, know when to shorten or lengthen maturities, and recognize which securities to choose for cycles of inflation, recession, and worse.

Conclusion

You have come to the end of this book, but you have reached only the beginning of your possibilities with Treasury and agency securities. With what you have learned from these pages behind you, ahead of you lies a long span of intelligent and versatile investing. You are well equipped to join those many investors for whom Treasury and agency securities represent nearly perfect investments.

As you saw from Section I, these securities are highly secure against default, are available in a range of useful maturities, and generally can be bought and sold in fully liquid markets. The direct obligations of Uncle Sam—bills, notes, and bonds—offer the greatest assurance of interest and principal and the broadest markets. You can purchase new issues of Treasury debt directly from the Federal Reserve without commissions, and you can buy and sell Treasury and agency securities efficiently at low cost from full-service and specialty brokerage firms.

Agency securities include a diverse array of types, maturities, and backing, so they require a bit more investigation than direct obligations of the Treasury. In some cases, markets may not be as liquid nor securities as abundant as Treasuries, but their often higher yields plus AAA ratings make them worth including in your portfolio.

Mortgage-backed securities, particularly pass-throughs issued by the Government National Mortgage Association, have become an extraordinary segment of the debt market. Also highly secure against default and widely traded in public markets, pass-throughs nonetheless require more sophisticated investment understanding than Treasury and agency securities. Their uncertain maturity, different method of principal repayment, irregular interest distributions, and other singular features shouldn't dissuade you from investing in pass-throughs, but they do require you and your financial counselor to understand and evaluate them more carefully.

Also, you don't have to be a direct investor to enjoy the benefits of Treasuries, agencies, and pass-throughs. Hundreds of mutual funds and unit trusts offered by brokerages and investment companies allow you to own portfolios of these securities with a consolidated investment. Indirect investment offers a number of advantages not provided by direct ownership of Treasury and agency securities, but you must be aware that their fees and costs may be greater than the costs of direct investment.

Section II showed how to manage Treasury and agency securities in your portfolio. Whether investing for capital stability, current income, or future accumulations, you can arrange maturities and choose the type of bill, note, or bond that meets your investment needs. In particular, zero coupon securities, noted for precise accumulations, are highly useful for retirement and tuition planning, and they can be structured to provide current income as well as future accumulations.

Finally, you saw how changing economies challenge your investment program. But with knowledge of an income investor's most significant tool—the yield curve—you can manage Treasury and agency securities not only to survive, but to prosper from inflation, recession, and depression. Treasury and agency securities can be investments for every season of life and every cycle of the economy. With what you have learned, you are ready to make the most of them.

Glossary

Accreted Interest: The difference between par value of a zero coupon security and purchase price. Also called original issue discount. Yearly accreted interest is the amount of accreted interest "earned" each year that you hold a zero coupon investment.

Accrued Interest: The amount of interest that a conventional note or bond accrues between interest payment dates. Must be paid by buyers and received by investors who purchase or sell Treasury and agency securities between payment dates.

Agency Security: Any of the bills, notes, and bonds issued by agencies and instrumentalities of the federal government.

Asked Price: The price at which a dealer in Treasury or agency securities is willing to sell securities. Conversely, the price sellers receive when selling.

Auction: The issuance of new Treasury bills, notes, and bonds at stated intervals by the Federal Reserve.

Average Life: The estimate of maturity for a pool of mortgage-backed securities.

Basis Points: A relationship between a bond's price and yield subdivided into hundredths. One hundred basis points equals 1 percent interest yield.

Bid Price: The price a securities dealer is willing to pay to buy a security. Conversely, the price sellers receive for selling a security.

Book Entry: Electronic record of ownership of Treasury and agency securities as opposed to receipt of a securities certificate.

Brokered CD: A certificate of deposit retailed through a brokerage firm differing from conventional certificates by its fluctuating market price and negotiability prior to maturity.

Broker-Maintained Market: A market for buying and selling Treasury and agency securities maintained by a brokerage firm.

Callable Bonds: Treasury bonds that can be redeemed by Uncle Sam five years before maturity.

Call Date: The date on which and after which selected issues of Treasury bonds can be redeemed before maturity.

Call Protection: The degree of security that an investor has against a bond being redeemed. Practically, the number of years between today and the call date.

Capital Debenture: A zero coupon security issued by the Federal National Mortgage Association.

Capital Gain: Sale price of a security minus purchase price.

Cash Flow: Amount of total payments, interest and occasionally principal, received as current income from Treasury and agency securities.

CATS: Certificates of Accrual on Treasury Securities. A zero coupon derivative issued by Salomon Bros.

CIB: Compound Interest Bonds. The derivative Treasury zeros from Kidder, Peabody.

Cliffing: A strategy of arranging bonds so that they all mature in the same year.

Competitive Tender: A method of purchasing new issues of Treasury bills, notes, and bonds in which the investor specifies the yield, and accordingly the price, he or she requires to purchase the security.

Connie Lee: Nickname for the College Construction Loan Insurance Association and the securities it issues.

Constant-Dollar Investment: Securities such as savings accounts and money market funds that do not fluctuate in price.

Convertible Zero: As it applies to the Treasury sector, a stripped Treasury zero that converts into a current income obligation five years before maturity.

COUGRS: Coupon on Underlying Government Securities. The derivative zeros issued by A.G. Becker Paribas

Coupon Yield: Also called nominal yield. A bond's coupon payment divided by par value.

Current Income: Cash-in-hand payments received from interest and dividends.

Current Maturity: The number of years until a bond matures, regardless of its original maturity when issued. Any bond has a current maturity of five years if it is five years from maturity date.

Current Yield: A bond's coupon payment divided by its market price.

Default: An issuer's failure to pay accreted interest when a zero coupon issue matures. Treasury securities are considered default-free.

Derivative Zeros: Zero coupon bonds created by stripping coupon and principal payments from a U.S. Treasury security.

Dollar Cost Averaging: A technique that takes advantage of fluctuating bond prices or net asset values of mutual funds by investing a fixed amount at fixed intervals.

Dollar-Denominated: Foreign securities that pay interest and principal in U.S. dollars.

EE Savings Bond: A zero coupon bond issued directly by the Treasury in par values ranging from $50 to $10,000. Purchased at half of par, EE savings bonds mature in 12 years and are eligible for extended maturity.

ETR: Easy Treasury Growth Receipts. The zero coupon derivative bond issued by Dean Witter.

Eurodollar CDs: Certificates of deposit held in U.S. dollars by European, British, and Eastern depository institutions and available to U.S. investors.

Extended Maturity: A provision whereby a bond continues to pay interest beyond its stated maturity.

Factor: A decimal between 0 and 1 that represents the amount of mortgages remaining in a pool of mortgage-backed securities.

Factor Book: A tabular presentation that shows relevant information about factors, value of remaining mortgages, and interest rates on mortgage-backed securities.

Fannie Mae: Nickname for the Federal National Mortgage Association and the mortgage-backed securities it issues.

Farmer Mac: Nickname for the Federal Agricultural Corporation and the securities it issues.

Federal Farm Credit System: Established by Congress to provide credit to farms and farm-related enterprises.

Federal Reserve System: The nation's central monetary authority and the Treasury Department's agent for selling new issues of Treasury bills, notes, and bonds.

FHA: Abbreviation for the Federal Housing Administration.

FHA Experience: An estimate of the average life of a pool of mortgage-backed securities in relation to experience tables developed by the Federal Housing Administration.

FICO: Nickname for Financing Corporation, an agency created to assist the S&L industry by retailing securities to the public. Also the nickname for its securities.

Fiscal Agent: The authority who is responsible for issuing new securities of federal agencies.

Flower Bond: A specially identified series of Treasury bonds accepted at full par in payment of estate taxes.

Form 1099-OID: An IRS form listing taxable interest on zero coupon securities. Required to be mailed to some holders of zeros.

Freddie Mac: Nickname for the Federal Home Mortgage Association and the mortgage-backed securities it issues.

Fund Family: An investment management company that offers several types of mutual funds.

Ginnie Mae: Nickname for the Government National Mortgage Association and the mortgage-backed securities it issues.

Good-til-Canceled Order: Instructions to a broker specifying that an investor is willing to buy or sell a security at a specified price until the transaction is executed or the order is canceled.

HH Savings Bond: A savings bond that pays semiannual coupon interest, unlike EE savings bonds.

Income Stream: A strategy of arranging bonds so that they produce a consistent series of payments.

Interest Rate Risk: The prospect that Treasury and agency securities will decline in price if economywide interest rates rise.

Intermediate-Term Bonds: Those maturing five to ten years after original issue.

IRS Publication 1212: The IRS publication that reveals the amount of phantom interest taxable per year on identified issues of zero coupon bonds.

Issue Date: Month and day that a security is initially issued.

Limit Order: Instructions to a broker to buy or sell a security at a specific price.

Load: Difference between net asset value and the price at which a mutual fund will sell shares.

Long-Term Bonds: Those maturing in more than ten years.

Margin: Purchasing Treasury and agency securities with money borrowed from a bank or brokerage.

Margin Requirement: The percentage of investment that may be financed using borrowed capital.

Market Order: Instructions to a broker to purchase a security at present market price.

Maturity: The date upon which a Treasury or agency security repays its full principal. Also the date a zero makes payment of all accreted interest.

Mini-refunding: Auctions of Treasury securities occurring in March, June, September, and December.

Mortgage-Backed Security: A collection of mortgages bundled into a single security and retailed to private or institutional investors as a single security.

Net Asset Value: The price paid to purchase and the price received upon selling shares in a bond fund that charges no load.

Noncallable: A note or bond that cannot be called prior to maturity. Many Treasury and most agency securities are noncallable.

Noncompetitive Tender: A method of purchasing Treasury bills, notes, and bonds directly from the Federal Reserve at the average price during an auction of new securities.

Note: The general name for a Treasury or agency security with an initial maturity of fewer than 10 years.

Original Issue Zeros: Zero coupon securities originally issued by a corporation, government, or governmental subdivision as zeros. A zero coupon security not created by severing interest and principal payments from a pre-existing bond.

OTC Market: Abbreviation for over the counter. The electronic network through which Treasury and agency securities are purchased and sold.

Par: Amount that a Treasury or agency security pays investors at maturity.

Phantom Interest: The yearly accreted interest that a zero coupon security is presumed to pay each year you hold it even though payment of interest isn't made until the zero matures.

Premium Bond: A note or bond selling at a price above par.

Primary Dealer: Any of 40 firms recognized by the Treasury Department as eligible to bid on Treasury and agency securities when they are initially issued and to make a market for secondary buyers.

Public Market: The listed exchanges through which zero coupon investments can be purchased and sold.

Purchase Price: The amount paid to purchase a Treasury or agency obligation.

Quarterly Refunding: Auctions of Treasury notes and bonds occurring in May, August, November, and February.

Rating: The alphabetical designation attesting to the investment quality of a bond. Treasury and agency securities are AAA-rated, said to be "investment grade."

RATS: Registered Certificates of Accrual on Treasury Securities. Another trade name for derivative zeros backed by U.S. Treasury obligations.

Reinvestment Opportunity: Ability to reinvest interest and principal paid by income securities.

Reinvestment Rate: Rate of interest earned by reinvesting interest payments rather than consuming them as current income.

Reinvestment Risk: The prospect that securities will not be able to pay higher rates of interest when general interest rates rise or retain previous levels of interest if general interest rates fall.

Sallie Mae: Nickname for the Student Loan Marketing Association and the securities it issues.

Serializing Maturities: A technique of arranging maturities of Treasury and agency securities, especially zero coupon securities, to produce current income or promote capital stability in a portfolio.

Settlement Date: The date on which investors must pay for Treasury and agency securities they have purchased. Also the date on which a sale of securities is officially recorded.

Short-Term Bonds: Those maturing within five years.

Split Fund: A mutual fund or unit trust that contains Treasury securities and other types of investments.

Spread: The difference between the bid and asked price in the secondary market for Treasury and agency securities.

STRIPS: Separate Trading of Registered Interest and Principle of Securities. A special type of derivative zero made possible by the Treasury Department.

Switch Privileges: Ability to shift a mutual fund investment from one fund to another sponsored by the same mutual fund family.

Target Fund: A mutual fund containing bonds that mature in a single year, giving the entire fund a terminal maturity in that year.

Tax Anticipation Bill: Short-term security similar to a T-bill that is accepted at par in payment of corporate federal taxes.

TBR: Treasury Bond Receipts. A derivative zero from E.F. Hutton.

Term Structure of Interest Rates: A graph representing the yield to maturity of Treasury securities at identified years of maturity.

TIGR: Treasury Investment Growth Receipt. A zero coupon derivative bond created by Merrill Lynch.

TINTS: Treasury Interest. The derivative zero issued by Shearson Lehman Brothers.

Treasury Bills: Obligations issued by the Department of the Treasury maturing in 13, 26, or 52 weeks.

Treasury Direct: The program through which investors may purchase new issues of Treasury bills, notes, and bonds directly from the Federal Reserve.

Uniform Gifts to Minors Account: A method of securities ownership whereby parents or other relatives may contribute cash or securities to children. Portions of returns generated by the securities are taxed at the children's tax bracket instead of parents' presumably higher bracket.

Unit Trust: Similar to a mutual fund. A portfolio of securities, including mortgage-backed securities, offered by a brokerage or mutual fund.

Volatility: Relative measure of a security's price movement during a specific time.

Weighted Average Maturity: The arithmetic mean of maturities of securities held by a mutual fund.

Yield Curve: A graph linking the term structure of interest rates and showing the general pattern of yields to maturity on Treasury obligations.

Yield Elbow: The point on the yield curve that indicates the year at which the economy's highest interest rates occur.

Yield to Call: The percentage a bond will yield to the date at which it is eligible to be redeemed by its issuer.

Yield to Maturity: The total percentage yield a bond will produce if held for its full term of maturity.

Zero Coupon CD: A certificate of deposit that pays interest only upon maturity.

Index